EUROPE'S POLITICAL COMMUNICATION DEFICIT

Sophia Kaitatzi-Whitlock

"... parlons franchement, une crise politique latente affecte l'Union européenne. Pourquoi? Parce que nous doutons de nous-même, nous ne nous donnons pas les moyens de nos ambitions affichées"

Jacques Delors, 30-06-1994

Published 2005 by arima publishing

www.arimapublishing.com

ISBN 1-84549-099-1

Printed and bound in the United Kingdom

Typeset in Garamond 12/16

Abramis is an imprint of arima publishing

arima publishing
ASK House, Northgate Avenue
Bury St Edmunds, Suffolk IP32 6BB
t: (+44) 01284 700321

www.arimapublishing.com

Acknowledgements

I would like to thank Sage Publications for permission to use material used in Chapter 5 previously published in the European Journal of Communication, and the Institut de l'audiovisuel et des télécommunications en Europe (IDATE) for permission to use material used in Chapter 6 previously published in its journal Communications and Strategies.

Thanks are also due to the State Museum of Contemporary Art in Thessaloniki, Greece, for kind permission to reproduce the cover picture by Ivan Kliun, (Untitled, 1921-1922, gouache and watercolour on paper, 35.4 x 26.6 cm) from the Costakis Collection.

Contents

Chapter 9

INTRODUCTION

Politics in the European Union have been conducted without an effective mechanism of political communication being set up to involve European citizens in the political process. EU citizens have thus become disaffected with Euro-politics and are often quite ignorant of what is being decided on their behalf. They have too often been kept in the dark about the facts, reasons and rationales which underlie policy decisions.

This book looks at how the economistic remit of the founding treaties of the EU, and of course the power of commercial media interests, has led from the 1980s onwards to the systematic liberalisation of the European media and their concomitant disastrous weakening as essential organs of public spaces for political communication.

In 1980 and 1982, the then institutionally very weak European Parliament (EP) called for a straight-forward measure for the establishment of an instrument for European political communication – the idea of a pan-European television channel. The largest and most decisive power shift ever to take place in the EU was played out on the backdrop of this initiative. With hindsight, one may argue that this policy was premature, for in fact the goal of fostering European political communication, and, who knows, perhaps also a sense of European unity, was rapidly undermined.

All the changes that followed, from the first Television Without Frontiers Green Paper in 1984 (which became the TWF Directive of 1989) onwards, in fact, effectively privileged economic forces over political ones. Control of the communications sector was handed over to market forces, notably to major players in the global media market, an abdication of authority which meant that politics at the EU level has become increasingly divorced from real power.

Commercial communications channels or media provided by non-profit organisations may serve a broad spectrum of information and entertainment needs, but they cannot be relied on to provide an adequate political communication framework for citizens, especially of one encompassing the size and nature of the EU unless this is prescribed as their specific mission.

The existence of a framework for independent political communication is a mandatory part of any democratic political entity. It comprises the entire set of platforms (TV channels, journals etc.), mechanisms and regulatory provisions (rules of conduct) that are indispensable to every democratically organised and constitutionally defined state. Such provisions guarantee the constant continuation and the smooth, un-hindered functioning of political communication. The model upon which such a system could be organised may be a matter for dispute, but the existence of such provisions and guarantees is so essential to the functioning of a democracy that, if they are contested or counteracted, the democratic nature of that regime is simultaneously called into question (Dahl 2000, Mouffe 2000 & 2005, Meyer 2002, Kellner 1990). Such a system can operate best when it is independent from both direct state intervention and corporate powers, but it cannot operate at all without the will and the economic support of the polity.

It has been wisely said that in a democracy it is process that renders essence. The way we design and organise the field of communications helps make politics broadly disseminated and comprehensible, guarantees a fair knowledge of the issues being contended, and encourages citizens to participate in them. If the political agenda is set according to the agenda of corporate media, it is controlled and manipulated, and politics ceases to be democratic. In this sense, politics can be organised in or out of the public communication domain.

The story of over twenty years of involvement in communications policy by the EU is a story of how priorities were totally inverted, with private media conglomerates coming to control the entire terrain. The rationale behind this was to allow 'national champion' EU media companies to compete successfully against competitors in the global terrain – to survive or perish. Bowing to this social-Darwinist argument, the all-important sphere of political communications was abandoned, and national state monopolies in the electronic media were swept away. A tentative, pan-European, electronic-communications space emerged in the form of the Europa TV experiment in 1985, but it was not duly supported; in fact, it was even subverted. This was all the better for the private, transnationally-broadcasting operators, who were thus left to control the terrain all on their own and to exploit the transfrontier market for 'attention'.

The 'democratic deficit' in the EU is thus related to the fact that in the entire Union no space has been made available for its multi-ethnic citizens to become involved in EU politics. Information has not been sufficiently provided for people to understand EU politics, nor are citizens provided with the means to participate effectively in political developments – failures closely related to the function of communication. There is already a great deal of literature dealing with various aspects of the *democratic deficit* in the European Union. But there are as yet no studies which explicitly attribute this democratic deficit to the deficit in pan-European political communication. This book argues that case.

Two key processes have changed decisively in the EU over the last twenty years. First, the audiovisual sector has come to be treated only as a commodity service. The second process has been to segmentalise and limit the residual control and actual practice of political communication exclusively to the national domain. This dual distortion has led to paralysis and deadlock in procuring, disseminating, and discussing Euro-politics at any level other than that of the Brussels enclave. This phenomenon is deeply subversive of the very idea of European political integration. European issues, conveyed by national-level public service broadcasters (psbs) and the local commercial channels that began to mushroom after 1989 were relegated to the national level, leaving European-level politics without coverage.

To the extent that power politics now takes place in Brussels, and to the extent that a European citizenship has been established, it is imperative that a coterminous and corresponding political communications space be readily available to us all. If, on the other hand, EU citizens are obliged to look at political events exclusively through the mirror of national and often nationalistic media, we can no longer reason in terms of a European political union or of European citizenship. Our attention is diverted from the real locus of politics. This, however, is indeed what European leaders have staged and are offering to their polity. They should hardly be surprised that referenda on the European Constitution have been negative. During twenty years of EU, communications policy-making European citizens have been mocked and derided. Throughout this period, citizens were sacrificed as objects of commodification to the powerful media moguls.

Through this initial aberration – the decision to hand over the entire domain of communications to private market forces – EU politicians endorsed, by the same token, the loss of their own power as well. The politicians fell into their own trap. The political class in Europe has been greatly weakened since the inception of this policy, and it is questionable whether they will ever recover.

Interest in European affairs is nearing extinction in many member states and the all-time-low turn-out in the 2004 Euro-elections was a clear confirmation of this growing disaffection. Political reporting on EU affairs is both inadequate and distorted, creating a vicious circle of indifference. The decision to keep politics in Brussels while limiting the communicative function to the national level, always from a limited national perspective, leads to absurd and politically destructive developments. It is evident that such a malaise cannot be handled individually or partially, because it is a truly central and structural problem. This is the way it has been designed. If the 'Euro-malaise' produced by it were ever to be cured, this could only come from another change of structure. Only then could politics return to centre stage and become meaningful to citizens again.

This Euro-malaise is now a widely acknowledged phenomenon. In response to the disappointing, if not alarming, anti-European climate which culminated in the referenda of 2005 that wrecked the project for the European constitution, the Commission, in October 2005, came up with the concept of the "Plan-D for Democracy, Dialogue and Debate". Among other ambitions, it aims to start a "consultation process on the principles behind communication policy" in the EU. Plan-D encompasses

> a long-term plan to *reinvigorate European democracy* and help the emergence of a *European public sphere*, where citizens are given the information and the tools to actively participate in the decision making process and gain ownership of the European project. (Commission 2005a: 2-3, emphasis added)

The current situation of the EU is unviable because it lacks community-forming ligaments. What is primarily required for any democratic polity is not the transfrontier supply of lowest-common-denominator programming but a common channel for public affairs. Yet, up to now, the EU has opted for abolishing its own 'nervous system', to use the apt phrase of Karl W. Deutsch (1963).

Chapter 1 explores what I consider the communications lacunae of the EU – its lack of a framework for political and civic communication and the source of Europe's democracy deficit. In Chapter 2, I analyse the key policy documents that marked the turning-point in European, communications policy-making, the 1984 Green Paper 'Television Without Frontiers' (GPTWF) that resulted in the Television Without Frontiers Directive (TWFD) in 1989. I present the rationale and the original policy steps of the Commission in 1984, when the ground was laid for this European communications impasse and for the politically dangerous condition outlined above. I argue that there was a fundamental error of judgment at the inception of this 'Flagship of the Single Market'.[1]

---

[1] It was the British Commission Vice-president, Lord Cockfield, who dubbed the Green Paper on TWF the 'Flagship of the Single Market' (Collins 1994).

The rationale deployed in this policy document clearly reveals the contradictory ideas and mutually exclusive goals which have carried Europeans to the deadlock experienced today. It promoted, in both overt and covert ways, a strategy for the 'privatizing of the political' through a restrictive, economistic framework for Community legislation. The controversies that were manifest at the time also show that fears were expressed then about what the EU might face and is actually facing today. The TWF is taken to mark a turning point and the end of an era.

The directive was subsequently criticised for abandoning some of the strategic options of the 1980s – such as emphasising rather than stripping away the political essence of communications. Logically then, after the adoption of the subsequent Treaty of the European Union, in 1992, one might have expected these shortcomings to have been remedied. Chapter 3 monitors the first revision of TWFD in search of such remedies. It critically assesses the policy review phase with regard to whether it amends any of the fundamental errors. It discusses the key issues for the revision of the 1990s and correlates the new constitutional environment of the Treaty of the European Union (TEU) that did not at all help to modernise and to *politicise* the economistically-trapped framework Directive. The question put is whether the newly-adopted European citizenship had been taken into consideration at all in order to alter some of the provisions for democratising television.

Every revision holds out the hope and promise for adjustments and significant amendments. Therefore, what are the promises in store from the currently ongoing revision concerning the missing element of political communication? Since the adoption of the Directive in 1989 considerable technological innovations have materialised. Network restructurings, including the phenomenon of convergence, have created yet another economic and technological arrangement. Furthermore, the sheer experience of having implemented the TWFD over the previous 15 years presents a different backdrop for this last revision. One of the most promising challenges relates to the much-needed and welcome potential for regenerating and democratising television, the most popular mass-medium *par excellence*. How are these challenges taken up by policy makers? The new constitutional basis enables EU decision makers to proceed to a thorough redefinition and substantial re-grounding of the role of communications in the Union. Is anything happening in that direction? The objective of Chapter 4 is to monitor and evaluate this second revision process – which is still ongoing. My concern is to examine whether, at this stage, ten years since the last revision process and amidst a number of severe crises for the EU, the political communication aspects are confronted and taken on board. More specifically, given the revolutionary advances in communications technology, the so-called 'control revolution', I focus on how Commission policy-drafters and Euro-parliamentarians respond to these challenges. Have they, for example, considered the advantages for democratising the EU through interactive-participatory television as a much needed platform for *political communication*?

After the forced liberalisation of the communications markets in the 1980s, what did reality and experience demonstrate with regard to the most central apprehensions about media power abuses and concentration? In Chapter 5 I monitor policy efforts on the political economy of the audiovisual sector and reveal the most spectacular case of non-decision making. I assess the thwarted attempt at controlling the concentration of ownership of media companies. Considering the promises made in the 1980's regarding, for example, diversity of broadcast content, what is the current situation? What impact has the abandoned policy on pluralism and media concentration had on the supply of diverse and pluralistic content? In Chapter 6, I turn to yet another media policy issue which reveals the 'hands off strategy' that was adopted by the Commission in regard to infrastructure and technology policy. This approach of effective retreat from policy is exemplified in the official devolution of decision and policy-making prerogatives to market forces. The case of digital, Pay-TV, by all accounts, appears to be another example of indulgence on the part of Eurocrats and certain neo-liberal governments.

Chapter 7 correlates EU policy in this field with international and global policy, political and techno-economic trends. Mapping the larger global context within which the EU found itself acting gives us a perspective on the difficulties it faced and the challenges for this *sui generis* agency to act effectively. This highly and rapidly globalising environment explains to some extent the political paralysis in the face of the inexorable march of global capital integration. Changes in the General Agreement on Trade and Tariffs (GATT) and the World Trade Organisation (WTO), in the International Telecommunications Union (ITU) and in global capital movements have been significant constraining factors that cannot be ignored. Is it the external or internal enemy that hampers developments? The chapter argues that the greatest sources of inability are to be found within Europe itself, in its crypto-nationalisms and the hegemonic role of certain member states. The ongoing economic and political controversies never cease to cause consecutive tugs of wars between the national and supra-national poles. Such phenomena severely hamper policy-making in the EU and indeed lead to policy impasses that are further reinforced by global and national undercurrents or explicit trends.

In Chapter 8, I go on to examine the missing image of the EU in the national media across the continent. Why are EU citizens reported to be so ignorant of their own Union? Why do journalists after fifty years of the European integration experience maintain nation-centric or even nationalistic perspectives? Yet, the synergy between television and the new media (the Internet) could help to provide the missing ground for a pan-European public sphere. The technology is available here and now to greatly empower a Union that is at present in a politically catatonic state. But, political elites appear negative, reluctant or hesitant, in effect incapable.

In this regard, I argue that the synergetic combination between mass media and interactive new media may ascertain the required quality of political communication of a regional union such as the EU. Both the element of interactivity and that of massive visibility – provided for by television – constitute preconditions for a working, Europe-wide 'interactive public space'. These benefits may only be obtained by adhering to pertinent 'must carry' rules and by promoting the innovative resource of interactive and participatory civic television (Kaitatzi-Whitlock 2006). A strategy like this certainly presupposes strong political will and concerted action: that the EU acts at last as a unified and a strong supra-state. Political leaders then would have to abandon their present 'hands off' attitude to technology and the media. It would require the Community to impose 'must carry' rules and adopt an altogether different, proactive approach to politics and to policy-making. A window of opportunity for the re-invigoration of the relationship between politics and citizens has been opened, but despite the ambitions of Plan-D, the signs of the revision process demonstrate the reinforcement of commodification and its prevalence over political aims.

In conclusion, I argue that we are faced with a situation in which the cultivation of a vital political role for the citizen is set against commercial exploitation. If the governing institutions of Europe do not act to rescue politics and its citizenry from subjugation to the priorities of commodification and privatization, the current 'euro-malaise' will continue to grow and will keep weakening these institutions, stripping them, eventually, of what remains of their legitimacy.

Chapter 1

POLITICAL COMMUNICATION – THE POWER TO CONTROL THE POLICY AGENDA

Politics can be organised in or it can be organised out of the sphere of public communication. This is indeed what distinguishes democratic from authoritarian politics.[2] The way we organise the field of communications constitutes the way we organise politics and the political sphere itself (Deutsch 1963, Barber 1984, Hanada 1999, Dahl 2000, Meyer 2002, Starr 2005, Garnham 2000: 165-189). Media policy is itself a medium of control which acts upon politics, and at the same time it is a product of the political process (Hanada 1999).

Hence, there is a dialectical triangular relationship between policy-making in communications, element (A), political communication in democracies, element (B) and democratic politics for legitimate management and allocation of state power, element (C). These three elements form a coherent triangle and are either mutually reinforcing or mutually undermining of each other, depending on the type of initiating move made by element (A). If the media through which politics should be kept transparent and open are not put in place or not adequately supported in reality, this is not a democratic politics.

If the media are allowed by (A) to be controlled or dominated by commercial forces, these forces will control the political agenda. As a result, the strategic function of control that each person and each people, in the meaning of *demos*, needs to possess over its immediate environment and condition is, thus, negated and they are deprived of it. By the same

---

[2] Historically, liberal democracies emerged and were developed as political entities linked intrinsically to a free press and related media systems. They were also distinguished by evolving into nation-states.

token, true political communication is effaced or reduced: mutated into a *quasi* political communication (such as infotainment).

Over the last 50 years a complex supra-national political structure has been developing which both unites the different nation states it is comprised of, but also supersedes them. This is a process of stage by stage voluntary Union forming. Over a process of about half a century most of the key institutions of the European Union (EU) have acquired a pan-European scope and validity. Yet, notwithstanding these developments, there is a marked deficit in the Union's means for political communication. In the EU, media still remain nationally entrenched and nationally oriented. This applies to nearly all of the transnationally broadcast media as well.

The EU as a political structure lacks a vital communication system corresponding to it. This is a crucial incongruity in the system. Nationally-based and locally-financed media focus on European affairs from a national or, often, even from a nationalistic perspective. National media serve different needs, which may be at variance with those linked to the EU dimension. They address citizens as Danes, Spanish, British, or French, etc. and not as European citizens. National political and opinion-forming actors take the blame for this resistance. But the "most powerful of these is the sociology and the structure of the European media. Contrary to a large number of policy sectors, this media has not undergone a significant process of 'Europeanization'" (Smith 2004: 12).

However, a 'Europeanized' media system should not be confused with the quantitative increase in the reporting on European topics in national media. National media – by definition – cannot be the components of the requisite and still putative pan-European communicative sphere. The concept of such media in the main is to address national publics. They thus "remain attached to national viewpoints, and communication habits" (Grimm 1997: 252).[3] This signifies that there exists – and that there will

---

[3] Yet, as shall be argued in Chapter 8, even quantitatively the under-mediatization of the EU supra-state affairs is itself greatly damaging the public perception and the understanding of Europolitics by Europeans.

probably always exist – a tension between the national and the supra-national levels. Such a tension is explicable; if however, what is manifest between the two levels may be characterized as a permanent and relentless antagonism, then evidently there are mutually destructive forces at work.

European Citizenship in a European Communications Vacuum

The idea of European citizenship was first proclaimed during the adoption of the Treaty of the European Union at Maastricht in 1992. Thirteen years onwards, the corresponding knowledge about its essence and its premises is default for those primarily concerned by it. Informat-ion resources, a relevant discourse or even ideology of Europeanism in regard to this new citizenship are markedly absent in the public symbolic and discursive domains. Meanwhile, institutional channels for legitimacy transfer from the national electorate to the EU level are too slim to make European citizenship an engaging or a meaningful concept (Scharpf 1997, Zweifel 2002). It is a citizenship that, for some reasons, one keeps quite silent about. As a result citizens themselves have no concrete knowledge about it. Or they may have a very vague idea or no notion at all about it. Yet, it is something which they supposedly possess.

In principle, all EU citizens enjoy rights to information and to communication. But how can these be applied and realized within the Euro-political domain? Are they perhaps of no practically significant value to us as Europeans? How, and most importantly, in exactly what common public domain or space are we to access, to enjoy and to exercise our active and passive information rights? What electronic media are readily available for citizens across the EU? Such questions persist and become even more acute, when considering the nature and complexity of the policy process in Brussels and Strasbourg. This has grown very complex, and, in the circumstances, it certainly is beyond the reach of and comprehension of ordinary citizens living in distant cities and regions. Yet, today all the technological means are available; one satellite position suffices to cover the entire territory of the continent, and broadband interactive and digital networks traverse the broader region of Europe.

Even if we focus on the less demanding *passive information rights,* we already observe severe dysfunctions, such as the low salience and visibility even of the key issues among the multitude of common, EU affairs. The gaps in regard to the exercise of *active information rights,* which are immediately linked to political participation, are by far the most huge and most severe. And these are, of course, more severe. Currently, there is no common platform other than the Internet to accommodate such needs, and this is not an ideal medium for a common and universally accessible publicness and visibility (Kaitatzi-Whitlock 2002, 2003). Still, today the Internet is accessed by less than half of Europeans. Meanwhile its demographic spread is constrained and biased in a number of ways Moreover, the range and frequency of its uses are often more limited than is suggested by 'creative statistics'.

Addressing the political crisis facing the EU currently (2005), which was highlighted starkly by the two dismissive referenda in France and the Netherlands, in May, Peter Golding pointed out that such crises convinced many observers that "the masses were both ill- and under-informed, and that ideals for an expanded and further integrated Europe had been baulked by popular ignorance and indifference" (Golding 2005). Golding, furthermore, quotes the chief European Commission spokeswoman, Françoise le Bail who admitted – through gritted teeth – "We accept that it is a 'no' vote…There is almost certainly an *information deficit* [4] and efforts will have to be made to explain things more clearly to citizens…" (*Guardian* May 31st 2005). The Commission communication on Plan-D best epitomizes this gaping black hole in European political communication.

---

[4] In Chapter 8, I elaborate further on the issue of citizens' ignorance and its causes. About figures on civil disatisfaction and ignorance; see also www.europa.eu.int/comm/public opinion/archives/eb/eb63/eb63 en.htm.

Faced with declining confidence in political systems, the Commission believes that it is important to ensure that representative democracy continues to maintain the trust and involvement of Europe's citizens. the latest Eurobarometer survey shows that public approval of the EU has steadily decreased over recent months. Whether in terms of trust, image or assessment of EU membership, all the indicators have fallen. A similar decline is seen in the public approval of and trust in the national political process. While membership of the EU is till supported by 54% of EU citizens, the image of the European Union has steadily decreased in citizens' eyes with only 47% of respondents giving a positive response. Trust in the European Union has dropped from 50% of citizens trusting the EU in autumn of 2004 to 44% in spring of 2005. (Commission 2005: 3)

So, the information deficit is officially admitted but the critical question remains: through what media networks are the EU institutions and other interested parties going to remedy the huge information gap that afflicts European citizens and polity and that has surfaced in such a pressing way? The commitment of the European leadership to the goals of Plan-D can be tested by this most crucial question. The Plan-D initiative (proposed by Commission vice-president Margot Waldström) says nothing about how this engaging civic role and the invigoration of democracy are going to take place.

What is the relevance of Plan-D, for instance, to the ongoing policy-making of the EU in communications? As shall be seen in the analysis of the current revision process of the TWF Directive (Chapter 4), the Commission does not propose any measures that resonate with its Plan-D. The claim to be aiming to remedy the malaise so lucidly diagnosed in Plan-D is paradoxical, as current policy on television, the most important and influential medium was totally irrelevant to the goals of Plan-D.

Notwithstanding the established ignorance about European citizenship by EU citizens, this idea has continued to preoccupy the elites over the last decade. 'European citizenship' was dealt with again and broadened in scope in the revision of the Treaties of Amsterdam in 1997, while the relevant articles were re-numbered in the next revision of Nice 2000. Articles 17 to 22 of Treaty of the European Community (TEC) deal with concrete rights and obligations attached to European citizenship.

These rights – as modified at the Treaty of Amsterdam – comprise:

(1) the right of free movement and of residence in the union (territory of members states) (Article 18),

(2) the right to vote and stand as a candidate in municipal elections (Article 19 §1),

(3) the right to vote and stand as a candidate in the European Parliament elections in the country of residence (Article 19 §2),

(4) the right of diplomatic and consular protection while travelling or residing in third countries (Article 20),

(5) the right to petition the European Parliament (Article 21 §a),

(6) the right of referral to the European Ombudsman (Article 21 §b), and

(7) the right of written communication with the institutions of the Community in any one of the official languages (Article 21 §c). Citizenship is, moreover, subject to the principle of non-discrimination on the grounds of ethnic/national origin.[5]

In spite of this array of 'rights' it is accepted that European citizens are deprived of essential competences (Chryssochoou, 2005: 89) More to the point, as can be observed there is no specific right coded in regard to communicating on civic and political affairs in the public media. Even

---

[5] (a) Rights (5), (6) and (7) do not derive exclusively from citizenship. They are equally provided to all persons (natural or legal bodies) who reside in the EU. (b) Election and voting rights and the right to diplomatic and consular protection while abroad are subject to relevant subsequent national legislation or to bilateral agreements between member states. See Appendix for full text of these articles.

though we are living in the era of communication and the so called 'information society' this omission is remarkable in one of the major western democracies. The implication is that 'public media' are in fact privately owned and controlled and only serve politics if it is profitable to do so.

Hence, there is no invocation, let alone 'constitutional' guarantee, in respect to citizens' access to existing or potential media (print, electronic, private or psbs) – to develop dialogue and debate and exercise their right to communication. But if the exchange of ideas is not given space in which to be implemented, it can hardly be expected to take place.

It is worth remarking that this fundamental notion was the locus of intense contention during the processes of the revision of the Treaties. Attempts were made, not unsuccessfully, to redefine the notion of citizenship for the European context, notably through its wider interpretation by the ECJ.

Despite all evolution in its scope and interpretation, however, the definition of citizenship remains linked, conditionally, with such economic considerations as the acquisition of work in the country (member state) of residence (Kaidatzis 2005). At a time of galloping and massive redundancies, and when employment becomes more and more precarious and ever more casualised, this condition is very damaging. According to its logic, citizens from say France are reduced to a position of denizens in say Denmark unless they are employed. Here again we are faced with the original constraints of the founding treaties, which never cease to stipulate in support of the economistic and against the political approaches. Hence, the 'fundamental rights and citizenship of the Union' are reincorporated in the text of the 'Treaty Establishing a Constitution for Europe' – despite some minor improvements – in this constrained form.[6]

This development reflects broader encroachments on the notion of citizenship as incorporating human, civil and social rights, which has become established during the course of the twentieth century. Pressures

---

[6] 'Treaty Establishing a Constitution for Europe', title II, Articles I-9 & I-10 respectively, European Communities, 2005: 19, Luxembourg: Office for Official Publications

in this direction take the shape of both official and unofficial, not to say hidden, agendas. Keith Fauks, in his article 'What Has Happened to Citizenship?' (1994),[7] explores such re-definitional exercises and the new meanings of 'citizenship', which seek to dissociate it from social rights and attach it to the notion of consumers' rights, particularly in the UK under the government of John Major. Such trends reflects tha fact that global sub-contracting, the production-lines of the 'global factory' etc. resulted in the effective globalisation of labour markets, challenging "prevailing definitions of national citizenship, culture and tradition" (Mazower 1998: 405).

At the EU level, such an exercise towards redefining this constitutive concept, by emptying it of its original, time-honoured and universally accepted content, demonstrates an attempt to make 'citizenship' suit the Treaty of the European Community, rather than making the Treaty correspond to an accepted idea of citizenship.

The need to clarify what form and content European citizenship could take is a top priority issue. This requires envisaging and accommodating the dual aspect of the European condition. Such a citizenship should then simultaneously encompass the generic European aspect along with the different national affiliations. In order for Europe to transcend its definition as an exclusively economic entity, the negotiation of a common political identity is a *sine qua non*. But this can never obtain outside a common symbolic and communicative sphere. This process requires addressing the issue of citizenship and its definition beyond monisms, unilateralisms, ambiguities and oscillations. Certainly European citizenship cannot be conceived of simply in terms of a formal status with a set of

---

[7] Consider also, in this regard, the more general tendency towards changing legal provisions and regulations via the path of redefinitions. Sometimes this path takes the form of new jurisprudence on old provisions. Article 10 of ECHR is a case in point. Another case of socio-political deterioration promoted through semantics or re-definitions is the concept of 'full employment' or 'employed'. This concept has undergone serial redefinitions so as to fit 'realities' in the labour market where redundancies are on the daily agenda (Kaitatzi-Whitlock 2000a). Another conceptual distortion can be traced in the Commission's term *e-government*, by which is actually meant access to bureaucracy.

nominal rights attached to it. It must entail identifying with a set of common political values and principles, which are constitutive of modern democracy and comprehensive of the European specificity.

However, as has just been observed, the conception of European citizenship that was adopted made citizenship conditional precisely on economic prerequisites. Furthermore, it was not attached to any new proactive and creative or formative civic functions and other vital institutions, such as institutions that would guarantee political communication functions commensurate with the Union. Thus, European leaders proclaimed EU citizenship, but, as usual, relegated the implicit and corresponding political communication tasks to national media, which, for their part, are reluctant to assume such tasks.

In this light, certain writers argue that the absence of both European political parties and of a developed system of communications media is adequate evidence that the democratic deficit cannot be resolved just by developing legal instruments such as a constitution (Grimm 1997). Indeed, such writers argue that to perceive of a "European demos would require a fully developed European-wide media system transcending the borders of national media and supported by the establishment of a *lingua franca*..." (Ward 2004: 21).

The issue of a common language is of course always one of the problems of the first order; however, it is not insurmountable. If we accept this view, we would have to disregard the operation of the EP, the year-long operation of Europa TV and that of Euronews, all of which, despite their limitations and their costs, represent successful experiments in multilingualism. Such a restrictive approach implies also that multi-lingual states such as Switzerland are not viable, which of course is not the case. In addition, modern technological advances facilitate 'simulcasting' in both a *lingua franca* and the national languages. Even though linguistic diversity inevitably makes communication difficult, this is not incompatible with European reality.

Sceptics about the potentiality of a veritable and functional European polity stress that in Europe there exist several *demoi*, not just one *demos*, and that a proper political union can never come into being. Weiler, among others, argues that the multiplicity of languages and cultures makes the invocation of a classical concept such as 'citizenship' in the discourse on European integration problematic, if not redundant. He reasons that, since the Treaty of the European Community set out to "lay the foundations of an ever closer union among the peoples of Europe" (Weiler 1997: 498), Europe consists of 'Demoi' rather than of one unified 'demos'. Consequently, "if there is no demos, there can be no democracy" (ibid: 502). In a more proactive and forward-looking, if not quite optimistic, approach one can take the existing situation as the starting point and examine what is feasible. "So, given the absence of or the incomplete nature of the European *demos*, how would it be possible for the EU to come closer to its citizens?" asks Chryssochoou only to reply that the debate of the last decade has brought to the fore the claim "to go beyond the condition of republics to a condition of the republic." (Chryssochoou, 2005: 88). He argues that the main objective here is the creation of an autonomous and self-reliant corpus of citizens whose members will be in a position to make their democratic demands at the level of the Union (ibid). He advances the view that the EU needs to create horizontal ties among the partial *demoi*. This in fact emerges as a precondition for the achievement of a higher level of the social legitimation (ibid: 86) the Union is in dire need of. This gives a pro-political view that millions of European citizens must enjoy the possibility of influencing the politics and the policies of the central political system.

The central point of the 'pessimistic rationale' is that, as things stand, "the EU is not democracy-capable because such a capability would require a *community of communication*, of experience and of memory (Zweifel 2002: 13, emphasis added). One can question the validity of this view on at least two grounds, one of which – the practically proven possibility of multilingualism – was just mentioned above. But acceptance of these evaluations, in fact, raises more severe logical and political problems. For what *demos* would accept that important political issues be decided at a level it has neither adequate information about nor control over? Would such an EU member state be *democracy-capable*? To accept the existing decision-making dualism and concurrently to defend a uniquely national citizenship is to accept the most severe form of *depoliticization* in contemporary Europe.[8] Between these two positions, the normative but more proactive approach of Chryssochoou, who encompasses associationist and republicanist[9] theoretical propositions, presents a potential *vade mecum* of how the EU might find a way out of its current impasse. The important element of this approach is that it considers the establishment of a *European public space* as indispensible. It also presupposes the reinforcement of the institutional capacity of citizens to actively implicate themselves in the democratic participatory role of claiming and influencing the entire integration process. Having said this, the current imbalance of power between economic and poltical agency in the regional and the global terrains remains the crucial hurdle that must be overcome.

A Framework for Depoliticization

In an attempt at interpreting these peculiar phenomena, it is perhaps useful to explore the theoretical and normative bases for an alternative relation between polity and communication within and at the EU level. Projecting common EU affairs in a unitary and universally-accessible public domain is crucial because, like it or not, Brussels is the decision-making centre for the entire Union. It is not merely the fact that decision-making in Brussels is under-mediatised (see Chapter 8). Nationally-centred

---

[8] Chantal Mouffe refers to citizens on the left who are suspicious of European Integration as they feel that the nation-state is the remaining necessary space for "the exercise of *democratic citizenship* which is put in jeopardy by European institutions. They see the European project as the Trojan horse of neo-liberalism and as endangering the conquests realised by social democratic parties. I do not deny that there is some ground for their distrust of current European policies, but their mistake is to think that they could resist neo-liberal globalization better at the national level" (2005: 127-8).

[9] For a discussion of *civitas* in the republican ancient Greek and Roman spirit but also in more modern versions see Crick (2002: 24-25) in Chapter 2.

approaches to political communication often lead to a disorientation of citizens. The combined effect of insufficient journalistic coverage and debate and the biased presentations of Europolitics through a limited local perspective eventually contribute to a much worse failure: *depoliticization.*

Irrespective of pro- or anti-EU feelings, what takes place in Brussels cannot be ignored. One cannot confuse the demand for the operation of a European political communication platform with pro-Europeanism. What is at stake is democratic politics versus depoliticization. If politics wins as opposed to depoliticization, the question of pro-or anti-Europeanism is open to discussion and acceptance or rejection. A European, political communication platform is an indispensable tool for political knowledge and participation, whatever camp one is in. But precisely because it offers the chance to air and discuss the possible options this latter is more conducive to the European integration project. Hence it is a strategic imperative for the future of the European integration project. So, the absence of an imagined common European identity as well as the waning commitment to EU citizenship result precisely from this still-missing *European public sphere* and the deficit in European *political communication.*

Television is still the most central medium in establishing mass and common visibility, in commanding attraction, and in capturing and maintaining popular attention. It is still the best medium for inducing new interest, and it is the most pervasive and accessible of all media. What is even more promising is that through digital interactivity, and under certain preconditions, a pan-European television system could emerge as a broadly participatory medium (Bourdieu 1997, Kaitatzi-Whitlock 2004).

Both agency and structural conditions must combine and interplay in the creation and the open negotiation of a transnational community or civil society. This is a reciprocal, systemic-functional process where agency cannot exist outside the system and system cannot operate without agency. The situation faced by the EU is exactly that. It created no structure for a system of political communication to operate within and welcome citizens onboard. So citizens (agency) do not attend, do not reciprocate, and do not respond.

Closely related to the integration problem is the concept of 'responsiveness' of one government, organisation or group to the messages and perceived needs of individuals or of other political and social units. This is an essentially cybernetic concept, denoting the probability of 'favourable' or adequate response within a relevant time, where favourableness adequacy, and relevance can be defined in terms of empirical characteristics of the system under study. (Deutsch 1963: ix)

To put things in the cybernetic terms of Karl Deutsch, the EU lacks the 'nerves of government'. It neither communicates its affairs to the agency which is coterminous with its system, which is to say the European citizenry, nor possesses a regular and transparent mechanism through which to receive, learn about process and absorb the incoming feed-back from citizens. Citizens are deprived of a feed-back mechanism. Other than leading to political dysfunction this causes indignation and, particularly at times of Euro-elections, this dysfunction is amply manifest.

Two assumptions are made here, grounded in the experience of recent decades. The first assumption is that there are many individuals and civil groups across Europe who wish to develop transfrontier activities, exchanges and ties, but lack the requisite network structures either to involve themselves directly in European politics or to engage in building up and developing broader communication bridges between them.[10] The second assumption made refers to the enhanced possibilities conferred by the emerging medium of *interactive television*. Television is the best medium for these civilian groups with a common visibility and for bridging the gaps of distance and of socio-cultural differences. As is argued by Pierre

---

[10] These broadly include professionals, members of unions or federations, education professionals, academics and students, regional and local community politicians, members of transnational NGOs and members of civil society organisations such as the European Association for Viewers' Interests (EAVI), the Bureau of European Consumers (BEUC), or more broadly activists in transnational movements, active members of traditional or innovative party formations, travellers etc.

Bourdieu (1997: 8), Television, under such different premises, could be an instrument for certain functions of direct democracy. But as can be seen also in Chapters 4 and 8, EU policy-makers have not so far demonstrated any clear political will to forge a new political communication terrain on ordinary generalist issues, let alone over an interactive television channel.

Given the possibility that the operation of a pan-European transnational TV channel could encompass such needs, the question is why do we, as EU citizens, not dispose of such a medium? The synergy between television and the new media, notably the Internet – at least theoretically and technically – could re-generate and greatly enhance the role of television. It could transform it into a participatory electronic public sphere, a politically valuable resource, a common deliberative and communicative space. Such a live electronic forum could function, among other things, as a means for communicating horizontally, in a real and symbolic interactionist way. In describing the function of television reception, Thomson observes a satisfactory "quasi-interactionist" service (Thomson 1995: 84-85). In terms of political communication, however, merely 'quasi-interactionist' services are hardly adequate, because, as is insightfully put by Judith Lichtenberg, citizens do not only need to speak (freedom of expression in a void) they also need to be heard (Lichtenberg 1990). For this need to be heard as well as the need to hear other fellow citizens, in a polity the size of the EU, specific platforms for political dialogue are required, as both actual and symbolic interactionist debates are indispensable.

Robert Dahl could not have put the matter more explicitly: he holds that democracy requires free expression for a number of concrete reasons, and subsequently he succinctly details each of these justifying and simultaneously explanatory reasons:

> To begin with, freedom of expression is required in order for citizens to participate effectively in political life. How can citizens make their views known and persuade their fellow citizens and representatives to adopt them unless they can express themselves

freely about all matters bearing on the conduct of the government? And if they are to take the views of others into account, they must be able to hear what others have to say. Free expression means not just that you have a right to be heard. It also means that you have a right to hear what others have to say.

To acquire an enlightened understanding of possible government actions and policies also requires freedom of expression. To acquire civic competence citizens need opportunities to express their own views; learn from one another; engage in discussion and deliberation; read, hear, and question experts, political candidates, and persons whose judgments they trust; and learn in other ways that depend on freedom of expression.

Finally, without freedom of expression citizens would soon lose their capacity to influence the agenda of government decisions. Silent citizens may be perfect subjects for an authoritarian ruler; they would be a disaster for a democracy (Dahl 2000: 96-97).

However, all these aspects of civil freedom of expression can only be implemented and satisfied if and when a political communication system is available.

Much earlier, Jürgen Habermas (1989) had set out the immanent, liberal-democratic criteria by which we can identify and assess the existence and the role of a 'public sphere' and its agencies. The term *public sphere* that Habermas coined and made famous is coterminous with political communication. Any public sphere worthy of the name has to fulfil certain fundamental preconditions. It must be available, and above all accessible. It must be open to all citizens for interactive participation. For the electronic mass media, in the past analogous prerequisites were embodied in the principles of 'universal access' and of 'internal pluralism'. Such principles delineated the issue of scope, the principles and rules for political discussion and communicative action, allowing also, thereby, some scope for the influencing of the political agenda.

Among the pioneering defenders of the 'universal access' principle was the Hutchins Commission Report[11] on Freedom of the Press, set up in the mid-1940s in the USA to assess prevailing conditions and to issue guidelines for policy. Even though not unique in identifying the persistent access problem in the American media of the time, the Hutchins Commission, according to Stepp (1990: 187),

> proved more potent than other complainants in promoting a manifesto for reform. Its recommendations – in particular, its call that "the agencies of mass communication accept the responsibilities of common carriers of information and discussion" and provide the diversity, criticism, and interchange necessary for society to thrive – became the building blocks of a 'social responsibility' doctrine. (ibid).

What distinguishes that era from the present one is that we are now experiencing a post-social-responsibility condition.

Crystallizing the Habermasian thesis, McNair (1995: 21) summarises the five core functions of communications media in 'ideal-type' democratic societies. They must: (1) inform citizens of what is happening; (2) educate as to the significance of facts informed about; (3) provide a platform for public political discourse facilitating the formation of 'public opinion' and *political will formation*; (4) monitor and scrutinize the role of governments and of individuals in public office and (5) provide a forum for the advocacy of different political viewpoints. These key elements of a functional public sphere were embodied in the codes that prescribe the role of journalism. Fulfilling these prerequisite roles allows the media and journalism to approximate to the ideal type of 'public sphere' (Habermas 1989, McNair 1998).

---

[11] Robert Hutchins was the chancellor of the University of Chicago when he was assigned to lead a Commission of 13 members for the investigation of the issue of the Freedom of the Press. The Commission's report went straight to the issue of *access* on its first page. (Stepp 1990: 186).

A pan-European, televised, public space remains still a potential. If it existed, however, it could pursue at least two key functions: firstly, to disseminate political information of a broad scope, and secondly, to accommodate participation in the exchange of citizens' opinions and messages in public deliberation and dialogue. The Europa TV project, bold and important though it was, failed in providing for such participatory, political communication functions. However, in today's' rich, interactive environment one may hardly overlook it. Such an electronic forum could create the ground for overcoming feelings of alienation or suspicion amongst Europeans or for procuring solidarity. Indeed, in the national context, the first objective has been pursued through the *principle of universality* [12] in the classical public service broadcasting (psbs) and through the 'must carry' rules. The second objective, although technologically precluded in the past, is currently realizable due to revolutionary innovations in communication processes and systems.

In terms of power, the most significant political arena in Europe today is undoubtedly located at the supra-national level. Most policy areas are under the direct or indirect control of supra-national EU decision making institutions. Those that are under the exclusive prerogative of national governments are correspondingly very few. Notwithstanding the primacy and the centrality of the supra-national level in power-brokering, however, a corresponding political communication framework of the EU remains severely deficient and underdeveloped. The questions that arise in regard to this deficient framework concern the options available to EU citizens to actually receive and share information and to participate in trans-national and wide-reaching forums beyond frontiers: to participate, in effect, in the formation of their own union.

---

[12] Universal access or the principle of universality stands for the requirement that all citizens, irrespective of their class or geographical position, receive the same type of communications services. In this sense this is a qualification of the principle of equality and is a prerequisite for the equal value of every vote. See also Garnham (1990).

Since its inception, the project of European unification is at a most precarious moment in its history. Umberto Eco (2003) registers his worries, arguing that the EU "will either become European or it will disintegrate". Indeed, in view of the recent series of crises (over the war in Iraq (2003), the dismissive referenda on the constitutional convention (2005) and the impasse over the next budget period (2005)) his arguments could hardly have been more pertinent. In a nutshell he considers that the EU is currently "between renaissance and decline". Fernando Sabater (2003) remarks, similarly, that the "European states are today less united than ever".[13] Studying the tensions between the nation-state, on the one hand, and the EU, on the other, Habermas (1998/2003: 99) considers that it is only the symbolic construction of "people" which "transformed the modern state into a national state". This implies that just as the national unification processes of the 19th century contributed to the formation of nation-states, today, appropriate and corresponding symbolic constructs can assist the construction of a unitary Europe, a continental union with cohesion and a common political and cultural identity.

National Media: Agencies of Europeanization?

In his essay the 'Post-national Constellation' (1998/2003: 139-142), Habermas argues that such a project as the building of a union in Europe is feasible under certain conditions. In his view, the present challenge facing the EU has crystallized into two major priorities: first, to impose re-distributional obligations on (the stronger) market forces, and secondly, to generate a new collective identity beyond frontiers and the limits of nationhood.[14] In regard to the second challenge, he suggests that such

---

[13] Articles by Umberto Eco and by Fernando Sabater, amongst others, were originally published in *La Republica* and in *El Pais* respectively, after Jürgen Habermas's call to European intellectuals to write about the future of Europe. I have used the translated versions published in the Greek press.

[14] The same arguments are updated and refined in one of Habermas's more recent articles· "Why Europe needs a Constitution", where he states· "National consciousness

34

political desiderata can only be brought about on the initiative of civil society or through the communications media (Habermas 2003: 139-142). However, both of these Habermasian conditions are failing today. The first failure is due to the growth of unbridled, globally-oriented, neo-liberal market forces that will not succumb to political demands. The globalization of "financial markets make it increasingly difficult for nation-states to preserve autonomy of action, yet markets – as a series of panics and crashes demonstrates – generate their own irrationalities and social tensions" (Mazower 1998: 405). Political power is moreover either taken over by entrepreneurs, the example of Berlusconi is the most striking but it is far from unique, or they are so divided that they are effectively knocked out vis-à-vis such forces as UNICE (Union National des Industries de la Communauté Européenne) and the global capitalists more broadly.

The second Habermasian condition is clearly related to the lack of a common communications space in Europe in the first place. As is amply demonstrated in Chapter 8, national media staunchly refuse to fulfil their elementary obligations to fairly represent current, public affairs and thereby to adequately 'cover' the 'topic of the EU'. Worse still, not only do national media fail to provide that primary kind of information needed, but they even undermine EU institutions and distort EU developments. Moreover, this applies not only in certain anti-EU countries (e.g. the UK), but even in such 'core EU countries' as Germany. As for the limits of the role of any civil society, it is beyond dispute that it also is predicated on adequate media coverage for its projection, visibility and its feed-back

---

emerged as much from the mass communication of formally educated readers as from the mobilization of enfranchised voters and drafted soldiers. It has been shaped as much by the intellectual construction of national histories as by the discourse of competing parties, struggling for political power" (2001: 16). He further argues that the adoption of a Constitution by the EU can function as a "unique opportunity of transnational communication, with the potential for a self-fulfilling prophecy" (ibid). However, as the course of events has shown, notably with the two recent (2005) referenda in France and in the Netherlands, the issue of the common constitution as handled by EU leaders has met with a rejection. In addfition, the fact remains that until recently most Europeans ignored its preliminary adoption on the 29th October 2004 in Rome.

with society. The existence and the welfare of civil society are conditional on the existence of independent and accessible political communications media. More to the point, for civil society activists to develop a significant role in the public affairs of the EU, the existence of *dedicated media* is indispensable. In these circumstances, for Habermas to argue this case is, to say the least, utopian.

In a more recent article, 'Why Europe Needs a Constitution' (2001: 16), Habermas sets out even more categorically the sufficient preconditions for "identity formation beyond national boundaries". These comprise "the emergence of a European civil society; the construction of a Europe-wide public sphere, and the forming of a political culture that can be shared by all European citizens". One can raise the obvious questions: are the EU communications policies of the last twenty years conducive towards or relevant to any of these preconditions? This book demonstrates that the EU's communications policies have thus far fought against and effectively counteracted such preconditions, and certainly that they frustrate the Union's declared goals of political integration.

Habermas explicitly mentions and anticipates a 'Europe-wide public sphere', yet he does not conceive of it in the sense that I propose here: i.e. of supra-national (non-national) media of dedicated and independent, pan-European channels. Instead, he considers that the existing, nationally-entrenched media could promulgate a sort of inter-penetration and a flow of exchange of views on common topical issues. This, however, seems an utterly unrealistic and insufficient media basis for the stakes involved in moulding and solidifying European identity.

Existing national media, some of which are also broadcasting globally, have not, so far, taken such initiatives of their own free will. Quite the opposite. Neither are they likely to, as, in their own self-perception, they see their role as "to sustain cultural diversity, *national citizenship*, language, culture and identity" (EBU 2002: 3, emphasis added). In addition, public service broadcasting channels (psbs) are generally on the retreat, despite their constitutional promotion in the Treaty of Amsterdam (1997). They are on the defensive vis-à-vis commercial channels and face a complex set of both identity and viability crises (Papathanassopoulos 2002 & 2005: 200-1). In an era of post-social responsibility, psbs, indeed, belong to the rear-guard of an *ancien régime* (Nieminen 2000: 131) with horizons that rarely extend beyond the boundaries of their country of origin. They cannot cater for needs that supersede the national definition.

As for national commercial operators, they could not be further removed from the goals envisaged by Habermas (2001). Due to an extremely accentuated and internationalised competition, they cannot be bothered with objectives like those suggested. In fact, they are far more preoccupied with their survival and prevailing strategies in a hostile environment. Hence, these operators often perceive such objectives as directly counterproductive, or even antagonistic, since Euro-politics does not rate highly as 'infotainment'. Such channels, by definition, operate under the constraints of mass-audience ratings (Kaitatzi-Whitlock 2004). This is why they would most probably react strongly against any demand to comply with such objectives, should EU leaders impose relevant 'must carry rules'. And anyway, the imposition of 'must carry rules' would presuppose a balance of power between political and economic elites, which does not exist at this moment.

The Stifling of Citizens' Communicative Needs

Decision-making at the EU level has brought major changes to the lives of Europeans and continues to do so. The ensemble of the EU decision and supra-governmental institutions themselves are not, however, readily exposed or vetted. They are not made accountable to EU citizens nor are they adequately brought into focus by existing media. *Accountability* itself is a derivative of ample and free media coverage and pertinent policy scrutiny. This lack of accountability is exacerbated by the very low priority given to European affairs and Euro-politics especially by commercial media. Politics in general is downplayed and EU-level high politics in particular, as they seem complex, 'dull', distant and unconnected to everyday life, and therefore unattractive. Immediacy is said to be a key criterion for 'saleable' news. Commercial channels, which have to sell viewer packages to advertisers, cannot risk including news about the intricate and distant concerns of the EU. Thus, they are either filtered out or stripped of their significance. Meanwhile, citizens are deprived of the power which would accrue from this knowledge. Thus, 'European citizenship' is reduced to just a rhetorical invocation.

But, just being informed is not enough. EU citizens also need to express their opinions just as they need the concrete means of implementing and fulfilling their active, information and 'communication rights'. These needs and the corresponding objectives, although today technically achievable and abundant, are frustrated politically. As is shown in Chapters 3 and 4, which deal with the revisions of the TWF Directive, no measures were proposed to cater for such needs. Hence, citizens are deprived of realizable possibilities of an interactive and pan-European public sphere. Members of civil society in the EU are still awaiting the regular possibilities to express themselves and also to establish and develop a dialogue amongst themselves, across borders and between countries. They require channels to participate in crucial debates.[15] Without such real opportunities for participation, citizens will, 'naturally', turn their backs upon a mechanism that operates under false pretences, with promises and rhetoric: a system which does not include them, involve them or respond to their needs.

The direct effect of this type of *mediatic deficit* is that citizens withdraw from politics and Euro-politics, thereby becoming more passive, more divided, less demanding and more easily duped. Meanwhile, bias accrues from the sheer partiality of news coverage. The habitual national or local prism that is usually preferred 'inevitably' continues to frame 'us' against 'them', the other nationals of the EU.[16] It is therefore crucial to identify

---

[15] See the recent pan-European survey, 'Broadcasting and Citizens', Baldi 2004, (ed.), based on the research study 'Citizens First', conducted by EACTV-Latimer and the now renamed the European Association for Viewers' Interests.

[16] See Schattschneider's discussion of 'the mobilisation of bias' (1960).

and highlight that such partial coverage, inevitably, generates a 'naturalised' partisan and therefore divisive approach. Such one-sidedness can hardly be tolerated by Europeanists or any benevolent critic who implicitly or explicitly takes into account the *common European interest*. [17]

Notwithstanding the lack of a pan-European outlook, one of the central and recurring rationales for justifying divisive policy options within the EU framework is the notion of *cultural diversity* [18] which is particularly notable in matters of media and cultural policies. This reflects the obsession of member-states with controlling symbolic, media and cultural affairs primarily at the national level. *Diversity* is a value *per se* but, in an entity that is explicitly and voluntarily seeking integration this can be not only exaggerated, but also falsely invoked.[19] Moreover, the greater threat to diversity does not come from within the Union.[20] Extreme emphasis on diversity in the endo-European context may well become a trap, as we are no longer just nationals of our closed nation-states and bearers of our idiosyncratic cultures. We share a common cultural heritage,[21] for example, a common constitutional tradition across the continent. Denial of this fact through any type of nationalistic introversion hardly with stands scrutiny.

This obsession, may indeed have a boomerang effect on the European integration process as, logically, strong communities cannot arise out of a Babel of extreme diversities or discrepancies. In other words, apart from a measured diversity we also need common understanding and a new

---

[17] Even though a contestable and a contested term, the notion of *'public'* or *'common interest'* or *'general interest'* – like the notion of public good – is implicit in any concept or practice of public policy production. See Apter (1977: 526-7). See also Stiglitz (2002).

[18] See for example the EP Report on Cultural Industries (2002/2127 (INI)), (EP 2002: 14/14).

[19] See Helman Heikki, 2001.

[20] Diversity of origin of TV, fiction programming has actually vanished mainly due to the near total domination of Hollywood contents.

[21] Over time, the reality has emerged that "Europe discovers that beyond the differences of its tongues and customs, its people partake of a common culture...Europe is becoming conscious of the existence of a European identity" (Berstein & Milza 1990).

'common' sense. So, given the urgent need for common trans-cultural and trans-linguistic political *fora* for the European civil society, the discourse of unconditional diversity is in fact undermining the process of community building.

Thus, if excessive diversity counteracts *Europeanism* then perhaps the slogan of diversity, in the European context, embodies an Anti-European strategy. The slogan 'unity in diversity' risks becoming a rhetorical ploy, an empty signifier. The preoccupation with diversity is currently strong at a number of levels notably that of the UNESCO. This highlights legitimate fears that have arisen out of the uncontrollable movement towards globalisation of markets. However, cultural diversity, seen globally, is different from the equivalent value in the EU, as the latter represents a voluntary Union of states.

Distinguishing the Whole from the Parts

Today we can clearly distinguish the pan-European level from the part-European levels, i.e. the national, regional-linguistic or local areas. We are at a stage where about 80%[22] of the legislation and decisions that shape our public and private lives originate in Brussels. Meanwhile, considerable financial resources, which are drawn from EU citizens' taxes,[23] are allocated at this supra-national level. Legislative measures once adopted at this level are usually transferred into the internal national legal systems often without due or extensive discussion. As EU legislation takes precedence over national legislation, it is not negotiated or exhaustively

---

[22] Kenneth Ducatel, Member of Cabinet, DG Information, Society and Media, interview with the author 28-11-2005. EU prerogatives for decision- and policy-making are high. These correspond to 70 to 80% of the national legislation that originates at the supra-national level. For instance, over 70% of Greek legislation derives from Brussels (Stangos 2004). This rate is higher for member states participating in the Euro-zone, the 'core' counties of the European integration.

[23] In 2005 the budget of the EU was 115.956 billion Euros, only 1% of the budgets of the 25 member states combined (www.Europa.eu.int/comm/budget/budget/_detail/index_en.htm).

debated at the national level. Policies are not examined thoroughly or discussed in the way they were in the legislating procedures of national parliaments, which are closer to citizens and more open to scrutiny and hence also to political dispute.[24]

Thus, at the EU level of decision making, we have no pertinent or adequate media coverage, while at the level of the final transfer and application of legislation (national), issues arrive 'ready made', beyond any contention and political controversy. Here, then, we are faced not only with discrepancies in the scope of politics between the two poles and levels, of EU and nation-state, but, effectively, with the structural depoliticization of political affairs.

It is worth remembering also that at the EU level, it is the Commission that plays the greatest role in drafting and shaping legislative measures, even though these are of course subsequently discussed and adopted by the European Parliament (EP) and the Council. This insulates real power politics from publicity and affects civil society negatively, as it diminishes its actual role in EU politics: constituent members are no longer able to follow or monitor the policy process, let alone intervene in it. So, what arises is a situation of formidable EU power without the corresponding accountability.

Consequently, this peculiar political structure, from which a corresponding media system is missing, is fundamentally incomplete, as this actively contributes to the alienation of European citizens and to excluding them from the options for direct involvement in Euro-politics. The damage is further accentuated by the fact that national media cover pan-European issues with a national bias. Thus, the EU emerges as a peculiar political entity and an actor, who is at once a very crucial power broker and at the same time also a system whose operations in the present continuous tense, remain outside monitoring and beyond the light of

---

[24] Related to this problem Laffan (1999) remarks the constant challenge facing the national political systems because they encounter the need to adapt to a normative and strategic environment which evades their overall control. (in Chryssochoou 2005: 69). MEXRI.

publicity. In day to day media coverage EU governmental institutions appear as the peculiar *political other*, an entity that enters into our attention span for short 'moments', particularly in 'snaps' about spicy intergovernmental fights at notorious Council meetings or summits. These are the best moments of the EU's momentarily heightened publicity.

Reasons Accounting for the Deficit in Political Communication

The multi-layered *media deficit* can be attributed to a number of sub-parameters. First, there is no unitary elaboration of a minimum, common, European thematology (media agenda) that concerns all Europeans, irrespective of nationality. As a result, most of the significant 'European issues' do not command adequate or appropriate media coverage for presentation, analysis and debate. Secondly, national media do not care to reflect and 'reproduce' news or significant commentary presented in the media of other member states, thereby initiating a very useful *interpenetration* of national media. Such a practice of a discursive *rapprochement* and of taking into consideration the views of other national citizens would contribute gradually to the recognition, understanding and to the acknowledgement of 'other fellow Europeans'. This resonates with the propositions of Habermas. However, such practice is not significantly developed. Thirdly, 'must carry rules', specifically in regard to 'a European contents thematology' have never been conceived of or put on the agenda in the context of the transfrontier media environment.[25] Fourthly, there is not single common Europe-wide network that provides information about European affairs in a unified fashion and that addresses such affairs also discursively, at a minimum, common level, perceptible by citizens throughout the Union. Thus, strictly speaking, the *principle of universality* is

---

[25] As shall be analysed in Chapters 2, 3 and 4 on the Television Without Frontiers framework Directive and its subsequent revisions, this never became a policy consideration in a Europe in the making.

not applicable on any single political issue, even the most central or the most vital, across the EU. Given this context, it is evident that national media are not solely responsible for this crucial default.

The institutions of the Union also compound this structural failure in provision of minimum, common information and communication in their own ways. Due to labyrinthine, dispersed, and occasionally even secretive, policy processes at the Community level, the relevant information packages addressing pan-European audiences are quite small. Accredited journalists routinely have access to information packages that are ready-made and supplied by the appropriate EU bureaucracy services. Problems of exclusion from the domain of information exchange more generally may be serious within the EU framework and are not discussed adequately at either of the two levels. The work of the Council of Ministers especially is fraught with too much secrecy, thereby manifesting a severe lack of transparency (Sbragia 1992, Zweifel 2002). This refers often to internal disagreements, not only between different governments, but also between EC institutions, notably members of the Commission and ministers: "Much of this interaction goes on within meetings of the Council of ministers from which external observers are specifically excluded" (Smith 2004: 6). The European Ombudsman, Nikiphoros Diamantouros, had to intervene in November 2004, in order to make the deliberations of the Council more accessible to EU citizens. This very effort to counteract problems of transparency and to guarantee 'rights to information', more than anything, else is a proof of this mounting problem.

Another indication of a lack of transparency can be observed in the case of a pan-European Eurostat survey which established that 95% of European citizens, in January 2005, attributed the enormous rise in the prices of daily consumer goods to the adoption of the Euro currency. It was revealed that Commission officials tried to conceal this particular survey finding, which was discovered accidentally and subsequently leaked to the press (*Eleftherotypia*, 14/01/2005). Thus, transparency and comprehensive information about common affairs and opinion are occasionally undermined by European institutions themselves. Moreover, the recent decision by the Commission to announce its regular calls for participation in funded programmes exclusively via the Internet is yet another case in point. This change, in fact, accentuates the digital gap and an already existing problem of unhindered universal access to significant information (Manousaki 2004), as active information mining is still the skill of a technologically and mediatically literate minority.

The combined effects of all these instances and factors contribute to the notorious *democratic deficit*. However, the most severe components of this consist of the accountability and the legitimacy deficits (Habermas 2001: 14; Zweifel 2002: 11-15, Kaitatzi-Whitlock 1996: 218). Significantly though, both accountability and legitimacy boil down to the deficit in political communication.

Media Deficit and Political Defeat: the Vicious Circle

The lack of common European public fora constitutes a deficient European, political-communication system that deprives citizens of common visibility, a platform for analysis, dialogue, understanding and the shared negotiation of their common concerns and problems. The low and steadily diminishing turnout in the last Euro-elections crystallizes a mutual disaffection between citizens and elites in the EU. The key to this disaffection is the absence of channels for direct, mutual and unhindered communication. But the paradox consists in the lack of common, European, public fora in an age of mediatic abundance and affluence in communication means and techniques. The deficit in dedicated media for a common, political communication in fact reveals something more significant: that not only Europeans but, primarily, their leaderships suffer from a severe identity crisis. There is overt confusion between claims to belong to Europe and actual, political behaviour sustaining it. The fact that abstention from elections was higher among the new, accession member states complicates the 'picture' even more. An *'imagined common European identity'* and a *'common European vision'* are more remarkably absent in those countries, as was demonstrated, critically, in the Euro-split over the Iraq war.

This has some overt and some covert causes and certainly also forebodes serious implications. Behind the absence of a common, European, public space and an entrenched segmentalisation of public spaces, lurk, on the one hand, national egoisms or techno-nationalist economic interests and, on the other, hegemonic globalising forces. The cause for absenteeism in the June 2004 Euro-elections is, at least in part, a result of this. What is more, there are no media with a sufficiently broad reach to counteract such outcomes in a common, transparent, multilateral and effective way, by civil society, by willing elite groups or by both. Undoubtedly, unless a common European public space is set up, also resolving *de facto* the problem of the common language, European citizenship will continue to remain a rhetorical referent, an 'empty signifier', devoid of any real meaning for the inhabitants of Europe, or any attraction and recognizable citizen prerogatives.

In Democracy, Procedure is Essence

In democracy, *procedure* constitutes the *essence* of day–to-day politics. One of the key and indispensable democratic *procedures* is to constantly inform people and constantly allow and invite citizens themselves to communicate their views and preferences about politics (Habermas, 1989, Lichtenberg, 1990: 110, Keane 1991: 176). The concept and the practice of dialogue among citizens are a *sine qua non* component of political communication, where the possibility of expressing ideas, disagreements or dissident views is guaranteed (Metaxas, 1979, McNair 1998).

Consequently, in democracies, to allow the reasonable formation of political will, to listen to and to consider the opinion of the people is not an option. It is mandatory. European leaders, notably the ministerial and the European Councils, and the EU policy-making machinery have so far omitted entirely this crucial, democratic function: Eurocrats and nation-state leaders, each for different reasons, have acted in concert to establish this European-scale vacuum. This vacuum and the absence of the most fundamental democratic processes are now threatening to suffocate the European Union.

In this chapter I have shown that in spite of the adoption of Euro-citizenship in the 1990s, the EU completely lacks a framework for European political communication. I furthermore argued that this lack is a constitutive element of the democratic deficit that plagues the EU. Moreover, I have argued that there is a dialectical relation among three fundamental and intrinsically linked elements which form a coherent triangle:

(A) Policy-making, specifically in the field of communications.

(B) Political communication in democratic politics, and

(C) Politics, more generally and democratic politics more specifically, as the source and means of state power.

I have looked into the relations between these three interlinked elements, starting from element (B) of my triangle, the lack in political communication at the EU level. I argue that (B) is negative and – more precisely – it is lacking because element (A) was originally designed so as to preclude (B). I shall go on to argue that since the relation between (A) and (B) is negative, then, inevitably both impact negatively also on element (C), politics as such.

The fact that these three elements are intrinsically linked to one another entails that we must necessarily examine this triangular nexus together and these pivotal elements in successive couples. Therefore, in the following chapter I shall go back to the origins of EU involvement in the field of communications policy, in order to trace the point in time and the specific link of transmutation of element (A) and to identify the reasons for this presumed, negative relation between elements (A) and (B) and (C).

Thus, along with the thesis that communications policy-making is the factor through which political communication, politics and the political are organised, I need also to clarify the *double specificity* of communications, as such, and in the concrete constellation of the *sui generis* supra-national actor under examination. It is indispensable that each type of polity identifies its particular specificities and that it acts upon them accordingly when constructing its fundamental structure. Hence, before embarking on the analysis of the crucial transmutation that marked the turning point in national and European politics, I need to clarify specifically the proper peculiarities both of the media sector *per se* and of the policy actor under examination. In combination, these twin peculiarities produce a *double division*, which unless taken into consider-ation result in a disastrous double split. Communication is a constitutive and strategic resource: the means of forming and maintaining community, polity and politics (Wiener 1949, Deutsch 1963, Morin 2001). Communication is a precondition in the participation in political affairs.[26] But it is also in part economic (professional or entrepreneurial) in nature, which gives it double nature: both political and economic.

These two specificities are in tension, indeed in conflict, a conflict which came to a head, notably in the post-satellite (1960) and the digital era (especially after 1969), when it became technologically possible to convert communications media into cash-cows which exploited for enormous profits on the global market. The advent of global media that could convert national political and cultural media into global profit makers created a mediatic duality that political orders everywhere have had to try to resolve in the post-satellite era. It became imperative for policy makers to clarify and to establish the internal hierarchy between these two competing natures of communication, and not allow the economic to overwhelm the political. This can be achieved via structural measures and effective regulatory checks and balances.

---

[26] According to Aristotle's 'Politics' so praiseworthy and indispensable was the participation of citizens in town-meetings that they received "a fee which puts a premium on attendance by the poor" Sabine & Thorson, 1973: 114).

The second duality arises from the very nature of the EU itself, which is an original, indeed unique, two-tier political constellation comprising, first, the national level (25 member states) and, secondly, the supranational EU level in Brussels and Strasbourg. This can be schematised as follows:

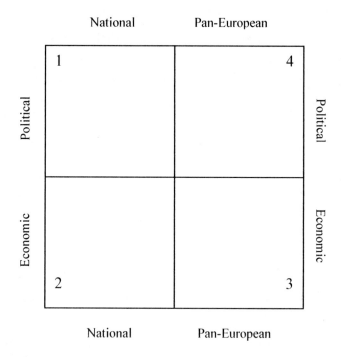

As will be shown in the analysis of EU communications policy-making, in attempting to Europeanize communications there was an important omission. Instead of preserving a fair balance between all four of these elements (the political, economic, national and supranational), Eurocrats focused only on economic aspects and thereby effectively handed over the communications domain to private control and commercial exploitation.

The politically strategic importance of communications means that its economic nature must be acknowledged, but kept under close observation and control. The economic cannot be allowed to suffocate the political.

But rather than maintaining the vital political communication function of the media at both the pan-European and the national levels, in the 1980s European politicians of both conservative and socialist parties in fact condemned political communication to near extinction and deprived themselves of even the most elementary visibility into the bargain.

Chapter 2

THE TELEVISION WITHOUT FRONTIERS DIRECTIVE
– THE 'FLAGSHIP OF THE SINGLE MARKET'

In the first chapter I argued that the deficit in a pan-European media system, and more concretely, the lack of a common framework for political and civic communication in the EU is a constitutive part of the democratic deficit of the EU. In this chapter I am going to explore how it became possible that this deficit arose, especially in regard to the supranational level, after the EC took charge of EC-wide, media policy. Over the last fifteen years we have experienced the consequences of the community's involvement in this domain. Paradoxically, and contrary to widespread expectations cultivated in the 1980s, the capture of this policy-making prerogative by the Community supra-state has not led to the creation of a pan-European communication framework for Europeans. The question is: why this is so.

On the basis of analysis and classifications in the first chapter I tried to clarify that in order to establish a sound, working, political-communication framework in Europe it is imperative first that both natures of communication (political and economic) operate at both levels of the political constellation (national and supra-national/pan-European), and second that the political nature of communication takes precedence and is supreme over the economic nature.

In this chapter I shall examine, in particular, the Green Paper on 'Television Without Frontiers' (GPTWF)[27] and I shall present and discuss its rationale, as this document was the true initiator of the European

---

[27] This Green Paper will be referred to as the Green Paper on TWF, the subsequent (1989) Directive as TWFD or TWF Directive.

communications policy in the audiovisual sector. The policy pursued was successful in that it accomplished its objectives. Yet it was concurrently politically destructive; in fact it became a veritable political trap, as it recognised only the economic nature and role of communication and effectively abolished the political nature and role for it, at both political levels. This Green Paper is at the source of all applicable policy in the audiovisual and the broader communications sector in Europe since 1989. It was grounded primarily on the relevant articles of the Treaty of the European Community (TEC),[28] and secondarily on the jurisprudence of the European Court of Justice (ECJ). The key role of the GP therefore requires particular attention and analytical 'unpacking'. I shall subsequently discuss the debate that followed the publication of this Green Paper and the Commission's first proposal for a Directive.

The actual Directive was adopted at a much later stage, in 1989, when a compromise between member states and between competing market and forces of civil society was successfully brought about. The Directive will not be discussed in its entirety, but will be evaluated with reference to its most catalytic and controversial provisions, notably in respect to the dual strategic shift: (a) from the political to the commercial control of the media and (b) from the national to the supra-national control of the policy agenda on communications media. Yet, as shall be documented in Chapter 8, the paradox is that although the control of communications policy (element (A) of my triangle) is in the purview of the supranational level, Brussels and Strasbourg are themselves effaced from media visibility, as reporting continues to be unilaterally nation-centred (Smith 2004, Brettschneider & Rettich 2005).

---

[28] Articles 59 §2 and 66 of the TEC provide for the freedom of movement of services within the Community. In this framework broadcast programmes are considered as 'services' i.e. commodities, for remuneration; hence the Commission was empowered to produce policies thereof. Articles 59 and 62 must be taken in conjunction with Articles 66 and 56, which refer to certain exceptions regarding public policy, public security and public health. The fact that this policy affects national sovereignty explains the 'minimum harmonisation' approach that was eventually agreed upon and which, as such, does not amount to a proper 'common policy'.

My aim is to explain how this key policy document and the subsequent framework directive itself laid the grounds for an exclusively market-led and market-driven system of communications in Europe, thereby transmuting the nature of it and curtailing the democratically, prerequisite, political nature of communication. I argue that the Directive that was finally adopted depoliticized public communications and supra-national public affairs, thereby contributing to the wider alienation of citizens from politics. The *sine qua non* of public, pan-European communication, element (B) of the triangle, was thus precluded.

The chapter will conclude by summarizing the findings that support the main thesis as laid out above. Additionally, it will be argued that this outcome was not only a defeat in purely political terms, but also in economic terms. The strategic shift of defining this sector purely in terms of economics, gave rise subsequently to a whole set of policies that have contributed to the weakening of the European audiovisual sector and thus to Europe's trade balance as a whole. In the end, a minority of European broadcasters, but particularly extra-European interests in both the hardware and software audiovisual industries, benefited from this process, which has thus contributed to the acceleration of global capital integration.

Setting the Premises for the Strategic Transmutation

Given the lack of political and cultural prerogatives of the Community and the urgent demand for policies in the area of communications, the Green Paper on TWF became the major catalyst in the broader, political and economic affairs of the European Community and in the audiovisual spheres of its then 12 member states. It forcefully advocated the need to tackle this sector from an *economic* angle, via the circumscribed framework of a contestable economistic approach, one which has nevertheless prevailed ever since. As Jacques Delors argued in good faith, "under the Treaty of the European Community, the EC does not have the means to impose a cultural policy. It will, therefore, have to tackle the problem from an economic point of view" (Jacques Delors quoted in Negrine & Papathanassopoulos 1990: 67).

The Green Paper on TWF was the matrix. It provided the discourse, the goals, the manner and the means for an EC-wide, strategic intervention into the pan-European, audiovisual sector. First, the economistic TEC framework was mobilised in conjunction with supportive ECJ jurisprudence on the interpretation of key TEC Articles. Secondly, internationally adopted principles with respect to freedom of information were invoked. Thirdly, the evocative power of 'integrationist ideology' and rhetoric was deployed quite heavily. Fourthly, the urgent need to develop a large, audiovisual, hardware, industrial policy was pertinently stressed with regard to new transfrontier media, such as satellites and cable. Concurrently, the neo-liberal rhetoric of the *external global danger* and the doctrine of the inevitability of price competition, as well as the urgent need for global competitiveness, were mobilised and strongly propagated.

In this atmosphere of neo-liberal hype and exhortation to imperative changes, in spite of the topicality and the sensitivity of the issue, the Green Paper did not properly elaborate on the *constitutional caveats* of the TEC regarding (1) civil rights, or (2) the need for political communication at EC and pan-European level, and (3) policy-making prerogatives and competences. In this way such structural, political prerequisites were allowed to slip off the agenda. This is particularly remarkable considering the fact that complaints about the democratic deficit were already then growing quite strong. Yet, the lack of these structural and political prerequisites was not deemed to be an obstacle or to become a policy priority. But if the Commission were to disregard issues of political communication element (B) what kind of communications policy was it actually pursuing?

In fact, the Green Paper on TWF was a precursor to the White Paper on the Single European Act and Market and reinforced an already prevailing economism. It is therefore not surprising that it was dubbed the 'flagship of the Single Market'[29]. It is noteworthy that it was drafted at the end phase of the outgoing 1984 Commission, whose president was Luxemburg's former Prime Minister Gaston Thorn, who throughout this period maintained – what turned out to be – a partisan relationship both with the Companie Luxembourgoise de Télédiffusion (CLT) and with ASTRA.[30] In this light, the negative integration theory became the key ground for the policy rationale of the Commission.

This meant that member states were asked to make concessions (a) of sovereignty, (b) of cultural self-determination and (c) of policy prerogatives on shaping the political sphere. These concessions were demanded in advance and only in the hope of promised, future, political and cultural measures and provisions for the political aspect of integration. Free-marketeers, by contrast, received their gains in advance without having to make any practical commitment to working towards political integration. As a corollary, the normally superordinate objectives of the national audiovisual and cultural orders soon came to seem subsidiary or even open to doubt. The naïveté of this approach became fully apparent after the GATS agreement of December 1993, during which the EC, under heavy pressure, in principle, abandoned its supposed commitment to the cultural importance of this sector, placing European cultural industries at the mercy of a global, competitive environment.

The European Parliament Strategy Backlash

The formal involvement of the Commission in audiovisual policy came in response to requests by the MEP R. Dury who tabled a motion for a

---

[29] The Single Market strategy is also referred to as The Single Market, SEM, SM and The Internal Market in official documents. I have mostly used The Internal Market in this text for the sake of simplicity.

[30] Gaston Thorn, significantly, later became the chairman of CLT. CLT was a founding member of the Association of Commercial Television (ACT). Both the Luxembourg governments and the CLT systematically promoted neo-liberal partisan policies aiming at a pan-European and later a trans-Atlantic and global market (Kaitatzi-Whitlock 1996).

resolution on television advertising in 1982, asking the Commission to pre-empt the cultural and social consequences of TV advertising. More concretely, this motion proposed stringent provisions equally applicable in all member states (EP 1982b). Acting from rather contrary motives, but in the same direction (in terms of intervening supra-nationally), another group of members of EP had later requested that a survey of existing national legislation on television advertising be carried out with a view to its harmonisation (EP 1982). Prior to that, in a 1979 resolution the EP had called attention to issues of misleading and unfair advertising (EP 1979).

The central thrust of the EP's position and call for the involvement of the EC in the field of communications policy was grounded on its belief in the essential role of political communication for community building. The Hahn Report of the EP argued that:

> Information is a decisive, perhaps the most decisive factor in European unification....European unification will only be achieved if Europeans want it. Europeans will want it if there is such a thing as a European identity. A European identity will only develop if Europeans are adequately informed. At present, information via the mass media is controlled at national level....Information and economics are closely interrelated – an obvious example being advertising – and consequently the involvement in European unification clearly adds a new dimension within the context of the treaties of Rome. (Hahn Report 1983: 7)

In effect the Hahn Report sought to transfer some media policy control from the national level (element (A)) and to bring some political communication role (element (B)) to the supra-national level. The problem was in the timing. This initiative took place at a premature moment, when no fully-fledged and constitutionally-supported political entity existed quite yet at the supra-state level. Those who supported it had a fine and, to the extent that they did not threaten all member-state control, a politically legitimate goal. They intended in fact to be constructive and fill in the EC's political communication gap. This required a supplementary change in the level of communications policy-making and this could only be safeguarded if prior political and constitutional guaranties were in place.

In response to the 1982 EP requests, and on the basis of the EP Hahn Resolution (EP 1982a), the DG X of the Commission produced an Interim Report in March 1983 entitled: 'Realities and Tendencies in European Television: Perspectives and Options'. That first report favoured a Europe-wide television channel as envisaged by the EP (Theiler 2001, Commission 1983). It also called for the building of European consciousness through the use of television as a forum for this objective (Sachpekidou 1990: 83-4, Theiler 2001). Moreover, it supported the European Broadcasting Union (EBU), which consists of national psbs. The 'Realities and Tendencies' Interim Report argued that satellite TV would have a fundamental impact on European culture and that, therefore, public policy choices should take advantage of this powerful unifying factor (Commission 1983). The Interim Report also warned of the danger that exogenous programming would inundate TV screens in Europe. Similarly, it warned that 'European identity and cultural industries would be damaged' (ibid: 33), unless measures were taken to forestall negative developments.

The Interim Report sought to exploit the 'empire-building' capacities which it identified in transfrontier satellite broadcasting. The implicit rationale was that this would free the flow of information and enhance trans-European cultural interpenetration. This policy was, moreover, expected to contribute to the strengthening of the then–nascent, satellite and cable, hardware industries, thus shaping 'European identity' without extensive deregulation.

But avoiding the unconditional commercialization of the audiovisual sector EC-wide would have presupposed, in any case, a prior revision of the TEC, so as to incorporate into it counterbalancing and binding political principles, as well as the appropriate legal bases and instruments to support those values. Such a project in itself presupposed necessarily a well-grounded, strong, political will as well as a consensus among the then 12 member states. But, as the thwarted Spinelli experiment for a European Union had just shown, neither precondition obtained.

For the history of the attempts to move forward a political union, it is quite significant that just four months before the submission of the Green Paper on TWF, the EP had adopted, with a broad majority, a draft Treaty for the Establishment of the European Union, formulated by the EP Committee on institutional affairs, under the chairmanship of member of EP Altiero Spinelli (Sachpekidou 1990: 75). However, this was a much too immature and over-ambitious a project, since no desire existed yet among the governments of the member states to that effect. Outside the EP there was no manifest will for a revision of the Treaties towards a political union.

From *Dirigisme* to Neo-liberalism

This debacle of the EP also impinged on the *dirigiste* sections of the Commission, which shared the same philosophy. The frustrated movement by the EP reflected negatively also on the prospects for the 'Realities and Tendencies' report. In view of this policy impasse in the *dirigiste* camp, Commission leaders undertook the drafting of a television policy, the Green Paper on Television Without Frontiers (GPTWF), which was now placed in the broader Internal Market framework. Its discourse was completely divergent, both from that proposed by the EP and from its predecessor, 'Realities and Tendencies', which was drafted by the *dirigiste* DG X of the Commission (Collins 1994: 50). Effectively, the only common element in the two documents was that both advocated pan-European handling of this policy area.

The Green Paper on TWF also made reference to the 'public interest' propositions of 'Realities and Tendencies', though those propositions were hardly compatible with its own proposal to liberalise the sector and to subject it to goals of broader economic exploitation. Nevertheless, this rhetoric and tactic succeeded in gaining political consent from the EP. Similarly, the Green Paper acknowledged the 'agenda setting' role of the EP, which was both welcome and reassuring to this politically still very weak body.[31] Even though it was the only elected institution at European level, the EP at that time lacked any significant decision-making prerogatives.

The harmonisation of television regulation thus got underway on the pretext of forestalling damage to the European industry from international competition. The free movement of services (including the commercial flow of information), being covered by the TEC and fervently canvassed by powerful commercial lobbies and political forces thus seemed unstoppable. But dislocating the audiovisual sector from the national basis threatened fundamental political and cultural safeguards and values. The device of minimum harmonisation was proposed as a substitute to 'secure' those values.

The only way to have handled this issue at a supra-national level, and respect both the political/cultural and the economic/commercial roles of the communications sectors in a balanced way, would have been to establish the necessary, constitutional, political system first, thereby guaranteeing all citizens' equal rights and freedoms at EC level before embarking on restructuring the framework of this sector. The system the followed was the exact opposite. The cultural and political roles, which could not be catered for under the economistic restrictions prevailing in the founding treaties, were thus excluded. Commercial, commodifying and democratically corrosive forces gained the upper hand.

---

[31] The role of the EP up until the Treaty of the European Union (TEU) at Maastricht was essentially limited to that of being a qualified consultative body. Both this and the Amsterdam Treaty (1997) considerably enhanced the policy-making prerogatives of the EP and augmented its competences. Apart from broadening and reinforcing its role in the legislative procedures, the EP has since acquired budgetary competences and may also monitor, control and approve of the Commission in terms of its composition and its handlings. Notwithstanding this empowerment of the EP, decision-making at the supra-national level is still largely controlled by the Commission and the Council.

The axioms of private rights and 'consumer sovereignty,' canvassed by such celebrities as Rupert Murdoch, prevailed even though such approaches are politically subversive. These rest on a private-choice view of public space, but as is pertinently pointed out "the logical terminus of rights-based freedom is the evacuation of [the] political" (Venturelli 1996: 121).

A split within the Commission took place in the first half of the 1980s which revealed politically divergent policy approaches and conflicting or hidden national agendas and interests. Collins (1994: 50-51) divides the Commission of that period into market-oriented DGs, such as DG III and DG IV, and *dirigiste* DGs, such as DG X and DG XIII. He implies, moreover, that while the former reflected British interests, the latter reflected the French political culture, national egoisms and national alliances and interests. DG X, for instance, advocated the opposite line of action to that pursued by the 'ultra-liberals' of DG III, but was completely sidelined during the preparation of the Green Paper on TWF. This split more broadly reflected the ideological battle between those seeking a balance of interests and neo-liberal privatization-seekers.

The Objectives of the TWF Green Paper

The stated objectives of the Green Paper on TWF were:

> [1] to demonstrate the importance of broadcasting for European integration and in particular, for the free democratic structure of the European Communities; [2] to illustrate the significance of the Treaty of the European Community for those responsible for producing, broadcasting and re-transmitting radio and television programmes and for those receiving such programmes. And [3]... to submit for public discussion the Commission's thinking on the approximation of certain aspects of member states' broadcasting

and copyright law before formal proposals are sent to the European Parliament and Council. (GPTWF: 1)

The first two objectives seem mutually exclusive. The first addresses viewers as citizens, while the second addresses them as consumers. Even if there were no conflicts between these two roles or attributes, to put them together like this is confusing. They should be clearly delineated and organised so as to function either in clearly separated zones of broadcasting, or in clearly distinct, but strongly regulated, types of TV channels: advertising-free or advertising-funded under limited com-petition. In this respect, the model of the British 'duopoly' could have served as a paradigm.

But there is an unresolved tension between these two initial objectives. The problem is that in advertising-funded channels, packages of viewers are treated both as consumers and as objects for sale to the advertised industry (Smythe 1977). In a commercially multi-channel environment with intense competition for the attention of viewers, the com-modification of the viewer (ibid) is intensified and the possibility of treating viewers as citizens almost precluded. Lowest common denominator, mass entertainment and infotainment serve to undermine political communication or a democratic political culture (Kaitatzi-Whitlock 2004).

To the extent that the EC did not manage to establish the importance of objective (1) neither the compatibility between objectives (1) and (2) in the ensuing policy process, and given the TEC framework, it followed that the second objective would prevail. Hence, the proclamation of this threefold purpose served merely to support the final proposition (3). This objective was designed essentially to legitimate EC intervention in this then 'virgin', yet fiercely coveted, area Community activity. The *ulterior goal* was the capture of this policy prerogative, to carry it to the supra-national level and finally put the communications sector under the exclusive control of market forces. The real objective was, thus, to re-set the agenda, according to the mould prescribed by the TEC and in an essentially different way to the one expressed in the previous Commission document 'Realities and Tendencies'.

On closer inspection, the first proposition, which launches the idea of European integration – via broadcasting policy – when compared to the second proposition, constitutes a mere 'vision' and a rhetorically 'sought after resource', as there is no legal or political basis for its pursuance (in the sense of an agreement or a commitment). Nevertheless, the ideology of continental integration commanded great rhetorical power, that is, it contained an ideological and sentimental charge which demanded commitment and had been warmly welcomed by Europhiles and Euro-federalists. By contrast, the second objective, well-grounded as it was in the TEC, was more secure.

Without minimal, constitutionally-guaranteed, citizens' rights at the EC level, the democratic rights theory (freedom of expression) enshrined in the first objective was inadequate. Consequently, the EC could not assume such responsibilities. The odd thing is that Green Paper drafters associate this civil and democratic freedom with the freedom of movement of commercial services, as guaranteed in the TEC (Articles 49, 50, 52, and 66)[32], and thereby succeeded in legitimising the whole project of intervening in this policy area. This tactic has been criticised as arbitrary, notably because it conflates two distinct categories (civil rights and economic freedoms) and was then used to advance "commercial rights" through the vehicle of individual democratic rights and freedoms.[33]

As a consequence, EC audiovisual, policy discourse was founded on three 'pillars'. First, the rhetorical, but legally and politically baseless 'striving' for European, cultural integration, "in particular for the free democratic structure of the European Community" (GPTWF: 1). This pillar is contested, because, at least at that stage, it belonged to the sphere of the imaginary. Secondly, it was founded on the inbuilt drive in the TEC

---

[32] These were ex Articles 59, 60, 62 and 66.

[33] Drawing on legal and constitutional jurisprudence Hoffmann-Riem, Zeri, Hesse and MEP K. Malangre argued against such a conflation of unequal categories, which also served to dichotomise the role of the media. See also Chapter 5 infra.

towards a common domestic market on a grand scale, free from tariff and non-tariff barriers, legally, ensuring the four basic freedoms of movement, including that of commercial services. Thirdly, it was predicated on the principle of freedom of (transborder) information flow, as enshrined in the ECHR. Remarkably, however, this was purposely but also arbitrarily paralleled and conflated with Articles 49 and 55 of the TEC, which dealt with the free movement of services and the derogations thereof respectively. This, then entailed that information was to be henceforth treated exclusively as a service, as determined in the TEC. Here, then, lies the crucial turning point in the internal hierarchy between the political and the economic role for communications, which is concurrently the internal hierarchy shift in the power between the political and the economic forces.

In the words of the then Commissioner Heinz Narjes, the purpose of the Green Paper on TWF was to examine the "significance of broadcasting for the progress of integration as a whole, and to demonstrate the relevance and application of the Treaty of the European Community to this field of activity". But most importantly, it aimed to limit "the efforts of those lawyers who might try to deny us any powers to act on it" (in Wedell 1985). Real objectives can be clearly distinguished from unrealistic ones if one classifies the objectives of the Green Paper into those which are legally and institutionally grounded and those which remain groundless. The first category belongs to realisable objectives, the second to the rhetorical. This clarifies the actual hierarchy of objectives, which also predetermined the winners and the losers of this crucial battle.

As a consequence, the premises and definitions of the TWF policy agenda were built into the circumscribing character of the TEC with its market-biased constraints. The key problem lay in the structure of the aspiring policy-maker which lacked commensurate means for some of the central stated objectives. Inevitably then, those objectives collapsed. Even if one accepts that these intentions were not simply rhetorical and were genuinely pursued by some policy agents (e.g. the EP), the outcomes of the policy process undoubtedly reveal the strength of that agency and of those 'objectives'.

Once the rhetorical objectives collapse, what remains are the real objectives. Taken in steps, these objectives were the following: first, to legitimate an EC (supra-national) intervention in this, politically, highly significant field. Secondly, to submit this field, which, at that time, presented extra-ordinary promises and potential for growth, to uniquely economic exploitation. Thirdly, to hand the sector over to the strongest commercial forces (globally fit national champions) for exploitation. The anticipated benefits were coveted by some significant, ,incumbent national-champion firms and certain new entrants in this growth sector, but also co-extensively by the advertising industry companies and those they advertise, thus placing the audiovisual sector at the service of the entire economy. As a corollary, the aim was to enlarge the size of the audiovisual distribution market by Europeanising it and by giving Euro-brands the possibility of greatly enhanced exposure. This was to provide new, totally unexploited ground to the advertising sector. As was pointed out, however, from an economic angle, establishment of a common market for broadcasting does have implications that go far beyond the broadcasting sphere (GPTWF: 37). In fact, these implications are the most severe, if not the most politically subversive:

> As an advertising medium, broadcasting organisations help to stimulate sales of goods and services in many branches of the economy. The cross-frontier broadcasting of advertising promotes cost savings and increase in efficiency. These economic aspects must not be overlooked, if from a cultural and social point of view, the role of broadcasting as a medium providing information, expression of opinion, education and entertainment is to be preserved. (GPTWF: 37)[34]

---

[34] "The Community takes the view – and rightly so – that broadcasting is an essential element in creating the single unified market in Europe.... At the moment, European broadcasting is a microcosm of the market fragmentation which we are now determined to remedy" (Cockfield 1986 9). Thus the most decisive argument for the Commission

Hence, in the rationale of the Green Paper, the essential prerequisite for the enjoyment of all the above-mentioned values was, inescapably, the commercialisation of the sector. The furnishing of this view in this way is of course reminiscent of plain propaganda. This implies that before the advent of commercialisation we lacked freedom of information. Dexterity, juggling between competing intentions and rhetoric served well both the implicit and the explicit purposes of the policy and the relative pacifying of opponents.

Freedom of Expression for the Highest Bidder

Efforts were made both in the policy discourse and in the broader debate to sell the good intentions and the benefits for all. The policy document was quite reassuring to those fearing the domination of commercial forces by stating that "[f]reedom of expression, however, cannot be the prerogative of the highest bidder..." (GPTWF: 3). Thus, it appeared that policy drafters sought to achieve two goals, both of which were deemed indispensable to the Internal Market: "to ensure that the circulation of broadcast signals and services... was not impeded in other member states and to harmonise Community broadcasting regulation so that competition between signals and services took place on fair and equal basis" (Collins 1994: 58). The essential objectives of the policy were to restructure the audiovisual sector via liberalisation and enlargement. This could only be accomplished by extending the freedom of movement and of commercial exploitation to cultural services. More importantly, however, the implicit strategic goal was the usurpation of the field of communications from politics and the subjection of it to the sole control of commercial and 'big capital' market forces.

---

was the enabling aspect of advertising and its beneficial impact on the (free market) economy (Commission 1984: 35-38).

The timing of the EC's intervention was determined by both external and internal factors, notably the need to boost new economic activity in a recession-stricken EC, through the opportunities offered by the advent of new technical outlets (cable & satellite). Thus, the role assigned to transfrontier broadcasting in the European, integration process fitted in with those industrial imperatives. The Green Paper on TWF restricted the scope of its proposals, allegedly because the TEC covered some areas adequately (e.g. competition), so that it saw no case for further specific harmonisation. Among the conspicuously neglected cases were the issues of concentration of ownership and content-development measures in media production.

A minimum regulation approach was successfully promulgated in order to reassure those member states or other forces that were alarmed by an extensive EC intervention. Community policy drafters thus conveniently avoided a comprehensive harmonisation which would have "to incorporate 'fair play' norms and protection of vulnerable consumers (e.g. children)" (Collins 1994: 58). As was blatantly stated by the drafter of the green paper Ivo Schwartz, "an approximation of most of these rules is not desirable" (quoted in Collins ibid).

Following the publication of the Green Paper, the Commission launched a *consultation process* which sparked off an extensive as well as very intense debate. Its 55 main points took up practical as well as political matters in justification of its envisaged policy. Clarifying, for example, why certain issues were taken up as sensitive or immature, and others not, occupy a large part of the document. The deliberately incremental, step-by-step approach was also selected as another means to secure the goal of a 'minimum harmonisation'. The underlying rationale was that thorny issues were best left to be dealt with 'gradually' or at a later date. In this way, thorny, crucial or essential problems were deferred for a possible, future solution (GPTWF: 4). The 'incremental' approach proved tactically extremely handy; for instance, an issue such as the right of access to broadcasting (establishment), could be circumvented as thorny, although the TEC provided for this freedom, by declaring that it was an immature issue. As was argued "the temptation to propose perfectionist solutions (should) be firmly resisted" (GPTWF §14 & §15). In fact, the right of establishment for satellite businesses was of little relevance, because audience markets could be penetrated anyway. Conversely, this approach would have alarmed many governments, thus diminishing the chances of adopting the anticipated Directive, and so failing in the fundamental objective, which was legally to demolish national-definition, audience markets and thereby to penetrate and access them.

Although the Green Paper stressed the 'new media' element of the audiovisual sector, it was evident that the policy was to apply equally to all media, old and new, including psbs. Indeed, all the more so, because the 'national definition' of psbs counteracted its rationale for transfrontier broadcasting and for the so-called European Audiovisual Space (EAS). Hence the coming Directive sought to re-arrange the entire audiovisual sector. Old regulatory systems had to be demolished and changed from the ground up in order to be streamlined with the transfrontier commercial services. Thus, behind the ideology of *'transfrontierism'* lurked fierce commercialism. Notwithstanding such ground-shaking changes, this was called a minimum 'harmonisation policy', as if there was anything to harmonise between states with advertising-free channels to those few states that had advertising-funded channels. So, although it was a matter of replacing the former by the latter, they still called this initiative a practice of 'harmonisation'. The epoch of *transfrontierism* dawned along with the legally-mandatory advent of commercialisation and the commodification of citizens as viewers/audiences.

In comparison to the position of the EP, the Commission's Green Paper on TWF sought to transfer media control from the national, political level to the supra-national level in order to subject it to commercial exploitation. The DG III, on the one hand, and the EP and the DG X, on the other, concurred in seeking to move control to the supra-national level, but diverged on the second aim. While the EP envisaged a political role and a contribution to the European integration project via communications policy, the neo-liberal section of the

Commission, which by now controlled the policy agenda, aimed to use it in order to depoliticise communications altogether. The crucial mistake of the EP was that it was in fact presuming on a "wished political will" (Sachpekidou 1990: 75) to use the audiovisual as a 'supra-national empire-builder' at a point when such a common will in this direction was obviously lacking.

Legitimacy via Dichotomy

The Community lacked express legitimacy to handle cultural issues. In pursuing its objective in the light of this fact, it developed an extensive and intricate argumentation. This hinged on the principle of the free flow of information and the Articles of the TEC about the freedom of circulation for services. The other strategic component was the pertinent ECJ jurisprudence. The role of the ECJ has indeed been seminal in providing legitimacy for the development of transfrontier, audiovisual-sector policies. Zweifel (2002: 142) argues that the European Court of Justice itself "may be making a move from procedural to substantive legitimacy". In support of this assessment, he presents certain criteria to qualify this type of move. However, it is worth bearing in mind that (a) the jurisprudence in question came about over twenty years previously and that (b) the ECJ was and is still considered to be among the EU institutions with the least legitimacy (Sbragia 1992, Zweifel 2002: 20). In the circumstances, I would argue that this *move* on the part of the ECJ happened, first, without due legitimacy and accountability and, secondly, at an enormous cost for the European polity and the public interest.

In the community's argumentation also belonged the 'grand', but vague and politically and legally ungrounded, goals for cultural integration, as well as 'European identity'. Indeed, the preamble of the EEC Treaty refers to the famous and much invoked intention "to lay the foundations of an ever closer union among the peoples of Europe". In fact, this much-repeated phrase could have been the incentive for a political agreement in that direction, but, as it stands, it is not a substitute for one. The Green Paper on the TWF argued that Article 2 of the TEC states that the Community's 'task' is to promote 'closer relations between the States belonging to it' (GPTWF: 28). The same comment could be applied here: this 'task', too, could form the basis for a binding, political commitment. Faced with this array of abstract propositions about intentions, future tasks and wishful thinking one may ask: hierarchically and structurally what comes first – the closer European political and constitutional union, or the establishment of the 'integration agent' of a legally/politically ungrounded television policy? Which constitutes the end and which the means? In this vein, the deliberate mistake was that this conception 'confused' *transfrontierism* for an agency of community building.

The Commission document, rather than tackling this problem or distinguishing means from ends, argued assertively that "television will play an important role in developing and nurturing awareness of the rich variety of Europe's common cultural and historical heritage" (ibid). In fact, it rather convincingly echoed some of the claims and the political ambitions procured by the EP, for example, in respect of forging of the 'common European identity'. It thus argued that "the dissemination of information across national borders can do much to help the peoples of Europe to recognize the common destiny they share in many areas" (ibid). What is worth highlighting here is that the goal of "dissemination of information across national borders" was furnished without specifying *how* and *over what media* and means or frameworks this dissemination was to take place. This implies, then, that policy makers expected this goal to accrue automatically and of its own accord

Two more elements are perplexing: first, the urgency in pushing forward the transfrontier policy, second, the timing of it all. One cannot avoid correlating this policy push with the deregulatory onslaught that had just been set in motion by the Decision of Judge Harold Greene of the US Supreme Court on divesting AT&T in 1982.[35] Why was this noble and

---

[35] "In 1982 a Justice Department/AT&T anti-trust suit was settled by a decree issued after lengthy hearings under Judge Harold Greene. It provided for the divestment by

vague intention invoked at this particular historical conjuncture and not earlier or, better still later, once the political constitutional frame of the Union was in place? What was the rush about? What would be at stake and what were the implications of an EC involvement in the cultural sphere under such confused terms? It was argued that the citizens of the Community would welcome the extension of the potential coverage and content of television, if the Community was in a position to view the opportunities offered by these broadcasting techniques as a cultural challenge, and to place them within the context of a broad plan for the future of Europe not based on economic precepts alone (GPTWF: 23).

Given the layout of this discourse, the plan for an EC intervention in the audiovisual sector created a nexus of fundamental fears and hostilities. The first fear was related with the clear political and cultural nature of the audiovisual, as a key part of political communication and the corresponding absence of political/cultural aims and safeguards at the Community level. The fact remained that the Community was politically underdeveloped (Sbragia 1992, Collins 1994, Sachpekidou 1990: 78). This meant that political-communication priorities might be completely phased out. For this reason cultural jurisdiction became particularly problematic after the adoption of the SEA. Yet the Commission arbitrarily brought together two distinctly different categories – that of politics (and its co-extensive the citizen) and that of the market/economy – in a constitutional void.

The Green Paper, moreover, pioneered the idea, which later (on November 20th 1989) became ECHR law and legal jurisprudence, that individual freedoms apply as much to corporate bodies as to individuals. In doing so the ECHR equalised still more distinct categories: "It is irrelevant here whether they are natural or legal persons, companies with or without legal personality, associations, cooperatives, or foundations, or public-law or private law organisations" (GPTWF: 8, see also Chapter 5).

AT&T of its 22 operating companies,... but the general effect was to allow others to compete in areas where AT&T had a monopoly, while allowing a leaner AT&T to compete in fields that it was not allowed to enter previously. (Cawkell, 1988:46)

Built into these indiscriminate and reductionist conceptions are potential or latent conflicts regarding the democratic rights of citizens. These rulings prejudiced the 'real interests' of citizens (playing on what could be seen as subjective ones) by giving them the same status as that of powerful corporations. The emphasis of the GP analysis is clearly primarily on the right of economic corporations and agents to communicate.

The 'right to communicate' was introduced by the European Parliament in order to support its initiative for a European media policy in the first place. Yet, "it soon turned to be used for the protection of the right of broadcasters to extent their reach beyond national boundaries" (Sarikakis 2004: 86). This signified effectively the *appropriation* of a universal, civil and political right by a powerful minority of media owners. This could not of course have occurred without the jurisprudential support of the ECJ and the ECHR, on the one hand, and without the express political support of the Commission and other community agencies that stood as significant allies to these broadcasters, on the other. This is shown by the emphasis placed in critical moments on the "significance of media flow focusing on the freedom of the broadcasting movement" (EP 1985a: 16). As a result, the *right to transmit and receive opinions* was cast as a right that belonged to broadcasters, and this peculiarly undemocratic argument was used to justify this policy initiative. This controversy in itself raised the question as to why the *'freedom of broadcasters'* should be the central argument in the advocacy of these changes, as opposed, for example, to freedom of speech as a universal civil right. It could hardly be justifiable politically and legally that broadcasters (as economic and organisation agencies), on the one hand, are invested with human and civil rights, but, on the other hand, they are not obliged by law, e.g., by 'must carry rules', to provide access to citizens for their own communication rights, and for political communication purposes more generally.

The policy drafters wanted thus both to liberalise the sector and concurrently to 'release' it from political constraints. With control of the sector transferred from national control to the European and global levels, commercial exploitation would be facilitated in the 1980s. Typically, at this level there were neither legally binding rules of conduct, 'cumbersome' political remits, nor applicable constitutions.

The weaker member states and public-interest advocates had great difficulty in counteracting the objectives of the neo-liberal camp. The pivotal role of jurisprudence was manifest in several instances. Prior to the sweeping proposals for liberalising the cultural sphere by the Green Paper, more cases of ECJ jurisprudence had paved the way for liberalisation and for 'negative integration'. Two court rulings, on the Sacchi case and on the Debauve case, established the right of the Commission to act (ECJ 1974 & 1980). The first decided that a broadcast was a *service* and the second ruled that television provides a *service for remuneration*, as provided for in Article 50 of the TEC. This critical jurisprudence gave the necessary legitimacy to the process and marked the *major turning point* that led to the subsequent "divorce of power from politics" (Baumann 2005). In this regard, it is worth pointing out that such developments were being pushed forward on both sides of the Atlantic. Significantly, these ground-shaking changes were set in motion not via political decisions but via Supreme Court decisions. On the basis of this jurisprudence the Commission argued:

> Nor is the right of establishment provided for in the EEC Treaty confined to industry, the craft industries, the distributive trades, banks and insurance companies... Under the system of the four freedoms, immovable cultural assets and, hence, radio and television broadcasting are treated no differently... It thus transpires that the activity of the Community has, since the outset, encompassed essential aspects of cultural life in member states. Even those who are culturally creative and creations 'belong' to the Community. (GPTWF: 6-7)

Democratic Rights, Freedom of Information and the Power-Shift

As has been seen, the neo-liberal section of the Commission developed extremely well-elaborated and well-grounded arguments in favour of the free flow of commercial information. These emphasised exclusively the supply side of the information chain, yet always in the name of citizens' choice:

> Freedom of information is a prerequisite to the exercise of the right of citizens to elect their parliament. Only citizens who can obtain information freely are in a position to assume responsibility for their democratic rights and duties. In all the member states, broadcasting enjoys a wide degree of independence from government. There is no state responsibility for the content of individual programmes and this is actively discouraged (ibid).

What we observe in this text is first, that individual citizens are isolated from their national citizenship and raised to a position of supremacy, secondly, that they are set against the power of the state in general and, thirdly, that operators and suppliers of information packages are depicted as benevolent suppliers, if not guarantors of freedom of expression. This rationale tends to obliterate or to supersede state responsibility in securing flows of political communication. It actively propagates the de-linking of information flows from such actors as nation states. Conversely, it advocates the extension of such independence to a supra-national level. However, while the Commission appreciates unilaterally the value of independence of information from state control, it seems to blatantly ignore the danger of information being controlled by the rising commercial media enterprises. This omission in the discourse of the Green Paper reveals blatant partisan attitudes and the fact that more complex aims and hidden agendas were at work.[36] The failure of the

---

[36] What could be gleaned from this 'monolithic' approach of the GPTWF was that it was modelling the EC policy on the deregulated and wildly competitive model of the USA.

Commission document to include anti-concentration measures or provisions about 'the right of reply', so as to protect viewers, is certainly not accidental.

In fact, such a framing of the policy discourse reveals a hidden agenda. In light of subsequent corporate moves and the relations of leading figures with media moguls, this hidden agenda is obvious. Gaston Thorn, Martin Bangeman, Silvio Berlusconi, Rupert Murdoch and his ally Margaret Thatcher, Kirch and Bertelsmann and their powerful ally Helmut Kohl, all had enormous stakes and interests at risk had the Green Paper even remotely hinted at such measures. What emerges is the transfer of such control from political agency (the member states) to the market, a move likely to subjugate information flows to commercial interests rather than securing the independence of information.

Moreover, given that the objective was to introduce an 'enhanced change' in the *status quo*, the statement that Europeans did receive varied information freely is paradoxical; EC intervention would in fact need to presuppose the opposite. Having stated that there is no state responsibility for broadcast content, which, at least at the time, was fallacious *per se*, and having argued for "independence of information" from state control, the Green Paper argued also that, in the case of satellite broadcasting, jurisdiction for channel control should lie within the transmitting state (supply side), rather than the receiving country or both (ibid). This then was yet another contradiction.

The fact that the Cassis de Dijon principle[37] was first pursued as a determinant of the oncoming Directive and subsequently successfully put in place, in respect of symbolic cultural goods, was the practical confirmation that communications were, in fact, being treated as

---

However, as has been shown by corroborated evidence, that system was afflicted by the most serious trends towards suffocating economic control and political power concentration (Bagdikian, 1983, Kellner 1990, Mosco & Wasko 1990).

[37] According to the Cassis de Dijon provision, member states cannot stop the sale of any European product/service in their territory on the grounds that it does not comply with the technical specifications of their country but should accept the specifications of the country of origin of the product.

economic assets and services exclusively. This approach obviated any possibility that the political nature of transfrontier information contents might be exempted from this rule. Thus, if a civil society organisation complained before a receiving, member-state regulator, against some transfrontier piece of broadcast on the grounds that it instigated chauvinism or violence, and if they demanded that it be discontinued, they would get nowhere. This is due to the fact that (a) information is a *free service*, and (b) legislation of the transmitting state takes precedence. This effectively meant that the most neo-liberal regimes in broadcasting regulation would be in the position to set the lowest common denominator standard for broadcasting norms.

Not surprisingly, this objective was in full accordance with the wishes of the associations of advertising agencies which "use European Treaties and conventions to support their assertion that the free circulation of advertising, based on the regulations in force in the country of transmission, should be the foundation of any future harmonisation" (Cuprie 1984: 9). In contrast to this, the EBU declared that "the law of the receiving country should predominate over that of the transmitting country (and that the former should be referred to, even if advertising was not originally intended for listeners in these countries" (ibid: 5). The theoretical and legal justification for cross-frontier internationalised operations lies in the principle of the free flow of information, but in the economic sphere this doctrine served the interests of hegemonic transnational economies paving the way for the penetration of foreign markets: "Several Western nations have used freedom of information as a rebuttal against regulation of DBS (direct broadcasting by satellite) activities" (Taishoff 1987: xi).

A Neo-liberal Manifesto For European Communications

In the Commission's Green Paper statement about "no state responsibility" lies nothing less than a *political manifesto*. This in fact can be seen as the beginning of the end for political control of policy-making in the field of communications. By the same token, this was the beginning of the end of "the divorce between power and politics" (Baumann 2005). The only persisting enigma is that the then-governments of member states of the Community came eventually to endorse, each for different reasons, the fundamental premises set out in the Green Paper, notably, those which made it the 'flagship of the Single Market'. It is difficult to imagine that statesmen could *abdicate* on the political control of the communications sector without realising the value of this loss. It is equally difficult to see how they imagined that Europolitics could operate without political communication.

The adoption of the central premises of the Internal Market as applicable to this key factor, that is, policy-making in communications – element (A) of the triangle- constituted a decisive mistake. This was not only due to the fact that it entailed erosion of national state responsibility, nor that it was handing a crucial element of state sovereignty to the Community level. It was primarily due to the *political immaturity* and extremely *economistic nature* of the Community, which itself actively assisted depoliticization from that moment onwards.

The worst damage – that could have and has been done – has been the depoliticization of policy-making in the field of communications. Control passed to economic and commercial forces rather than political ones, suspending a very real element of political power and prerogative from national state level without it being replaced by an equivalent political responsibility at Community level.

So a double shift of communications policy-making prerogatives occurred: first, a movement of displacement of it from the national to the supra-national level, and secondly, a displacement from the political forces to commercial forces, but under the protection of Community law.

This development, then, did not occur only because of the lack of an EC political/constitutional framework. If that were the problem, it could have been resolved either through a positive reception of the Spinelli initiative or through deferring the decision to have a Community-wide policy on this field later. It thus transpires that the lack of pertinent constitutional articles for the audiovisual in the TEC was merely the pretext for the Europeanising of communications policy-making in order to subjugate it to hegemonic market forces.

It was an intricate case of high–level, neo-liberal politics that paid off to the utmost for those pushing for it. This ideology and politics that was fostered within the Commission was compounded by the EC's constitutional/legal caveats. It moulded a policy-agency role of intervention in favour of commercialisation rather than the opposite, without obviating the 'actual' underlying 'conflict' (Bachrach & Baratz 1962 & 1963, Lukes 1974). European civil society never learnt or was able to perceive any of this intricate process at the time of its occurrence. Those forcefully in favour of deregulation and strongly against European integration (for example, the UK under the Thatcher government) were in the vanguard of this course of action. The timing of this policy intervention was, therefore, not accidental but strategically selected. Given the EP initiative for a political union, if free-market forces had not acted quickly, while the pretext of a constitutional caveat was still in existence, the potential for the process of the political union might have developed, thereby curtailing their options.

This, then, was the chosen method for subjecting the entire, strategic sector of communications to the control of commercial forces and removing it from the political sphere. The corollary of this reasoning presupposes that citizens do not sustain the political system, but are detached from it. This proposition clashes with and is refuted by the constitutional orders of member states. The citizen, who is an integral part of democratic politics, may participate in the political system and influence communications' policy only as long as it is under political control. Obviously, citizens have no power to influence communications policy when this sector of policy has been marketised and privatized. When political communication is precluded because commercial channels predominate with the supply of 'saleable' only infotainment, citizens cannot learn sufficiently or grasp politics and complex political affairs let alone influence them. Additionally, it is not in the interests of commercial channels or among their priorities to disseminate political communication material. In short, citizens are disempowered, as there is no system to guarantee their political agency when the prevalent system for communication and its control are in the power of privately-owned commercial structures.

The Internal Market framework is an exclusively, market-criteria system, solely controlled by the relevant DG of the Commission, which, moreover, is a mechanism superordinate to national governments. Simultaneously, the Commission itself is not a politically accountable institution to the electorate of EC/EU. Given such discrepancies and caveats in terms of political accountability, the invocation of citizens' rights is just another case of applying rhetorical ploys. Hence, the placement of the audiovisual sector in the Internal Market framework disempowered both citizens and governments, because the essentially political nature and role of communication, by definition, is not *recognizable* by that framework. The Internal Market framework deals only with economic elements, such as the control prerogatives channelled to media operators and owners and to content exporters. As is argued by Gareth Locksley,

> The CEC has located a dilemma. Its aim is the free flow of information and TV programmes through member states for political objectives which will provide substantial economic benefits. But it sees existing broadcasting organisations as a potential obstacle to the desired end. These organisations are frequently the main bastions of national culture. The CEC's intervention will extend the role of the market in the provision of cultural services. (Locksley 1987: 201)

The eventual outcome was a dual redefinition of the role of broadcasting that is fraught with implications. First, broadcasting as a public-service good accessible to all citizens, irrespective of their class, wealth and geographical location (Garnham 1986) was supplanted by broadcasting attached to policy-making and the tentacles of cost-efficiency. The latter kind of 'good' is price-marked, and its availability is conditional on the number of viewers it can obtain (price competition). Thomas Meyer elaborates on the economic and 'demand' aspects of this industry. Products that fail to satisfy the targeted mass viewers

> may be refined if it seems worthwhile to do so; otherwise they are simply taken off the market, and, further, that the media have an extremely limited capacity to transmit a full and complete picture of the nearly limitless wealth of events that comprise political reality, so they always have to pick and choose what they will feature and how they will present it. (Meyer 2002: 28)

As a result, diversely-sourced scheduling withers away. The second area of redefinition was related to EC law: "In the absence of express provision to the contrary in the Treaty, a Television signal must be regarded as provision of services" (GPTWF: 105). Hence, in order for the Community to tackle the issue at all, it had to see broadcasting stripped of its cultural aspects, merely as a service in accordance with Articles 49-55 of the TEC. So, as Commission president Jacques Delors himself put it, the EC must tackle the problem from an economic angle. This, then became the trap into which all three interlinked elements of the dialectical triangle of *democratic politics* (A) (B) and (C) stumbled.

The Inbuilt Bias

The bias in favour of commercial stakeholders – notably broadcasters and the advertised economy – can be gleaned also from the specific issues that were included and highlighted or omitted in the Green Paper. Broadcasting content, broadcast advertising and a limited co-ordination of copyright laws covered the entire scope of the specific issues proposed for discussion. By far the largest space of these specific issues was taken up by advertising. Conversely, among the obviously missing specific issues were proposals for 'must carry' rules to safeguard some form of political communication regarding the much-heralded objective of European integration. Equally missing were any specific issues in respect of rules of conduct to safeguard pluralism and concentration of ownership. These omissions point to a significant neglect of political values and the disregard for common political interest.

To start with, advertising-funded channels had to be authorised: it was made mandatory that such channels be available in all member states.[38] Overall twenty points of the Green Paper addressed the various aspects of broadcast advertising, and most significantly advertising was praised and presented as positively "desirable because it serves the general interest (sic)" in the form of revenue, market stimulation and consumer information (GPTWF: §19). On commercial intrusiveness, it was wishfully asserted that its disadvantages must outweigh its advantages. Other central and contentious issues included the permissible time for advertisements and the points prohibiting certain products to be advertised such as tobacco products and alcohol (ibid §20).

The pre-emptive application of the Cassis de Dijon (mutual recognition) principle suggested that a possible derogation of this principle in the cultural and political domain of communications was inconceivable The Green Paper effectively treated this *sui generis* political sector not only in economic terms, but even just like any other sector of the economy. This consequently also implied that notions of citizens' rights and plurality of information were empty words, since the information at issue is solely controlled by the rule of price competition, which *per se* is an impersonal and an unaccountable mechanism focusing on the exchange-value of information. By contrast the political system, where the category of the citizen intrinsically belongs, may or may not

---

[38] This policy proposal was a direct outcome of ECJ jurisprudence which had ruled on the freedom of advertising services to benefit from the relevant freedom of movement Articles of the Treaty.

manage all aspects of it (allocation, distribution etc.) well, because of its particular character, but it is at least accountable and subject to change.

As regards the risks related to advertising-dependent broadcasting, the Commission's document admonished that significant competitive distortions should be avoided between channels exclusively funded by advertisements and undertakings with mixed funding. As to how this should happen, no advice was given. Advertising was also presumed to be separated from other kinds of emissions, thus excluding so-called 'grey' advertising. Sponsoring was to be safeguarded but without 'influencing' the producers and the content of programming. Wishful thinking was not infrequent in the nearly 400-page document. The fourth section of the document comprised eleven paragraphs (§44-54) aiming to harmonise national legislations on copyrights. The ambition was to supplant these with a new, unified set of rules, since nationally defined copyrights can be barriers to the trans-border movement and exploitation of works. In the place of national territoriality, the Commission proposed EC-wide territoriality combined with an adequate increase in remuneration so as to overcome fragmentation.[39]

Among the general issues one set of rules referred to the moral welfare of minors and consumer protection. These measures addressed significant and valued aspects of quality. Yet, none of these relate to political communication concerns. Significantly enough, there was even no mention whatsoever of the least civil 'right of reply'. This is the most minimum and solely–defensive, civil communications right of access to channels' broadcasts, in case of screening offensive material against individual viewers. The relevant provision was eventually imposed at a much later stage

---

[39] The Green Paper introduced limited time-cover for rights-holders. In cases of re-transmission, suing by rights-holders could result in criminal penalties. The alleged objective was for the proposal not to result in the expropriation of works without compensation, nor to render works inaccessibly expensive for entrant broadcasters. Copyright protection can become a barrier to transborder movement of programmes. Yet, it also is a property right protected by the TEC. So, an EC-wide approach to this issue had to take place with the political cooperation of those concerned. In a changing, general framework works could have been rendered competitively disadvantaged over rights acquired for the entire continent e.g. for works exported by Hollywood.

thanks to an amendment by the European Parliament. This omission too indicates, then, that policy drafters were completely uninterested in or negligent of civil aspects and political communications values.

Meanwhile, although general reference was made to the importance of measures for programming production, no specific proposals were articulated thereof. Yet, supposedly, the creation of a common market for EC audiovisual production was seen as the essential step in fending off the dominance of the big, American, media corporations. Worthy of note here is the following: "This is yet another area where the establishment of a Community-wide market will allow European firms to improve their competitiveness" (GPTWF: 33).[40] In view of this statement of the GP, the absence of proposals on programming is flabbergasting. In addition, as was shown by the implementation monitoring of the first period of the Directive, this could not have been a grosser miscalculation. Contrary to ostensible objectives, the invasion by Hollywood products was in fact astronomical.

Overall, it was amply evident that all that the Green Paper drafters were concerned about was the opening up of the space for transfrontier distribution of information and entertainment products. What was certainly not in evidence was a comprehensive, overarching and balanced policy. Understandably, then, such blatant shortcomings in the key policy document sparked off legitimate fears that the EAS could become the most favourable, distribution carriage-way for supplying Hollywood-made material to Europeans, thereby, securing the most lucrative 'global market' for the USA.

The Avant-Garde of Neo-liberalism

Commission Vice-president Lord Cockfield characterised the Green Paper on TWF as *the flagship of the Single Market* (Collins 1994: 57). Indeed,

---

[40] The reality of course is quite the opposite. If the transfrontier EAS was profitable for any ones this was primarily for the American, show-business industry.

this very significant linking with the Internal Market signalled the fundamentally economistic profile of this original policy document. Essentially, it revealed the seminal role of the Green Paper itself in setting in motion the commercialisation of the audiovisual sector and of commodification of citizens in all EC countries. It was accurately characterised as the "most striking initiative in the media field to date" (Collins 1994: 17). This appreciation must be taken in conjunction with the assessment that the politically unaccountable Commission "is always in a position to sway the outcome" (Noel 1988: 24), thereby controlling the agenda more than any other EC institution.

Thus, the Commission, under the leadership of neo-liberal politicians, some of whom later became industrial leaders in this same sector, succeeded in pushing the audiovisual, the political/cultural sector par excellence, into *laissez-faire* through a double transformation and restructuring. This original Commission document can be blamed as the foundation for squeezing the political communication role of television totally outside the agenda. Through its singularly restrictive market criteria sealed the future options of EC governance.

Although the EP at that time had merely a consultative political role, its consent to this Commission policy document was crucial. By enshrining the Commission's struggle to gain legitimacy for its supra-national intervention in favour of narrow economic interests and against the political interests of all, it (also directly undermined its own status and role. Politically and culturally speaking, this represents the beginning of a rapid erosion of the political management and control of audiovisual affairs. Furthermore, both economically and politically this has exposed the sector, and the EC itself, to the danger of domination by global, predominantly extra-European, interests with disastrous effects for the European audiovisual economy in both hardware and software sectors.

Advertising was cast for the strategic part. Indeed, this choice defined the fronts that were formed in the ensuing battle over Europe's audiovisual affairs, which cut right through the audiovisual industries of the 12 member states. Contrary to Commission claims (GPTWF: 42), a new regime was to be created, challenging and dismantling the *status quo* of psb monopolies and nationally delimited markets. Wedell (1985) argued that the GP drafters, in their anxiety to prove loyal to the spirit and remain within the ambit of the TEC – which in itself reflects an old if not an altogether obsolete regime – have side-stepped the major policy issues of the future. With hindsight one may very well concur with this estimate. Thus, politically valuable objectives were discriminated against while the economic ones were favoured and provided for by the Green Paper.

Transfrontier Television Without Pan-European Communication

A hot debate followed the publication of the Green Paper. The arguments advanced dissected its implicit and explicit objectives and their short and long term implications, which were political, legal, economic and socio-cultural in character. The most controversial issue concerned the Community's right to enter this field at all and the tacit re-definition of powers between the EC and the member states that this implied. Due to the severely neo-liberal approach several governments felt threatened – if not ambushed – and reacted defensively. The debate hinged also on the scope of the proposed instrument and prompted considerable changes to specific issues. Yet, it failed to alter its fundamental nature and objective which was to permanently enshrine a neo-liberalist, market structure. Establishing the Internal Market of broadcasting amounted to just that. This was in pursuance of the 'imperatives' of the economy, which dictated penetration of the cultural sphere.

Legitimacy was among the principal issues of contention. The Community's[41] intention to enter this national cultural and political field made many forces, notably smaller member states, suspect the Commission of infringing national sovereignty, as a key policy area was

---

[41] 'Community' here obviously refers to an agglomeration of EC interests involving market players, member states, the Commission and the EP. These forces taken together constituted a substantial enough majority to support such a significant move.

claimed with dexterity by Brussels. The political/constitutional void was, moreover, intrinsic in the policy package, precisely because of the predominance of economic features. Opponents notably argued that the Council of Europe and even the EBU were more appropriate bodies for dealing with cultural politics (Negrine & Papathanassopoulos 1990). These two organisations were incumbent players in the European audiovisual field and it was thought that advantage should be taken of their experience. As a matter of fact, the ministerial convention of the Council of Europe, on media policy, of 1986 at Vienna, was willing to assume responsibility for transnational regulation of this sector (Sachpekidou 1990). The advantage of this was that it was politically accountable, as Council of Europe regulation had to be ratified by each individual signatory government before becoming legally binding.

However, such a policy preference sought to maintain the 'national system' and to put a brake on globalisation. Since the legislation of the EC takes precedence over Council of Europe legislation the formers' intervention in this domain was sought after and was finally achieved. Nevertheless, the Council of Europe also adopted its Convention on transfrontier television, which is very similar to the TWF Directive, almost concurrently with the adoption of this Directive.

Depending on the strengths and the weaknesses of each country in this sector, EC countries were divided into two major categories: ultra-neoliberal and protectionist. Conflicting economic interests and goals surfaced among member states but also between market forces and 'social partners'. The issues that sprang up were too many and too thorny to be tackled smoothly. Both institutional and non-institutional bodies (particularly interest groups) provided their feedback to the Green Paper and responded to the Draft Directive. The outcome of the first round of the debate was a proposal for a Directive that came up in 1986. The most significant change brought about by the reaction against the shortcomings of the Green Paper addressed measures on production, notably the European programming *quotas issue*.

Arguments against EC intervention reflected a fear of structural changes that would undermine sovereignty and cultural self-determination (Dupagne 1992). Transborder TV, as proposed by the Commission, was broadly challenged: "The UK House of Lords' Select Committee... noted that practically all submissions on TWF had contested the Commission's (and the EP's) right to exercise jurisdiction over broadcasting" (Collins 1994: 56). Fears that local and regional programme contents were threatened were also raised in Germany, where psbs were under the control of the federal Länder (Porter & Hasselbach 1991: 144-170). Germany originally opposed the proposal heeding the Länder level prerogatives. Indeed, the exclusive Länder jurisdiction on broadcasting policy was an issue in the country's Constitutional Court.

Those countries that had no stake in an 'international' audiovisual industry (either hardware or software) had everything to lose and nothing to gain. If the audiovisual came totally under the Internal Market framework, then EC governments would be expected to be overseen and monitored by the superordinate Community system, at a cost to their sovereignty and cultural/political self-determination. In such a case a simple and unilateral commercialisation would apply. Loss of national control would be compounded by the fact that 'constitutionally irrelevant' agencies would be dealing with public interest domains. In addition, media policies would no longer be locally designed, agreed and chosen but produced by the most rationalised and competitive global system, thus actually undermining local diversity and production. This 'blackmailing' into a losing position was at first rejected by many, particularly, the minor, member states. In fact the worst of these fears materialized soon after the adoption of the Directive in 1989:

> International bodies usually work on a system of give and take. States try to achieve what they want by influencing other member states either by offering something in return – 'we will vote for you on issue X if you support us on issue Y' – or by threatening to cause trouble. In the latter category three tactics (in order of

stringency) are: 'threatening to block progress on other, unrelated issues; threatening to boycott future meetings; and threatening to withdraw'. (Hartley 1988: 17)

Thanks to the horse-trading inter-governmentalist fashion of decision making at EC level, eventually, member-states' governments, despite the dissent of some persistent 'nationalists', were carried along. The alarming rhetoric of Commission officials, including Jacques Delors, was brought to bear. Even state leaders, such as François Mitterrand[42], were mobilized in the general push for common action: "American images, together with Japanese technologies, greatly dominate the European market...If we do not attack now, the cement of European unity will start to crumble" (François Mitterrand quoted in Negrine & Papathanassopoulos 1990: 67).

The draft proposal, in its striving towards harmonisation and in applying the relevant ECJ jurisprudence, was bound to enshrine advertiser-funded channels, indeed to make them unavoidable and ubiquitous. This virtually dictated radical, political choices to those countries that rejected that option until then. Thus, the Internal Market and EAS brought with them liberalisation and deregulation of a purely political nature to certain member states. This was bound to create not just supply specialisation, but to accentuate the problem of one state depending on the information systems of another, thereby interfering with its editorial choices and programming.

---

[42] France was in a potentially precarious position over the TWF policy but had a lot of stakes in the concurrently running HDTV and standards policy. France was, moreover, feeling confident at that time that it could influence and harness intra-EC politics. Compulsive rhetoric alone cannot, however, explain approval of such a major and nationally 'sensitive' issue by those member states that evidently had everything to lose from its adoption. The theory of 'subjectively sharedcommon interests' of Keohanne and Hoffmann comes as one explanation. The very nature of the inter-governmental policy actor was itself instrumental in the promulgation of such a control-allocative decision.

Commercial Transfrontierism

Advertiser-funded channels, combined with control over the channels being granted to the country of transmission, was a major blow to small member-states without satellite or audiovisual, export industries. This division pitted media-weak member states against the big and media-powerful among the twelve. In the pan-European environment the conflict between the audiovisual industrial states and 'non-audiovisual' states was reinforced by the economic benefits expected if advertising revenue (Euro-brands) were to move from member state markets to transnational services.

The issue of channel control by the transmitting state was a major controversial issue. The objective of the Internal Market was to be served by the mutual recognition principle of control from the originating country, as well as by the operation of satellite and cable emissions expected to be advertiser-funded. The dubious and economistic (ordinary goods) definition of broadcasting as a 'service', stripped it of its intrinsically cultural-political features. It, crucially, gave jurisdiction of control to the transmitter. This forcibly imported' deregulation would then negatively affect constitutional orders that sought to use the media as a political/cultural resource for political communication. Certain member states had developed audiovisual systems that empowered citizens to take part in the management of the system (Germany, Sweden). This concretely embodied citizens' real and actual interests, in Lukesian terms, since citizens have a say in media systems' organisation and function for attaining social goals. Its extinction or replacement by 'consumer choice' (which, even when valid, happens only at the end of the broadcasting chain), endangered those real interests. Indeed, as actual developments demonstrate (see Chapter 8) such real interests are by now encroached upon.

Thus fear of an intra-European 'cultural imperialism' grew in countries such as Belgium and Denmark. The throttling of linguistic, cultural diversity and of national heritage was feared by the non English-speaking member-states in the face of an invasion of cheap, American, TV programming. Various surveys show that viewers were more attracted to national programmes than to foreign ones. The Bureau Européen des Unions de Consommateurs (BEUC) Council was of the opinion that culture should essentially be protected at national level (BEUC press release, 10.6.1986: 6).

On the other hand, there were objections against undesirable and unwanted regulation of editorial freedom. Under the draft Directive... the EEC would require the British government, under pain of legal sanction, to order the BBC to allocate its money to programmes of a certain kind. "The Government would have to instruct the corporation to broadcast more of this kind of programme and less of that. We find that an unacceptable proposal" (BBC Director General in Collins 1994: 64). This is quite a significant aversion against the potentiality of applying 'must carry rules' by a policy actor other than the government of the member state in question. The role of nationally-organised broadcasting was in jeopardy: a fundamental transmutation of that role was under way. A real interest was in danger, set against the provision of a multiplicity of channels. So, the BBC accepted 'must carry rules' stemming from its own national regulation, but it repulsed the European equivalent as an infringement. This, to say the least is a very 'elastic' conception of *editorial freedom* as much as it is also nation-centred. It is the kind of narrow-minded claim that ignores citizens' needs to be able to learn and appreciate their Europolitics, since belonging to the EC was an already-chosen reality and not an option.

The freedom of movement of services was anchored in the TEC. Meanwhile the 'freedom of consumer choice' argument was seized on by the opponents of centrally-run state or *quango* monopolies. The implication was a shift in the controlling agency of the audiovisual sector. Control was removed from the political order (elected locus) and located in private, commercial, 'non-elected' and distant loci. This entailed that the trend was to give the same status to the electronic media as to print media. There are however significant differences between print and electronic media, in production methods, in the expenditure required to enter the market, and in their immediacy and impact on the viewer. The distance between production and reception is also a significant factor. Most importantly, electronic media operators 'borrow' from citizens such public property or global public goods as airwaves and public territory for their operation.

The cycle of consultations with the permanent national representations (COREPER) officially launched the formal policy process. On the basis of such consultations the Commission tabled the first proposal. Following the submission of the Commission, the EP adopted in October 1985 – by a qualified majority – its resolution on the creation of a framework-regulation in favour of a Community audiovisual policy based on the TWF Green Paper (EP 1985).

Thus we observe that the EP responded affirmatively to two divergent Commission inputs – the interim report 'Realities and Tendencies', of 1983 and its opposite, the Green Paper on TWF. Yet it 'emphatically' supported the options of the former which stressed the role of transborder television for 'democratic development' and for a 'European consciousness' (Collins 1994: 84). Nevertheless, the EP's oscillating stance and its haste to locate this sector's control at the supra-national level, at that historical conjuncture, actually assisted that unique opportunity and helped the opposite camp in its efforts to deregulate and control television and the domain of communications more broadly.

The EP thereby granted an uncritical strategic endorsement to the whole project of *commercial transfrontierism*. The EP saw this policy as crucially related to the future development of the EC itself. Considering the danger of a *de facto* formation of irreversible and uncontrollable structures, and of missing the chance to realise a common policy in this field, the EP urged the Commission to proceed with a draft Directive taking into consideration all views expressed in the debate (EP 1985).

The EP preceded to the adoption of yet another resolution concerning the economic aspects of the audiovisual sector (ibid). This generous support lent much needed legitimacy to the Commission's intervention in this field without any guarantees of political safeguards. This movement by an essentially weak and consultative (at the time) assembly, seems intriguing. This stance suggests that the EP underestimated the enormous transferral of power from the public domain to the private that it was assisting to. It also indicates that it did not grasp the long term and structural effects of that act on politics and power brokering more generally. The furore raised by the momentum for a European integration and unification, but also the self-interest of the EP which, being a pan-European institution, was urging to play its own part to the full, may to some extent explain these political misjudgements. In whichever case, for European unionists EC-wide, audiovisual policy had come to be of key importance.

Towards a Minimum 'Agreement' on the Draft Proposals.

Once the EC's legitimacy to enter into this domain was determined and secured, the die was cast and these general concerns were appeased. This was confirmed when the Commission proceeded to submit its first Draft Proposal on 30.4.1986. Whether and why one should establish transfrontier TV in Europe ceased to be the main issue. Henceforth the debate hinged instead on what measures should be included in a policy document, the first of its kind (a supra-national Directive in the audiovisual sector). The EP examined the draft proposal of the Commission in the relevant special committees (on media, legal affairs and citizens' rights). The report of the media committee was submitted to the EP plenary on 4.12.1987 which, on the basis of the Barzanti report, adopted its draft amendments at its plenary session of 19/20.1.1988. Informal policy influences came from the consultation with other interested parties invited by the Commission. Threatened interest groups such as the EBU and the BEUC were among the participants.

Subsequent to the submission and circulation of the first draft Directive (1986) and after the first round of consultations, several changes took place. Most important of these was the broadening of the definition of the term European. Secondly, in an attempt to mollify the opposition and to win the case for harmonisation of copyright, the position of the rights-holders was reinforced. Thirdly, a new chapter was added to include the provision for the right of reply, and finally the distinction between domestic and transborder transmission was deleted (Sachpekidou 1990: 114). However, the key characteristics of the drafts, that is the minimum scope of harmonisable provisions and the explicit introduction of the stricter at home rule, which was devised to provide enough flexibility to have the instrument accepted by its fiercest adversaries in the Council, remained unchanged.

The 'Right of Reply' was a provision proposed by the EP, and it had a history of appearing and disappearing between the various stages of the debate and decision-making process. Finally, it received a position in Article 19 of the approved Directive. The destiny of this 'civil right', however, would always remain conditional on editors' and broadcasters' internal codes of ethics. In addition, the proliferation of local, regional and transnational channels made its monitoring extremely difficult, in fact, impracticable.

The Commission tabled its amended proposal on 6.4.1988. Only a year after this date was the Council able to adopt a Common Position (on the second draft proposal) on 13.4.1989. In the course of it the Council dropped the provisions on copyrights from the agenda for lack of agreement. Similarly, it dropped the regulation of radio programmes thus narrowing the scope of the Directive considerably. The EP then approved, by absolute majority, the amendments of the Barzanti report on 24.5.1989. Then the Commission re-elaborated the draft on 26.5.1989, and presented its final proposal to the Council of General Affairs, which, however, failed to reach an agreement on its subsequent June convention, because a majority could not be found, and it had, therefore, to extend the formal decision-making process by one month, according to the then applying Article 149.[43]

Had the Council not reached an agreement by October 6th 1989, the proposal would have to be rejected (ibid: 56-57). Due to Parliament's second reading amendments,[44] the Council could not but adopt the provision for a majority of European programming quota. Alternatively, given the disagreements in the Council, it could have abandoned the instrument altogether. The French presidency and its wish and pride not to fail totally with this long-drawn policy 'rescued' the situation. The French made the Directive possible by giving in (Dupagne 1992) and accepting the ambiguity in the crippling phrases 'where practicable', 'gradually' and 'by appropriate means'. As though this did not suffice to totally incapacitate the quota's provision in practice, 'the German delegation insisted on obtaining a written statement on the part of the Council and the Commission, qualifying the provision on quotas as 'politically binding'. This statement, included in the Council minutes, was interpreted by the Germans as 'not juridically binding' (Maggiore 1990: 35).

Eventually, just three days before the expiry of the extended deadline the Council reached the compromise agreement to adopt the Directive on TWF (*Agence Europe*, 4.10.89: 7). As matters turned out, the Directive as adopted looked quite different in scope. It did not contain all the provisions foreseen in the draft Directive, while new provisions entered at the final stage. Yet, the strategic victory of the neo-liberal section of the Commission was that it was caged structurally in the correct commercialising framework. In the circumstances, no provisions were

---

[43] Article 149 was abolished and the relevant provisions in the revised TEC are dealt with in Article 202 and beyond.

[44] The Single European Act (SEA), among other things, enhanced and strengthened EP prerogatives in the policy-making process. According to Article 202 (ex 149) the EP was allowed second reading amendments for all Directives. Yet the EP acquired more effective prerogatives and decision-making role after the adoption of the TEU and the Treaty of Amsterdam.

tabled for 'must carry' rules of any sort, let alone about the appropriate and adequate journalistic coverage of European political affairs.

TWF Directive: The Pan-European Instrument of Commodification

Notwithstanding objections and conflicts raised in the policy process, the member state governments with the exception of Denmark and Belgium voted for this Directive, which, in its final form, should logically have served particularist interests mainly if not exclusively. The question that arises is why the majority of governments agreed to it. Apart from the policy 'ethos' of bartering on the package deals[45] involved in this policy-making process, but also in the Internal Market and 'Europe 1992' rhetoric, the 'subjectively shared common interests' thesis may explain the adoption of this policy by those member states whose stakes were in fact only risked by it. Rhetoric and confusion compounded such subjective beliefs.

The legitimising rationale of the Directive's preamble mentions the three original tenets with which the Commission launched its GP on TWF in 1984. The Directive was legitimised by Articles 47 and 55 (ex 57 & 66) and not Article 308.[46] Had Article 308 (ex 235) been chosen, it would have meant a possible breaking away from the strict Internal Market framework and a possible holistic approach, thereby taking heed of the cultural/political specificity of the sector. Such a hypothetical prospect would of course entail a unanimous political will for a common,

---

[45] The most instrumental contributor to the adoption of the directive has been the proposal of specific package deals throughout the policymaking process. These allowed member states to gain leverage and foster alliances for their cause, without endangering the entire process (Dupagne 1992: 117).

[46] Article 308 (ex 235) of the TEC states "If action by the Community should prove necessary to attain, in the course of the operation of the common market, one of the objectives of the Community and this Treaty has not provided the necessary powers, Council shall, acting *unanimously* on a proposal from the Commission and after consulting the European Parliament, take the appropriate measures" (emphasis added).

audiovisual-sector policy without the hidden traps of minimum harmonisation versus mutual recognition.[47]

Albeit at the eleventh hour, the Commission successfully brought its amended proposal to the final stage: it eventually became EC Law in 1989. The Directive's seven chapters and twenty-seven Articles were the result of prolonged battles and painstaking compromise, political dexterity and heavy lobbying from the regionally and globally, most powerful and vocal market and political forces. Eventually, as Article 27 decrees, the Directive was referred to the member states. Significantly, the EP proposal for a regulatory agency to oversee the co-ordination and the harmonisation in practice, like other EP proposals, was rejected by member states reluctant to allow a supra-national EC agency to usurp such authority. This in itself reveals the ineradicable inter-governmentalism and the national egoisms prevailing in the EC. An 'alignment on the weakest rules' between the twelve partners, juggling with vague terms, permitted a minimal and fragile agreement in regulatory terms, which however was structurally subversive.

Throughout the period of gestation, the Commission steered the agenda along in a firmly pro-Internal Market route. The paradoxes of a policy which aimed to satisfy so many diverse and competing, objectives (diversity, freedom of choice in programming, respect for national and regional nuances and European integration, economic exploitation) without any sacrifices are blatant and intriguing. The ensemble of these features rendered it automatically contestable. The dual regime of regulation being stricter at home[48] and looser at the transnational level is not only unrealistic but also completely unacceptable in competition terms. Given the assimilative powers of the market-place, stricter rules tend to be supplanted by less stringent ones.

---

[47] The legal basis for the Directive was Article 202 (ex 149) of the TEC (Sachpekidou 1990: 115).

[48] See Article 3 of the Directive (point 1): 'Member states shall remain free to require television broadcasters under their jurisdiction to lay down more detailed or stricter rules in the areas covered by this Directive.' (TWFD).

Competition for audiences rather than for quality of programmes caused an assimilative, market conduct which converted the 'stricter at home' rules into boomerangs. The end result with regard to broadcast content was that in the long term it became monolithic. It was this rather than any legal ambiguity that established a serious disharmony between member states with export potential in media services and those without. The belief that all parties would ostensibly be either pleased or appeased was built on confused grounds and on false premises, and proved dangerously fallacious. A gestation period of five years made this 'toothless Directive' (Tunstall & Palmer 1991: 17) a bitingly damaging instrument for the broad political and cultural interests of most Europeans, but extremely lucrative for a minority of others.

Acquis Communautaire: the Free Flow of Advertising

The victory of the TWF Directive consisted in establishing *free transborder flow of advertising*, while concurrently commodifying citizens and thereby in commercialising a politically strategic sector. Hence, the multifaceted deficit in essential information and reciprocal, pan-European communication that we have been experiencing ever since, was conceived and engineered when the EC managed to penetrate this highly political area of policy-making in the early 1980s and notably when drafting the Green Paper on TWF as part of the Internal Market strategy.

Twenty years since the launching of the Green Paper and fifteen years since the adoption of the Directive itself, one can make a number of observations as to which objectives were accomplished and which were frustrated. Overall, from the general European perspective, there are no positive effects, whether one looks at political or at economic objectives. Indeed, the broadcasting policy at community level caused the most thorough and severe political damage. This occurred without delivering any positive results to the economy of this sector. Economically, the only beneficiaries seem to be (1) the advertised (in the economy at large), (2) the advertising industry, as well as (3) global and Hollywood, product-exporting companies. Ever since its adoption, the quantity of programming has proliferated, the quality dropped dramatically and the position of viewers has deteriorated.

Purely politically, the privatization of control of this sector is now causing a pervasive depoliticization, an inter-European cultural alienation and an opaque ignorance. There are two distinctive sources of depoliticization: the first is due to the privatization of the political domain of communication and the framework and vehicles for political communication. The second is due to the masterminded effect that, while crucial decision-making processes all take place in Brussels, television viewers are directed to fix their eyes on national news and current affairs programming. The politically schizophrenic situation that has evolved entails that viewers limit their viewing to events of national scope, while in fact crucial decisions take place at the superordinate European level, and these certainly demand a 'wide-angle lens' to bring them into focus.

Europeanisation, however, was evasive even on the most attainable fronts. Market fragmentation was never remedied. European broadcasting is still a microcosm of a fragmented and alienated Europe. Crucially, the end result was further dependence and vulnerability for the European, audiovisual sector. Pan-European channels did not attract any lasting, political support. Transnational, mainly thematic, channels covering linguistic and cultural zones predominate in the realm of satellite, transfrontier broadcasting.

In 1981, fully advertiser-funded channels existed only in Luxembourg, the UK, and Italy. Over two decades later, psb monopolies are just about surviving, while advertising has become the prevailing mode for financing broadcasting services. Advertising has thus been made into the main regulator of content. With such a pivotal minder and a significant lever for the 'European conception of culture' what need do we have of such public policies? The troubles with political absenteeism, citizens' protests and reactions are not possible to hide, however. Democracy confronts us with the problem – sidelined, if not obliterated – of the real interests of the citizens of Europe. Democratic, communication rights and participatory forms of media organisations are anything but guaranteed; indeed they are radiant in their absence. When private interests are *de facto* the sole regulators and suppliers of information, such rights seem eccentric. The shift towards the free flow of advertising was successfully imposed, thanks to powerful, economic pressures and legal dexterity in aptly invoking the four freedoms of the Treaty of the European Community as interpreted in ECJ jurisprudence. For Commission proponents, the free flow of advertising was the cornerstone for the creation of a new, economic space, to give global industry a European springboard from which to take off.

In the triangle formed by (A) policy-making, (B) political communication and (C) politics that I pointed to in Chapter 1, I have tried to demonstrate how and why (A), rather than forging political integration, is effectively undermining both (B), and (C). I have shown why the existing framework continues and will continue to undermine politics in general, both at the national and at the supra-national level. The subsequent revisions of the TWF policy, which are monitored in the next two chapters, provide more evidence of the effect of depoliticization, as global commercial forces increased and solidified their grip over this strategic sector.

Chapter 3

REVISING THE TWF FRAMEWORK DIRECTIVE

The first revision of the TWF Directive (TWFD) turned out to be another long and painstaking process. It started in 1993 and was completed in 1997. Politically, the most significant element of this process was that it began just after the proclamation and adoption of 'European citizenship', which itself had resulted from the Treaty of the European Union (TEU) that was adopted at Maastricht in 1992. For the political optimists this was a promising conjuncture.

In this chapter, I discuss the options that have materialised in order to provide for and solidify citizens' communication rights in light of the furtherance of these developments. Communicative functions could have included measures to support collateral political functions, such as the elections for the European Parliament. They could also have included other, novel, political objectives. This putative scenario in fact raises the issue of broadening the scope of the policy.

I then discuss the factors that inhibited the re-grounding of the TWFD policy, with the aim of adjusting this policy in line with citizens' needs and the possibilities opened up by the TEU. I go on to present the issues that were raised in the process of the revision and those which prevailed. These policy issues were predominantly related to economic matters, though cultural self-determination also became a matter of controversy. In analysing these aspects I elaborate on the inability of Europeans to agree among themselves or to gain any ground in the formidable attack launched by the Americans in the communications industry. Finally, I discuss the failure of community policy-makers to even consider the possibility of introducing some basic 'must carry rules' to safeguard a role for a minimum level of political communication in the emergent Union.

European Citizenship and the Revision of Communications Policy

Central in the political debates on Europe during the 1990s was the need for the EU to advance mechanisms in order to forge ahead with the 'ever closer union'. This took *inter alia* the form of demands and concrete initiatives towards a common defence and security policy. Political unification or closer integration were once again very much on the agenda.

One of the concerns in view of the revision of the TWF Directive was the possibility of broadening the scope of this policy. If a broadening were opted for, the next key question was what direction should broadening go towards and what additional aspects should be incorporated? Could for instance the recommendations of the De Clercq report, which directly refer to safeguarding political communication, become part of the TWF Directive? Moreover, within this context it was reasonable to argue that the newly acquired European-scope citizenship, in conjunction with the right to stand for and to vote in European Parliamentary elections, under certain conditions (Papadimitriou 1999: 137), should have necessitated the creation of an array of appropriate political communication support mechanisms.

As things stand now, there is an all but total communicative and informational void about the rights that are attached to European citizenship and those which stand outside the existing national media. This is problematic on a number of criteria. As European citizens, we are entitled to vote for MEPs not just from our own countries but also from other EU member states. We can also stand as candidates in third member states (TEC, Article 19 (2)). The obvious question that this particularity raises is: how can we possibly learn about these other candidates, if an overarching political communication system (channels and relevant content flows) is not in place? An Italian citizen might opt for voting for a green party in Germany or Sweden. But how can s/he learn about the political programmes of such parties and candidates? Could a militant political body bring the EC to a constitutional court for not fulfilling its fundamental political obligations in regard to adequate political communication? Why is such elementary knowledge denied to European citizens?

In order to justify its politically amputating and economistic approach, the Green Paper on TWF in the 1980s argued that "in the absence of express provision to the contrary in the Treaty, a television signal must be regarded as provision of services" (GPTWF: 105). However, in the 1990s, two significant changes did occur to eliminate that absence: first, the proclamation of the Citizenship of the Union, which brings with it some fundamental attendant rights and obligations – some explicit and others implicit.[49] Secondly, the explicit call for cultural action "including in the audiovisual sector" by Article 151 of the TEC. [50]

---

[49] About European citizenship and the rights attached to it, see Chapter 1 and Appendix.

[50] *Article 151* (ex -128) of the TEC:

    1. The Community shall contribute to the flowering of the cultures of the Member States, while respecting their national and regional diversity and at the same time bringing the common cultural heritage to the fore.

    2. Action by the Community shall be aimed at encouraging cooperation between Member States and, if necessary, supporting and supplementing their action in the following areas:

    — improvement of the knowledge and dissemination of the culture and history of the European peoples;

    — conservation and safeguarding of cultural heritage of European significance;

    — non-commercial cultural exchanges;

    — artistic and literary creation, including in the audiovisual sector.

    3. The Community and the Member States shall foster cooperation with third countries and the competent international organisations in the sphere of culture, in particular the Council of Europe.

    4. The Community shall take cultural aspects into account in its action under other provisions of this Treaty, in particular in order to respect and to promote the diversity of its cultures.

    5. In order to contribute to the achievement of the objectives referred to in this Article, the Council:

    — acting in accordance with the procedure referred to in Article 251 and after consulting the Committee of the Regions, shall adopt incentive measures, excluding any harmonisation of the laws and regulations of the Member States. The Council shall act unanimously throughout the procedure referred to in Article 251;

    — acting unanimously on a proposal from the Commission, shall adopt recommendations.

The ensemble of these two significant changes should logically be adequate in order to remedy the original aberration that was supposedly derivative of the missing legal basis for a more holistic approach. That legal constraint could have been considered eliminated by the provision of Article 151. Additionally it could be argued that the attribution of citizenship conferred extra political obligations to offset the seriously disturbed balance in the field of communications.

Hence, the adoption of the Citizenship of the Union could be said to be a step, albeit a hesitant one, towards political unification. In this sense, it could also be seen as partly filling the gaps of the original TEC. As we have seen in Chapter 2, these gaps were successfully exploited to mould an exclusively economistic approach to the role of communications in society and in the polity, setting in motion the process of commercialisation of electronic media.

The proclamation of European citizenship could, thus, be significant for the future shape of communications policy-making. Notably, this was particularly crucial for implementing the long-standing demand of the EP for a European sphere of political communication (Kaitatzi-Whitlock 1996, Sarikakis 2002). In fact, it could be taken as a prime opportunity to redress the mounting imbalance of power between political constituencies and market forces. Similarly, it was an opportunity for intra-sectoral adjustments and for achieving a balance between hegemonic and weaker market forces, notably, operators and controllers of content distribution vis-à-vis European producers of contents and artists. In short, the TEU provided the opportunity to correct the structural aberration of placing communications policy in the Internal Market framework.

In Search of Space for Civic Communication

Within this context and in view of the up-coming revision of the TWFD, one could anticipate a re-grounding of the entire communications policy framework so that civic communication facilities were readily available in this Union in the making. Indeed some would argue that such a re-grounding was mandatory, if this European regime meant to be consistent with its claim to being democratic. The self-conception of the EU is that it "aims to be a fair and caring society" and that "all EU countries are committed to peace, democracy, the rule of law and respect for human rights, and [even that] they work together to promote these values in the wider world." (Commission 2005: 91).

According to liberal political philosophy and to all democracy theory, the provision of public political communication and of a framework for civic dialogue are preconditions for any democratic polity (Bobbio 1993, Dahl 2000, Barber 1984, Popper & Condry 1993, Starr 2005, Garnham 1990, Keane 1991, Dahlgren 1995). Meyer holds that "(t)he norms of democratic politics, as they are applied to pluralistic, law-governed polities, demarcate a broad spectrum of possibilities within which there is ample room for different models of *democratic participation*" (2002: 4, emphasis added).

My concern is, by investigating the evolution of this phase of communications policy, to establish just what form democratic participation could take for holders of the new European citizenship. If the 'broad spectrum of possibilities' for democratic participation "holds true even in cases where competing political actors try to yoke the constitutional framework of their respective commonwealths to their own political projects" (Meyer 2002: 4), why should it not hold true for the EU of the 1990s? And furthermore, what would such a citizenship be worth?

The installation of communications (audiovisual) policy – via TWF – in the Internal Market framework was not simply a case of "yoking together constitutional frameworks", but a major political aberration. The notion of European citizenship 'granted' to Europeans by the TEU could have been used as a vantage point for the veritable revision of this policy in order to redress the notorious imbalance and to provide concrete and practical possibilities for a European kind of political communication and corresponding communications rights and facilities.

According to Meyer there are three theoretical paradigms that enable us to define alternative approaches to participation in real politics. These include: (a) the model of democracy as a marketplace; (b) the model of participatory democracy[51] and (c) the model of democratic civil society. "All of them can legitimately claim to have specified what democracy in modern societies mean in actual practice." (2002: 4-5). To be sure, the supra-national formation of the EU is a *sui generis* case. But, it certainly calls itself democratic. Indeed its ambitions extend to the democratisation of other political entities, notably in Central and Eastern Europe.

Various advocates of the EU, depending on their views and criteria, would have no difficulty in classifying the EU in some of the three models of democracy above. Arguably, the 'market model of democracy' rather fits the EU's contemporary outlook. But even this paradigm cannot do without political communication. Having elaborated on the key features of each of the three models, Meyer concludes that none of these three types of democracy can operate without some form of *political communication*. Hence, is the EU model in fact democratic?

All of these models are compatible with the normative claims of Western democracy even though controversies might arise concerning their feasibility. They all concur in stipulating that comprehensive, reliable information about – and drawn from – the political has to be made available. What distinguishes them is the extent to which they insist on having something more: an additional public space for dialogue, deliberation, and consensus-building. All of them assume that *citizens will have complete, undistorted information about the most important political issues* as well as about the intentions and programs of the political actors who represent them. The participatory and civil society models, respectively though in different ways, further assume that there should be an extensive system of opportunities for participants to communicate

---

[51] For a discussion of the democratic participatory potential and the social legitimation of supra-state politics at the EU level see Chryssochoou 2005.

and try to achieve consensus, and that they should have a role in shaping decisions about political affairs that concern them. (Meyer 2002: 8, emphasis added)

As it turned out, the new Article 151 of the Treaty of the European Community (TEC)[52] welcomed the deployment of cultural and audiovisual policies proper by superordinate EC decision-making institutions for the first time. In fact this Article calls on the Community to bring "the common cultural heritage to the fore" by undertaking action "including in the audiovisual sector". This explicit reference to the audiovisual made up for the missing legal ground that the economistic TWF had been predicated upon back in the 1980s. Characteristically though, the prospect of superseding the economistic approach in communications and in audiovisual policy-making came up against another typical hurdle: the requirement for a 'unanimity vote'. This meant that for any change to occur each member state had to endorse it. This apparently democratic guarantee was the best way to ensure that nothing was done. Supra-national inter-governmentalism seems to be ideal for stalling decisions and for producing 'non-decision-making' (Bachrach & Baratz 1962 & 1963). This also suggests that the invocation of a lack of a legal basis, back in the 1980s, was merely a pretext, since a full-blown policy could have been grounded on Article 308 (ex 235) of the TEC. What was really missing was a true political will to this effect.

Decision-making hurdles such as the unanimity vote can cancel out even the most desirable policy. The possibility of addressing the political communication structure provided by the TEU was one such policy. Lack of will is of course often translated into lack of true power. Whichever might be the case the final outcome frustrated one of the most compelling relevant counterfactuals of European Union democratisation. Consequently, diagnoses of political crisis and accusations of Europe's

---

[52] Article 151 (ex Article 128) as amended by the Amsterdam Treaty and renumbered by the Nice Treaty,

'democratic deficit' did not appear to have any sobering effect on political and economic elites.

Compounding this lack of political will and ability to change, neo-liberal forces were in the ascendant once again. The adoption of the Bargeman Group Recommendations at the Corfu Summit of 25-26 June 1994 resulted in the prompt announcement of the Commission's *Action Plan on Europe's Way to the Information Society* (APEWIS, Commission 1994a) in July. This new framework embraced the audiovisual sector, seeing it as one segment of its 'globally coherent' (sic) ensemble of policies (APEWIS: 1-10). This was one of those grand, not to say pompous, EC strategies.

At the backdrop of the new Article 151 of the TEC, the 'embracing' of the audiovisual sector by APEWIS constitutes another adverse political manifesto, very similar, in effect, to that contained in the Green Paper on TWF of the 1980s. Yet, the German Commissioner for Telecommunicat-ions and Technology, Martin Bangemann, succeeded in launching and having his greatly inflated Action Plan endorsed (Kaitatzi-Whitlock 2000), thereby inspiring a new wave of delusion about European dynamism, something obviously much needed after the debacle of the HDTV project (Kaitatzi-Whitlock 1998).

APEWIS claimed control of the audiovisual sector in view of the trend towards convergence in the broad fields of information, tele-communications and culture. Significantly, putting audiovisual policy under the umbrella of APEWIS meant in fact its firm re-entrenchment within the economistic Internal Market framework. This approach extinguished all hope for a balanced, holistic or democratising media revision policy. The discourse concerning official policy documents never raised the issue of establishing a mechanism for European-wide political communication. This applied even to the European Parliament, whose overall input, though positive and in the public interest, was reactive rather than proactive.

It is noteworthy that the preparatory processes for the first revision of the TWF directive also overlapped with the workings of the De Clercq report (1993). This was submitted in 1993 and had elaborated on including aspects of political communications. It focused again on the potential of politicising the communications policy of the EU. Significantly, the report and its recommendations once again addressed the issue of addressing European citizens responsibly and informing them fully. However, the proposals made were considered "too audacious" and were eventually dismissed by a hesitant college of Commissioners (Smith 2004).

All this meant that the scope of the revision would not be broadened in a democratising and political direction. It is worth recalling that it was in response to such a demand from the EP in the early 1980s that the implication of the Community in this policy field started. The omission is particularly significant despite the fact that prerogatives for a cultural policy were available now. Article 151 of the TEC which specifically refers to the audiovisual sector had been put in place and a Europe-wide political communication policy could be based on that constitutional provision.

That the Commission opted to continue with the economistic approach of the Internal Market framework signalled that the tenets of the internal market were to be 'permanently' applied to the audiovisual sector. Guided by the White Paper of 1993, the main emphasis was on free movement of services, a new 'global understanding' and the responses of the market to opportunities for growth.

In this light, the Commission was expected to strike a balance and produce a new synthesis for a policy review pursuing the new objectives, but also addressing new challenges and problems. These had a dual character: one, defensive, aiming to protect and strengthen the audiovisual production sector, and the other, further liberalising and broadening the scope of the Directive to cover such new services as tele-shopping, thus further intensifying the commercialisation of television as a vehicle for the growth of the economy at large. But politicians, although prepared to further alter the role of the media, hesitated to endorse the protective and developmental measures proposed.

Protective Measures versus More Commercialisation of Television

By 1994 the TWF Directive had been applied and tested for five years and the collected experience was to be used as a ground for future corrective steps. Preparations for its revision started in 1993 in response to two clearly discernible realities. The first related to inadequacies and failures diagnosed in the Directive, notably the explosive trade deficit in audiovisual programming. The second referred to the development of new economic, political and technological challenges. There were notably, numerous infringements reported, caused particularly by the confusing articles relating to (a) jurisdiction and (b) quotas. These in combination counteracted some of the key objectives of the Directive and even the goals of the internal market. Failure to boost the production sector, combined with the onslaught of GATS liberalisations and the further transmutation of the role of the media set new legal, economic and political challenges.

The preparatory phase in the TWF revision process encompassed four overlapping processes: (1) the drafting and publication of the Think Tank Report (TTR 1994), (2) the drafting and issuing of the Green Paper on Audiovisual Programming in April 1994, which was shaped in the light of the White Paper on Growth, Competitiveness and Employment[53], (3) the consultation process with industry representatives which culminated in the Audiovisual Conference of June-July 1994, (4) the monitoring of the implementation of the Directive and the submission of the assessments on monitoring.

---

[53] The Delors White Paper on Growth, Competitiveness, Employment: The challenges and ways forward into the 21st century was being drafted during the final phase of the Uruguay Round talks of the GATS agreement and in the light of the G7 meeting in Tokyo (1993), where an accord was struck to conclude the liberalisation of services.

The Think Tank Report

DG X commissioned the Think Tank Report on the Audiovisual Policy in the European Union (TTR) in the autumn of 1993. This Think Tank started work under the chairmanship of film director A-P. Vasconcelos and submitted its report in March 1994.[54] The TTR was greatly influenced by the prolonged controversy between the US and the EU and certainly by the outcome of the GATT talks that ended with the accord on the liberalisation of services known as GATS (December 1993). Generally, the TTR diagnosed a severe crisis in audiovisual programming production and advocated an indispensable strategic transformation of the sector as a remedy. It advised a departure from a subsidised economy and an advance towards a self-sufficient economy, yet without resorting to a shock therapy of complete deregulation (TTR 1994: 33). Two ills were identified as afflicting the sector: first, the absence of structural frameworks in the existing configuration of instruments and the media industry, and secondly, policy omissions. The report recommended coherent political and industrial action to help Europe recapture its own market, a move which was seen as "a right which can be called natural" (ibid: 15).

Basically the TTR recommended emulating the industrial policy blend of the US system, notably in regard to copyrights and financial and distributional mechanisms. It argued that compliance with the quotas would be meaningless if 'European works' were not defined precisely. It was remarked that the audiovisual, alone of all large industrial sectors, had not only failed to acquire a transnational outlook, despite the talent, the market opportunities and the money available, but had also regressed into national markets rather than becoming international in its orientation (ibid: 17). The reason for this trend was thought to be 'lack of confidence and strategy'. As a result all these assets were "of less benefit to (Europe) than to the USA" (ibid: 15).

---

[54] The other members were Michele Cotta, Peter Fleischmann, Enrique Balmaseda, David Puttnam and Gaetano Stucchi.

Thus, the TTR emphasised the key importance of distribution, promotion and financial control, while condemning nationally fragmented systems and policies. Its overall proposals were undoubtedly maximalist. They presupposed an EC constitutional system which did not then exist. More specifically, they presupposed the abandoning of 'minimum harmonization' and the capacity for supra-national regulation. These European film makers and cinema experts thus questioned the crippling inter-governmentalist nature of EU decision-making and the fact that 'minimum' regulation was opted for and well-entrenched. It was argued for instance that "finance for the distribution element of the strategy would necessarily have to be made available at the level of the EU and overseen by a regulatory body operating at EU level." (ibid: 46). The sums envisaged were also exorbitant when compared to the meagre funds committed to the MEDIA II programme and to its predecessor which were supposed to support EU producers. If the envisaged network for distribution were actually to achieve viable competitiveness, it was argued, each consortium would require funding of about one billion European currency units (ECU). However, public funding of this order could not be committed. As for providing funding, why would any enthusiastic entrepreneur ever want to risk so much capital if, thanks to liberalisation, s/he could get the requisite 'product' a lot cheaper without risk?[55]

The TTR report was quite critical of the Commission in that it concurred that the EC policy had led to a condition where "the single market only exists for American films" (ibid: 20) and that "the fall in attendance in Europe has only affected European films" (ibid: 21). These programme production professionals admitted a plain and bitter truth: that the EC audiovisual sector simply "cannot compete with the world's leading industry under conditions of equality" (ibid: 17). In order to "claim back our

---

[55] European broadcasters avoided dependence on foreign supply by entering into transatlantic alliances and investing in American cinema, for example Credit Lyonnais, which inherited MGM and which was supported by the French state. This was also the case with Francis Bougygues's Cibby 2000, studio Canal+, Polygram (a subsidiary of Philips), Kirch's Neue Konstantin, Berlusconi's de la Penta, and the Berliner Bank, which invested USD 100 million every year in American films (TTR, ibid: 26).

industry", TTR proposed competitive tenders and the rigorous appraisal of business plans, including the operation of credits and a unification of the fragmented distribution mechanisms (ibid: 42-43). Automatic aid, even when rewarding success, could not obviate the need for structural mechanisms, notably pan-European distribution networks able to intervene 'upstream' in the production of films (ibid: 27). It was therefore seen as imperative that the paralysing fragmentation of national support systems be remedied (ibid: 22). These experts then were desperately calling for serious interventionist public policies at a time when EU leaders spoke of 'global coherence', as the terminology of the G7 group dictated, and when they promulgated the wildest forms of 'hands off' *laissez-faire* policies.

The priority and strategic importance of this sector cannot be limited to rhetorical statements TTR claimed that if it was not to lose out again on the second wave of expansion, when the consequences might well be lethal (ibid: 19), a coherent reflection of this 'strategic priority' in the political action and in the assignment of public resources which were thought to be temporarily needed (ibid: 17) was called for. The criticism against the strategy opted for by the Commission was at its sharpest when the TTR concluded that to "leave (the audiovisual industry) in the hands of the market would mean purely and simply condemning it to disappear rapidly" (ibid: 17).

Even though the Think Tank consisted of professionals with the remit to consider sectoral aspects and shortcomings, it nevertheless stressed that "the audiovisual sector is also an essential instrument to consolidate the European integration process." (ibid: 16 & 60). This was an interesting element as by this time the 'integration theme' had almost disappeared from official policy discourse.

The Focus on Contents and the Programming Industry

The Green Paper on the European Audiovisual Programming (GPEAP) of 1994 was launched in the aftermath of a host of important – both general and specific – developments and transmutations: first, the TEU and the small window of possibility for an alternative media policy; secondly, the negative referenda against the TEU, which marked citizens disaffection with Europolitics; thirdly, the formidable clash between the US and the EU and the latter's defeat in the GATS agreement; fourthly, the notorious retreat and U-turn in the infrastructure and the HDTV strategy of the EU and its subsequent shift towards wide-screen and advanced TV (multimedia and interactive); fifthly, the quantum leap achieved by digital compression, and digital technology innovations more generally; sixthly, the significant self-organisation of market forces in the Digital Video Broadcasting group and their acquisition of a formal status in matters of policy formulation at EC level; and finally, the climate leading up to the adoption of the APEWIS, proposed by DG XIII and leading UNICE (Union National des Industries de la Communauté Européenne) industrialists, streamlined and identified with the interests of international partners such as the USA and Japan.

Just like the Think Tank Report, the Green Paper confirmed the negative diagnoses about the declining programme industry[56] of the continent and the challenges facing it. Other than that, the main contribution of the GP consisted of a torrent of well-put questions. However, questions alone hardly make an affirmative basis for policy. Thus, with regard to the policy options, the basic problem was formulated as follows: "How can the EU contribute to the development of a European film and television programme industry which can be competitive on the world market, forward-looking and capable of radiating the influence of European culture and creating jobs in Europe?" (ibid: 14). A ready answer for this was to be found in APEWIS which pointed out that with regard to the development of infrastructures and applications of the Information Society, the EU "intends to play a full role

---

[56] Definition: "By programme industry, is meant the industry producing cinema and television programmes. Within the second category the main emphasis is on the production of stock programmes (fiction, cartoons, documentaries) which can be screened repeatedly and are thus the basic ingredients of catalogues" (TWFD: 15).

in harnessing and using the new technologies" (ibid: 8). Interestingly, however, it was also stressed that "there were some contrasting, not to say conflicting, views on what instruments should be used to implement the Union's audiovisual policy" (ibid: 9).

This remark obviated the fact that the GP had absorbed into its policy discourse certain critical points that were raised by the TTR and the latter's warnings and overall diagnosis. So, in effect this Commission policy document was actually blaming previous EC policies for this decline. The fragmentation of distribution structures along with the parallel support systems operating in each member state were equally blamed for the utter introversion of this industry. However, given the prevailing philosophy in the Commission at this time, the Green Paper did not incorporate the TTR's maximalist recommendations. But, ignoring its warnings about the lethal and unequal competition between US and EU producers meant that the EU was opting to let its production industry die.

> The European market has been among the fastest growing in the world with a current market growth rate of 6% a year in real terms that is being sustained even in today's recessionary climate. The US has benefited most from growth in Europe, increasing its sales of programming from USD 330 million in 1984 to USD 3.6 billion in 1992. In 1991, 77% of American exports of audiovisual programmes went to Europe, of which nearly 60% went to the EC... while the European Union annual deficit with the US in audiovisual trade amounts to about USD 3.5 billion. (TTR: 16)

Apart from the utter economic failure, the flagrant political issue arising here is the following: is European integration feasible on a cultural industry which absorbs and screens 77% of US export goods mainly from Hollywood? Can these symbolic contents become the material for constructing the 'European identity', so often invoked in the documents of the 1980s? Economically, these figures suggest that US gains and corresponding EC domestic trade deficit grew ten times between 1984 and 1992. These unprecedented losses highlighted at least three elements: (a) the almost criminal fallacies of the 'flagship of the Single Market' strategy for the audiovisual sector on the part of the partisan Commission of the early 1980s; (b) the total – and arguably intentional – disregard of the strategic importance of the content-software production sector at that same period; (c) the Commission's sole concern for the industrial and commercial interests of a handful of companies that controlled distribution.

In view of this sheer cultural takeover, it is critical to compare notes and recall the false policy pretences of the previous decade. Therefore, it was propounded that "this is yet another area where the establishment of a Community-wide market will allow European firms to improve their competitiveness." (GPTWF: 33). In the face of such a gigantic failure, it must be assumed that either the Commissions acted on completely false pretences back in the 1980s, or that it was entirely incompetent.

It may also be recalled that in its Green Paper of 1984, but also in its original draft Directive – a point strikingly taken by many analysts – the Commission ignored the production and programming aspects of the audiovisual. Only after a decade of supra-national policy-making in this field, after exorbitant losses and the entrepreneurial practice of domestic big players buying up foreign software catalogues, did it dawn upon Brussels analysts that the software-side of the industry was of strategic importance.

This demonstrates that the Commission for the first time looked at its role from the point of view of content production and its professionals in the Green Paper of 1994. This, however, happened far too late, at a time when the intra-sectoral balance of power had tipped irreversibly towards the broadcasters who were happily opting for cheaper American contents. Nevertheless, professionals in the audiovisual sector hoped for an eleventh-hour change, placing their hopes in a non-existent political will and commitment. Past EC policies were distribution and hardware dominated "even though this might not be the intention," a good-willed TTR (ibid: 18) pointed out. Notwithstanding past missed opportunities, the future held a great deal in store for programme-makers, the Green Paper also optimistically maintained. Digital compression of bandwidths and, hence, channel proliferation was counted on for increases in demand. This revealed negligence of the fact that the key scarce resource in this industry are the 'packages of viewers', and that programming is merely the bait for a given number of these. So the remedies of self-blinded drafters suggested that programming: "must be competitive in an open worldwide market; it must be forward-looking and be involved in the development of the information society; it must illustrate the creative genius and the personality of the people of Europe (sic); it must be capable of transforming its growth into new jobs in Europe" (ibid: 7).

In terms of timing, swift action was deemed indispensable if the EU was to strengthen its audiovisual policy. Otherwise it risked being overtaken by technological change and further liberalisation (ibid: 9). "Without European partners in the programme industry, (operators) will have no choice but to forge transatlantic alliances with the transfer of resources as an inevitable consequence." (ibid: 22). To whom might such invocations be addressed? Certainly not to those European entrepreneurs whose explicit business strategy was actually to forge the feared trans-atlantic alliances. "The most powerful operators on the world market are seeking to control the most important programme catalogues." (ibid: 7).

The real question was: how could these operators be stopped from forging transatlantic alliances when in fact this was already their prevailing strategy? Hence, rather than harnessing the centrifugal trends of operators who earn in Europe yet invest outside it, politicians – by regulating them instead of incessantly liberalising – urged the operators to self-regulate. These invocations once again reveal the effective inability of public policy initiators to act and to harness the industry. But, policy drafters' delusions were unlimited: "All parties will have to be mobilized to rise to the challenge of the future. Application of the subsidiarity principle is essential for the definition of a European policy when action is planned in areas which are not within the exclusive jurisdiction of the Community" (ibid: 30).

It is worth pointing out yet another crucial discrimination. Of all the components of APEWIS, only issues to do with the audiovisual content were not subject to decision-making by qualified majority procedures. This made the audiovisual sector cripplingly special in terms of non-decision-making. This particularity subjects it to blackmail and to ultimatums from both political and industrial actors opposing relevant developments. It exposed the audiovisual sector to various ulterior motives (e.g. bartering and compromise for the settlement of irrelevant problems).

As a matter of fact the supra-national EU policy-making level was the ideal locus and the instrument for perpetuating the domination of the interests already benefiting from the transatlantic alliances highlighted by the TTR through induced policy paralysis. The GP concurred with the TTR: in the TV sector the explosion in programming demand has failed to benefit the trade of EU programme production, "which remains locked into fragmented national markets." (ibid: 11). Instead, programme budgets have shrunk. But rather than blaming uncontrolled liberalisation, the GP blamed the 'laziness syndrome' of European producers.

The GP naively estimated that the revolution produced by digital bandwidth compression in frequency availability would considerably alter the balance of power between broadcasters and programming professionals. It was erroneously thought that channel proliferation leads to economies of scope: hence under certain conditions there could be demand for diversity. "But many opportunities will arise for programmes geared to limited and specialised audiences...: exploiting cultural diversity (sic) can be turned into an opportunity to be seized" (ibid: 15). The combined opportunities of the market amounted to a new industrial imperative. Not only talent, "but also industrial structures of the critical size were needed to secure the necessary financing and to constitute programme catalogues" (ibid: 16). So, producers and professionals had to mobilize and respond to market requirements.

Unlike the TTR the GP did not propose measures regarding either structural changes or developmental incentives. Instead endless open-ended 'methodological' questions were posed (ibid: 32-41), which again suggest the manifold constraints placed upon the policy drafter. The persistent problem was the inability to forge solutions through regulation and appropriate incentives owing to the long-prevailing imbalance of power between the sections of the industry.

Conflicting Factions at the European Audiovisual Industry

The 1994 European Audiovisual Conference (EAC) became the battleground for intra-sectoral confrontation: a watershed between illusions and feasible policy remaking. The subjection of the audiovisual sector to APEWIS complicated things further. It involved transcontinental links and the transatlantic diffusion, the enmeshing and merging of capital interests. The concept 'European policy' was thus blurred as boundaries were neutralised. Contrary to APEWIS and other key policy documents[57] of the 1990s, a decade before, policy discourse then depicted the EU as a competitor of the US and of other G7 members as well.

Different 'languages' spoken at different EC policy levels and professional groups were thus incompatible. The language of the European Audiovisual Conference (EAC) was laced with such terms as 'competitors' and 'enemies', notably referring to the USA. But, if European policies were no longer distinguishable from the global projects of the G7 and the WTO and if, as Mougeotte, vice-president of Association of Commercial Television (ACT), put it, there is no European programming to speak of, what was the relevance of such policies at EC level? Such an approach was perfectly served by non-policy-making outcomes and by endless procrastinations in decision-making.

---

[57] The sudden spirit of 'cooperation' with just recently 'hostile' competitors transpires also from the *Council Resolution on a framework for EC Policy on Digital Video Broadcasting* of June 1994 (Council 1994a) prompting dialogue with them (See Chapter 6).

Pinheiro spoke of the "need to act now" because "the audiovisual sector is not excluded from GATS'... progressive liberalisation" regime (EAC, 30.6.1994). This was an ominous development for an industry in decline and in deficit, as it would not be long before the US Department of Trade (USDT) and the Motion Picture Export Association of America (MPEAA) pressed anew for market access concessions. Europe had only "a brief respite" (ibid). It was the nearly unanimous opinion of the EAC Conference that any inaction, delayed action or contradictory strategy regarding programming could be fatal for the audiovisual sector. But as we have already seen dramatic terms like 'lethal'', 'fatal' and 'disastrous' were very frequently invoked, yet in vain.

There was a 'virtual consensus' on four crucial points: 1) that the audiovisual, as a growth industry, offers possibilities for job creation, 2) that the safeguarding of cultural diversity requires positive (integration) measures for the programme industry, 3) that digital compression accentuates the latter's strategic role and 4) that the EU must act quickly, if it wants to strengthen it (ibid: 7). This last assumption was the weak link. The requisite political will was absent, thus reinforcing a framework that paralysed proactive policy production. But the virtual consensus was not total, and these four points were not the entire story. Pinheiro exposed the contradictions and conflicts reflecting the divergent interests that fracture the European audiovisual sector. Lack of political will was a reflection of such divergent interests and of the double agendas of hegemonic member states. This alone invited failure.

Here lay the root cause of the EC's inability to impose and effectively implement any policies, making it essentially a 'nominal Union' in the audiovisual sphere. Economic interests with stakes in the international market would never sacrifice profits for the sake of the general good of the 'Union'. Owing to its key importance, to internationalisation, and its extremely fast growth-rate, which far outpaced the policy-making capabilities and dysfunctional rhythms of the EU, this sector crystallized this conflict of interests.

Commission President Jacques Delors in his keynote speech admitted that

> There are a lot of contradictions to overcome. First of all is the contradiction inherent in the doctrine of free exchange. Though it is a lever for prosperity and peace it cannot be likened to the fable of the fox in the hen house. The golden rule of the market must prevail instead. This stipulates that each one must have his chance. Is this the case for Europe today? Is the EU strong enough to have a presence in the WTO and to impose a minimum of rules of the game at the global level? These questions must be addressed by you, but also by our governments. (EAC, 30.6.94)[58]

The conclusion from Delors' position was that effective measures for the protection of this deficit-ridden market were indispensable.

There was then a distinct contrast between Delors' assessment that the EU was not strong enough to co-decide the minimum global rules and the new Commissioners Bargeman, Oreja and Monti, who 'optimistically' called for such rules in the Directive's revision proposal of 1995. On his part, Mougeotte, vice-president of ACT, represented that miniscule, but most powerful, part of the opposition which dissented and obstructed the 'consensus' of the conference. He claimed that the "European work is a myth", and that European audiovisual production consists merely of the sum of national productions. Like all myths, he said, it continues to feed collective spectres (EAC 2.7.94). He then resorted to the oft-repeated populist and neo-liberal axiom of his predecessor Rupert Murdoch: "Le public a toujours bon goût; le public a toujours raison" (ibid) and

---

[58] *"Tout d'abord le libre échange... Le libre échange est un facteur de prosperité et de paix, mais il ne peut pas être assimilé à la fable du renard dans le poulailler. Il faut que tout le monde ait sa chance. C'est la règle d'or du marché. Est-ce le cas pour les européens aujourd'hui? Se sont-ils dotés des moyens d'être présents sur les marches, sont ils assez forts pour imposer demain au sein de l'Organisation mondiale du commerce un minimum de règles du jeu? Telles sont les questions qui sont posées non seulement à vous mais aussi à nos gouvernements, et cela renvoi encore au Livre Blanc.'* (Jacques Delors, 30 June 1994).

demanded that the relationship between producers and operators be freely negotiated rather than regulated. He rejected a) supplementary quotas, b) 'reductionary' definitions of the 'work', and c) further constraints on advertising. These de-regulatory demands, however, surely do recall the fox in the hen house. Since quotas were considered indispensable by programming producers (Schoof & Brown 1995: 331), this defined the intra-industry tug of war between operators and programme producers.

Interestingly, Mougeotte also insisted on another controversial issue. He demanded that channel control jurisdiction remain with the transmitting state rather than be transferred to the receiving states (ibid). This again revealed whose interests were behind the first Green Paper of 1984, which starkly and incessantly advocated this policy. But why should the vice-president of ACT be terrified of the control of jurisdiction not staying with the transmitting state if he was so confident that "le public a toujours bon goût; le public a toujours raison"? Thus, the ACT tabled its own agenda at the EAC. This agenda counteracted, if not prohibited, any plans for corrective regulatory moves to satisfy the general European interest, which he rejected as a "collective fantasy" (*phantasme collectif*).

Similarly, Levy (of Polygram) claimed that "European distribution is meaningless without a product which attracts European audiences" (ibid). He also noticed some "most surprising omissions" in the GP, for example on copyrights. He in fact went on to threaten that if there were no copyright laws "we would ensure that Polygram got out of the entertainment business tomorrow."[59]

This is the type of 'threat' that European politicians have had to face in torrents from industrial leaders, ever since the advent of the 'techno-economic paradigm shift' (Kaitatzi-Whitlock 2003). Indeed the strategy of threats led European governments, notably those of the social-democratic

---

[59] Levy qualified his remark by noting that "sadly even the most recent European legislation on copyright weakens considerably the legal status of film producers and is penalising European companies to the benefit of our competitors in the United States" (ibid). This position is in fact shared also by the TTR. The cause of the onset of the strategies and tactics of threats to national governments must be sought in the origin of deregulation.

parties to accommodate, to 'behave' and to subjugate themselves to all sorts of industrial imperatives and ultimatums. Tragically for politics and for political constituencies of all kinds, this practice and all-too-facile accommodation to threats have led to a "divorce between power and politics" (Baumann 2005).

Any reform to counter this should provide that "economic rights granted to artists, directors and others should always be assignable to the producer" and that "the principle of presumption of transfer of rights of artists to the producer should be part of European Law" (ibid). On his part, CLT director Jean Stock lamented the inadequacy of the European programming on offer. This remark was expedient of course to 'justify' ACT broadcasters to turn to extra-European sources for programme-supply (ibid). Thus, the EAC exposed irreconcilable conflicts of interests projected in the prospect of revising the largely unimplementable TWF Directive. The key policy dilemmas and the conflicting options were elucidated. Most crucially the ACT's rejection of any regulatory redefinition – let alone of re-grounding – of the Directive set the tone.

The Abortive Proposal of the Pinheiro Administration

In the face of these irreconcilable conflicts it is small wonder that the revision proposal failed to materialise, as scheduled, in the autumn of 1994. Quite simply, attempts by the Pinheiro administration at DG X to submit it were thwarted by market forces and their political and governmental allies. It was eventually submitted at the end of May 1995. Tentative, unendorsed versions had, however, circulated in the interim period, revealing the troubles of formulating a policy. Consecutive adaptations of the proposal were made in order to make it acceptable to the most vocal business and political interests including certainly those of the USA.

The 1993-1994 DG X change of approach towards the programming sector (Commission 1994: 21) recognised both its serious problems but also its potentially dynamic role for growth. This shift was facilitated by the radical recommendations of the TTR – not fully endorsed by the DG X – which stressed that Articles 4 and 5 should refer only to stock programming (excluding flow programmes), that there be a separation between a national and a non-national European quota, and that operators be made either to invest in or to pre-purchase programming from independent producers (TTR: 38-39).

These straightforwardly protectionist recommendations vindicated, in fact, French Culture Minister Jacques Lang's rejected proposal of 1985, to link quotas with an obligation for investment in European production rather than attaching them on screening. This would have entailed an overarching EU commitment to the industry as a whole and not just to advertisers and broadcasters. It would have taken into account the particularities of this market and the fact that the audiovisual industry is "hardware driven but software led" (Tunstall & Palmer 1991). The DG X's shift of policy focus in favour of the production sector found no intra-Commission political base or support. This was clear from the unjustified delays and intra-Commission wrangles, but also from later further reductions and changes in the revisable provisions.

Rather than being disturbed about the future, Eurocrats lamented over lost ground. Pinheiro repeated the well-known, fateful story. The Single European Market "exists for operators from across the Atlantic, but it does not seem to exist for our own operators. US production accommodates very well to our market while we have been unable to do so" (Pinheiro, 02.07.94). On this exhortation he concluded that: "Action is, therefore, required from our side" (ibid). The Commission was preparing to submit a timely and "honest proposal" (Troussard 1994).[60] Yet, it was more than evident that the difficulties encountered by the Pinheiro administration in submitting its revision proposal on time were the first clear indications of the severely adverse policy undercurrents.

The 'maximalist' Pinheiro amendment to Article 4 provided for a majority of screening time for European programming or alternatively

---

[60][8] Troussard, DG X, interview with the author 28.08.94.

50% of investment in programming by broadcasters. Typically, in the revamped proposal this last figure was dropped to 25% to appease ACT. Similarly, the finite duration (ten years) for the quota measures was added later in 1995 to suit the demands of ACT and other external pressures, in line with the spirit of GATS. Having been held back from adoption at the announced time, the first revision proposal became also entangled with procedures for the change of the Commission due at the end of 1994. So, the issues of wasted time and of timing in policy-making began their adverse countdown once again. Notwithstanding this squandering of time, it was argued, that the revision of the TWF Directive presented the opportunity for a response to a rapidly-changing, competitive, communications environment (sic) as well as for amending the inconsistencies of the original policy.

Revamping the Revision Proposal to Suit the ACT

In a spirit of urgency and 'global coherence', the APEWIS had announced that "the 1989 Directive must be reviewed" and that a "proposal will be submitted in the Autumn [of 1994]" (Commission 1994a: 7). Yet, this was not to be. As we have seen opposition, disagreement and strife within the Commission against the Pinheiro proposal were widespread. This led to a reorientation and a retreat on that 'ambitious' policy revision. Leon Brittan, the British external affairs Commissioner, and the EC strategist of the GATS debacle, the new Commission President Jacques Santer (also former Luxemburg Prime Minister, like his predecessor in both positions, Gaston Thorn) and Martin Bargeman, Industry and Information Society Commissioner, were all explicitly against the quota provisions of the Pinheiro proposal (Frangos 1995). Jacques Santer went even as far as stating in a 'Herald Tribune' interview that quotas were artificial and that they could not last for ever (ibid). Not surprisingly, then, the Pinheiro proposal was thwarted. The new administration received a renewed mandate by the European Council in December 1994 to propose a revision.

The novelty of the new Commission was that it launched a draft policy resulting for the first time from a cooperation between three General Directorates of the Commission (DG X, DG XII and DG XV), and between Commissioners Oreja, Bargeman and Monti, respectively. In light of a strong trend towards convergence between the various sectors of the communication industries, this reflects the effort to streamline the audiovisual with the hardware and the internal market DGs. This approach also marked a new pragmatism in relation to the accelerating developments in the rising domain of information. Though entrenched in the framework of APEWIS, the new revision proposal could not totally sideline the policy discourse that was produced by the TTR, the 1994 GP and the EAC.

The Bordeaux ministerial Council reconfirmed certain key guidelines: (a) development of a competitive European programming industry within the framework of the information society, (b) respect for national identities and linguistic diversities, and (c) development of the audiovisual sector which should aim to create employment in Europe (ibid: 1). A pragmatic reductionism was also observed in these guidelines. From the perspective of my examination it is remarkable to note the absolute absence of any guidelines with reference to the classical repertoire of invocations of the 1980s: (1) the building up of European identity, (2) the promotion of European integration. Moreover, in spite of the recently proclaimed European citizenship, no special mention was made concerning this matter. This is perplexing, to say the least. This significant aspect of European developments, European citizenship, was not strong enough to give rise to communication rights nor to broadening the scope of the directive. Indeed, in combination with the emphasis laid down in guideline (b) about respect for national identities and linguistic diversities, the absence of communicative rights stemming from European citizenship amounts to its symbolic abandonment.

Marcelino Oreja, the new Culture Commissioner concurred with this assessment in his, summary of the "important results" conferred by the TWF policy. These comprised: (1) the assurance of free circulation of broadcasting services, (2) the establishment of a single base for advertising, (3) the protection of minors, and (4) the promotion of the European industry (Commission 1995c). Citizens were not the protagonists in any of these important results. Neither were political concerns the issue. Interestingly though, particularly in regard to the fourth 'important result' it has been estimated that the TWF policy, more than any other single policy, has contributed to the boosting of the Internal Market (Peterson & Bomberg 1999) and the European economy. Given such compelling results, the Directive merited a certain place "among the *acquis communautaire*" (ibid). With the exception of the defensive measures in regard to the protection of minors, all other accomplishments referred to economic interests, notably those satisfying the industries of advertising and the advertised. The TWF policy was certainly a great success story for these private interests. But, what about European public interest? Or, what's in it for European citizens?

In this climate of triumph over the promotion of the most powerful transnational private interests, it is not surprising to discover that all revisions focusing on broadening the scope of the Directive referred to a further step in commercialising the medium of television and in boosting the same private interests. This was to happen by (1) including revision provisions on tele-shopping, (2) extending the time allowed for advertisements, (3) allowing new types of breaks into programming flow, etc. As for the provisions on the promotion of European works, these were to be satisfied with some 'refinement' of existing Articles 4 and 5.

Quotas "are not an ideal measure", however, they are considered "necessary" (ibid). But quotas may balance out conflicting interests within the sector only to the extent that overarching commitment to that effect exists. The novelty of the Oreja proposal certainly reflected the GATS provision for a continuous liberalisation and a review of the 1993 agreement within five to ten years from its adoption. The EC was already on the path to streamlining its policies with GATS general rules. Quotas should cease in ten years, because by then they would have served their purpose, it was suggested. The proposed limited duration of quotas might work "to please all"; that is, this compromise might appease both the ACT and MPEAA on the one hand, and the producers, film makers etc. on the other. Notwithstanding the underlying wish to please all, the immediate reactions from both fronts were stormy. Given this disapproval the only remaining 'value' of this compromise was to contribute to endless policy disputes, thereby delaying or incapacitating decision-making (Commission 1995c: 3).

At the Bordeaux Council of 8.2.95, no majority was reached in favour either of strengthening or of reducing support for the European programming industry. This elegant stalemate no doubt reflected the fact that quotas were desired by producers but were opposed by private broadcasters on principle (ibid: 2). Thus the status quo of the original TWF regime prevailed. Interest was shown by certain ministers in the mechanism of investment quotas endorsed by Oreja himself, albeit as an "optional alternative" to screening quotas (ibid). Nevertheless this was the first time that the Commission officially promoted such a mechanism. Unanimity, allegedly, emerged concerning the necessity for common and uniform standards. "If there is to be a regulatory system of programme promotion, it must be applied in a uniform manner so as to avoid distortions of competition" (ibid: 2).[61] But such unanimity is worthless at *ad hoc* meetings and even at ministerial common positions because it has been shown to evaporate when it actually comes to deciding on conflicting issues.

The Controversial Issues

The scope of the revision of the Directive became a bone of contention between diverse market interests. Telecommunications operators offering audiovisual services claimed their GATS-given right to deregulation. They contested any broadening of the scope of the new Directive, seeking to

---

[61] *'S'il doit y avoir un système réglementaire de promotion, il doit être appliqué de façon uniforme de manière à éviter les distorsions de concurrence'* (Oreja, ibid: 2).

enjoy exemption from the rules of Articles 4 and 5. Yet, the mere operation of un-regulateable, point-to-point Video on Demand (VOD) services constitutes a distortion of competition against operators broadcasting in the clear. So the latter 'justifiably', yet 'impracticably', sought to correct this unfair competition by including VOD services in the TWF Directive.

The pressures from converging sectors were felt most in this proactive chapter of the Directive. The transmutation of a service from one that is broadcast, to one that is narrow-cast or individually received over a telephone line poses economic threats which must be faced. If the same film is enjoyed through these two different media, broadcast television and VOD, different rules apply: this cannot be legally and economically sustained for too long. Different rules create competitive disadvantages against the regulated broadcast sector but benefit the unregulated one (telecoms). Given the fact that broadcast programmes were universally received, while VOD can only be obtained against payment, advantaging VOD works directly against citizens' real interests, especially in terms of repertoire scope and quality standards. Given that in the long term such un-regulateable services undermine universally and in the open received services which have a distinct cultural and political role, citizens' real interests have been jeopardised in multiple ways. But the convergence of the two sectors is corrosive also in terms of trade balance.

Regulation on political economy criteria could unify divergent regulatory regimes as between telecommunications and television. This presupposes a transition from 'imperative' to structural regulation that would entail obligations in relation to investment quotas upon all types of operators. Proposed changes in Article 1 (widening of the scope of the TWF) excluded new services, notably VOD, from the definition of 'radiodiffusion télévisuelle'. This was inevitable, in spite of favouring companies such as British Telecom, which already provided films by telephone. Firstly, VOD is an individual, 'point to point' service; secondly, its regulation along broadcast media would have made no difference because it is impossible to monitor either quota applications, or content more generally, in practice; thirdly, its inclusion would have contravened Article 10 of the ECHR; and fourthly, it alienates the purpose of the quotas, which was to strengthen the audiovisual industry rather than to police flows of information to individual subscribers.

Tele-shopping was a novel kind of service. The common element with traditional broadcasting was that it claimed use of the same transmission media. But, since this practice represents a private transactual relationship between the seller and the buyer, it should be distinguished from public broadcasting. It could be located in telecommunications frequencies and regulated separately, that is outside frequencies for cultural and political broadcasts, along with other new services. In other words, it should not be permitted that yet another private commercial activity colonize the electronic public sphere, thereby driving more political and cultural symbolic exchanges out of the public domain. Nonetheless, the establishment of tele-shopping[62] functions in public broadcast frequencies and zones, through a special policy provision, added yet another instance of a policy-induced privatizing of the public communications domain. This necessarily also entailed the corresponding squeezing out of public communication contents from publicness. Put in other words, who cares about safeguarding political communication functions when there is money to be made through advertising and tele-shopping?

Revision of Article 2 aimed to resolve the issue of jurisdiction. It stipulated that only one company headquarters should apply. Following some litigation due to controversies and confusion that arose between receiving member states and operators transmitting from other countries, in the revision of 1997 (EP 2005) some derogations were introduced to allow receiving member states to stop emissions on the grounds of public health and order, that is, for the protection of minors and for fending off incitement of hatred, sexism and racism. This reflected not only the abuses arising from too much deregulation and the logic of 'lowest common denominator' that prevailed, but also a certain vagueness in

---

[62] In line with revision proposals, this new service should also be made to contribute a levy towards the development of programming.

Article 2 of the Directive (e.g. the UK Broadcasting Act of 1990 creating a haven). Article 2bis explicitly allows for the possibility of intervention by receiving states in case of violation of applying laws. Thus receiving state jurisdiction re-entered the agenda following relevant abuses by broadcasters. Receiving state prerogatives were spelled out. This provided that the Cassis de Dijon principle could not be applicable in cultural matters. It was particularly inapplicable when combined with the 'stricter rule at home' principle. Article 3(2) stipulated that member states could sanction violations of this law as they wished. But this would lead again to distortions of competition and to dis-integrationist trends, as it allows for divergence of rules.

Those who managed the revision struggled to retain elements of flexibility while also being stricter (sic) (ibid: 8-9). The problem of political cost assumed perverse dimensions at the supra-national level. Notwithstanding denunciations of crucial ambiguities in the original Directive that caused conflicts of interests (Commission 1995c: 4), attempts were supposedly made to 'reassure' all parties. Thus, the simplistic, false and disastrous logic that nothing need be sacrificed, was repeated. But ambiguities can hardly be remedied by trying to be both strict and flexible.

The proposed revision did actually eliminate the notorious phrase 'where practicable' that had unqualified the quotas articles – yet the phrase managed to make it into the final text of 1997. A new line of division was created between thematic and generalist channels, thereby fuelling the conflict between traditional and 'new' channels. It is clear that 'a quota system grounded on transmission time is convenient for generalist channels but not for thematic channels'.[63] The intention was to introduce investment quotas (thus remaining loyal to pledges for structurally boosting the programme sector) at all costs without damaging the interests of thematic channel operators too much.

---

[63] "Le système lui-même, basé sur le temps de diffusion, ne convient pas aux autres que les chaînes généralistes, alors qu'apparaissent en nombre croissant les chaînes thématiques." (COM-17.3.1995: 4).

This was said to constitute an improvement which added flexibility by offering the option of programming budget-investment rather than the screening quota (ibid: 2).[64] But thematic channels were required to contribute a mere 25% of their programming budget to investments in European audiovisual works as opposed to the 50% screening quotas imposed on the generalist channels. This penalises generalist and favours thematic channels, thereby establishing further unofficial derogations. Moreover, the 25% proportion of optional investment was a reduction from an earlier 50% proportion (Pinheiro proposal). This meant that citizens' real interests would once again be compromised.

This rationale was unsatisfactory not only because it introduced inequalities but also because it undermined the goal of promoting European works. Besides, if one considers all the exclusions of programme type and time applying in the quota provision – that is news, sports, games, advertising and teletext – all that is left on a generalist channel is pretty much a 'thematic channel programme': that is, the programme zones containing European audiovisual works in terms of fiction and documentaries (and current affairs if not classified with the news programming). The net effect of introducing this new distinction amounts to discrimination between types of channels and distortion of competition for audiences to the advantage of thematic channels (usually conditional and hence socially exclusionary). This entailed organising out the interests of those who cannot afford subscribing to pay-per-view (PPV) channels.

This exercise in 'flexibility' which was also described as realistic because it "reflects the actual practice in the market" is questionable (ibid: 9).[65] If the proposed reduced 'refinements' were in harmony with current conditions of the market, and if the EU was being diagnosed as

---

[64] "...que le système pourrait être amelioré, sans qu'il ne soit fondamentalement refondu, par l'ajout d'une option d'investissement, pour les chaines thématiques" (COM – 17.3.1995: 2).

[65] "Des niveaux d'obligation (soit proportion majoritaire du temps de diffusion, soit 25% du budget de programmation) (sont) réalistes et en harmonie avec les pratiques actuelles du marché" (COM – 17.3.1995: 9).

facing a severe import imbalance and a deficit, what did this new measure contribute to strengthening the European audiovisual programming sector? The fact that thematic channels were treated unduly favourably in relation to generalist channels would strengthen the trend of opting for them. Such 'side-effects' would lead to further, ostensibly un-intended, structural changes which would cause the decline of both generalist channels and of the principle of universality. Consequently, such favouritism concealed the undermining of citizen's real interests for free-of-charge access to politically meaningful information.

However positive and in line with technological achievements, this potential might further disadvantage those national markets unable to sustain such multi-segmentalisation. Considering that there is already a clear split between the strong, information-exporting member states, and the weak, importing ones, this step would increase the cleavage rather than be conducive to cohesion or to an even and equitable integration within the EU. On the contrary, this option risked further positive disintegration moves, both within the EU audiovisual industry and within the EU polity more generally.

In Article 6 the scope of the term 'European works' was further broadened to include any co-productions agreed with third countries subsequent to bilateral agreements as long as the majority of the capital is European controlled. Article 7 introduces essential distinctions between different transmitting systems, favouring VOD and new services with respect to waiting-times before broadcasting cinematographic works not explicitly covered by contractual agreements.[66] Once again, here we observe a blatant favouritism for the few operators that deal in VOD and in the new digital forms of sales. Interestingly, some of these such as telecommunications service providers come from outside the broadcasting field. Furthermore, it is quite evident that this new type of

---

[66] Video on Demand channels may require only six months before providing the screening of cinematographic works, Pay-per-view may wait 12 months, while the rest of the media must wait 18 months. Thus, the specially boosted VOD market-in-the-making will antagonise the video rental market.

service may be operated from overseas, thereby favouring global electronic trade and, conversely, undermining traditional local markets.

An increase of advertising time was granted to channel operators to appease the ACT. The political economy of this measure entails simply the intensification of exploiting individuals as 'the saleable packages of viewers' to the advertised companies. Seen from a political perspective, it is evident that this practice undermined an already precarious position of viewers as citizens. Thus, notwithstanding Article 151 of the TEC, both the original directive and the 1997 revision conceived of broadcasting as a private service subject to supply and consumer demand rules. Conversely, this approach ignored the wider political issues such as pluralism involved in it (Radaelli 1999: 125).

This increase in advertising time damaged, furthermore, the interests of newspaper owners, because "there is a very close relationship between the increase of the advertising market share held by TV and the decrease of the share held by the press" (Commission 1993g: 12) thereby infuriating the members of this federation. Not only was the survival of the print media threatened, the ENPA argued, but "the result would obviously have serious repercussions on pluralism, since advertising represents the main source of revenues for the press" they claimed. The crux of their point was that "the Commission cannot adopt rules that would worsen the existing imbalance in the distribution of the advertising resources." (ibid: 2). From a political communication perspective this is a very valid point as the medium of newspapers, with the exception of tabloids, admittedly carries the main weight of political information and of providing some form of public sphere to the citizenry. Critical comparison is however due here. This same federation of newspaper owners, only some months earlier, when considering the option for 'concentration of media ownership' regulation were among the very few who advised the Commission not to propose any measures relating to the protection of 'pluralism' (see Chapter 5).

Defeating All but Industrial Policy Goals

There seemed no light in the tunnel of the revision of the TWF Directive. Neither the French nor the Spanish presidencies (1995), both keen to procure a solution, managed to get their conciliatory revision proposals accepted by the governments of member states. Conflicting or divergent interests, diffidence and fears reflecting developments in the Union at large accounted for the paralysis. The EP, usually a keen advocate of public interest and the balancing of interests in the audiovisual domain, delayed delivering its Opinion (1996). Leading MEPs reported on the utter confusion in the legislative body of the EU regarding revision. "Regression to the status quo" was suggested for fear that if revised, the Directive would in fact do more harm than benefit the general interest and domestic programming production. This was due to irresistible threats, pressures for further deregulation[67] and stern opposition even to moderately proactive revision proposals.

This, then, is to admit that the effective control of the communications policy-making agenda was entirely in the hands of a handful of media moguls and of UNICE (Confederation of European Industrialists) and the equivalent global bodies.

In his EAC keynote speech Jacques Delors, famous for his slogans and aphorisms, said that the destiny of Europe passes through the audiovisual sector. He was right and the audiovisual is really a litmus test for the EU, in the sense that there is no polity without a corresponding system of political communication to acknowledge it and provide for it. In this respect developments in the audiovisual sector seemed ominous, and I should add, have proved ominous since. "Let us talk frankly, a latent political crisis afflicts the EU. Why? Because we doubt ourselves, we do not grant ourselves the means for our declared ambitions" (Delors, 30.06.94).

---

[67] Luciana Castellina, MEP and president of the Culture, Media Youth and Sports Committee of the EP, interview with the author, 4.11.1995, EIM/European Audiovisual Forum Conference, Elounda, Crete.

Regulation and deregulation *per se* are neither good nor bad. They are instruments which depend on the conditions they are used in and the uses they are put to. All agreed that the programming production sector of the EU was deficient. All agreed that it was an integral and vital factor for the viability and growth of the entire audiovisual sector. All agreed that it required strong incentives, both structural and financial, to lift it out of deficit. Yet, the process of revision, repeatedly designated as an urgent priority, was stalled and inconclusive. The condition of the audiovisual programming market dictated well-targeted, protectionist measures but the EC was "forced into a deregulation" which undermined its very existence and which can only help its competitors. The paradox is that although structural and conduct regulation was almost unanimously recognised as indispensable for the regeneration of the European audiovisual sector, nevertheless, deregulation was actually being pursued.[68] This, then, is proof that it has been a fatal mistake to subject communications policy to the perpetual constraints of the *laissez faire* strategy.

Behind this paradox lay three different forces: first, European and Europe-based multinational companies – broadcasting and telecommunications multimedia operators with global and diversified aspirations; second, certain member states governments which backed expansive, pervasive and thriving global entrepreneurs, and which were against a complete EC integration; third, the international exporting programming industry, notably that of the USA, consistently aided by the USDT, and the US Department of State (Wasko 1994). Compounding the cumulative muscle and activity of these three forces were the growing strategic transcontinental alliances among these same industrial and political

---

[68] This is because it leads to big profits for a handful of globally-active operators and to astronomical short and medium term profits for the American programming industry represented by the MPEAA and the USDC. The Holy (or Unholy) Alliance between these two groups of interests strongly opposes any contrary political measures by the EU. Such a radical structural revision of TWF would simply redistribute wealth and power in a way which would be manifestly undesirable to both the ACT and the MPEAA. Any tightening of Articles 4 and 5 would mean lost profits to them, though it would grant a breathing space to domestic producers and operators.

interests. The interlinking between the latter two categories was by way of rapidly growing centrifugal transatlantic business alliances.

The threat to the European project lay not in those alliances *per se* but in the manifest powerlessness of the EC to harness them or to tie them to European obligations, as the US and Japan do with their companies. Global capital integration, combined with technological innovation, further entrenched this global capital consolidation and detached local and regional communities from their own cultural autonomy and growth (TTR 1994: 18-19), deprived them of their right to self-projection and created unemployment. There was thus a clear discrepancy between stated objectives and real outcomes. Dis-integration, tacitly or openly pursued by certain actors, was reinforced by the lack of a timely and effective pro-EC policy, through frustratingly lengthy decision-making processes.

Cash Cows or Communication?

A politically attentive policy-making on communications would have necessitated a major and distinct strategic reorientation, putting communications in the service of the polity and of society as a whole. But the original strategy of subjugating the audiovisual media to narrow economic and profit-making activities was never really in question. In the long process of revising the TWFD, political communication for and at the European level was linked to it. Given the parallel assignment by Pinheiro to the De Clercq Committee in 1992-1993, and the recommendations of that report, this was odd, making a mockery of European citizenship. Both in terms of style and procedure and in terms of essential outcome, the revised Directive was an item of utter disappointment. In fact in many instances, it represented a regression, for example in further commercialising the medium of television and pushing it further into the control of the advertising barons.

Into the second decade of EC communications policy-making, what could be observed in the revision process of the TWF was a sustained and firm rebuffing of any political objectives. This policy activity exploited concerns of a political nature to establish itself at EC level. However, as has been analysed in the previous chapter, the original strategy was conceived and pursued in the interests of economic agencies.

The whole original policy had taken off on the claim and the promise to safeguard means for pan-European political and cultural voices. Quite the contrary to those original invocations, this framework policy was rapidly advancing towards positions that corroded even the existing pre-existing national safeguards for political and cultural communication. So, this movement was a disconcerting shift away from political and cultural priorities and towards industrial and commercial imperatives in the following stages of the policy process (Sarikakis 2004: 178, Iosifidis et al. 2005: 105). Given the disagreeable and increasing loss of legitimacy by EC institutions, it is striking that Brussels elites obstinately avoid encompassing distinctly political objectives in their communications policy which since the TEU has been possible.

No member state and certainly no group of member states intended to accept a change in the status quo merely on the grounds of the proclamation of European citizenship. This attitude in itself revealed the little or no importance attached to this overarching citizenship, which raises problems of credibility and legitimacy. It also raises fears about manipulation of citizens' pro-European feelings and aspirations. This then was a second round of policy-making that prioritised exclusively industrial and commercial objectives at the expense of political ones. Not surprisingly then citizens rebuff such policies and this political system as such.

From the Eighties to the Nineties the same powerful groups and personalities used all their power, dexterity and authority to prevent the emancipation of the field of communication from its role as a money-spinner. Distribution channel owners, the global advertising industry and the advertised industries fought with every possible means to continue exploiting television exclusively for profit. Those politicians in the Commission, in the EP or in governments of member states that attempted anything against this triangle of vested interests failed completely. And this situation is the best illustration of the "divorce between power and politics". Even to mention 'political communication' for European citizens and its corollary, the 'must carry rules' sounds odd to many. In Mark Mazower's words: "Europeans accept democracy because they no longer believe in politics" (1998: 404).

The nature of the European decision-making process as enshrined in the Treaties and the policies emanating from the supra-national level "disable the potential for democratic communicative structures to be built and for democratic accountability to be nurtured by ceding to national interests of the member states" (Ward 2004: 131). In fact, quite a few analysts (Sbragia 1992, Scharpf 1997, Venturelli 1998, Zweifel 2002, Ward 2004) argue that even if EU institutions were willing to be democratised, the structural preconditions on which authentic democratic processes can be grounded are still lacking.

In this vein, it is accurately highlighted that still today there are hardly any "European parties, no European political leaders and no European-wide media of political communication" (Ward 2004). As these are the prime components for democratic politics, their absence means that no European-wide controversies may develop. But what is democracy without the option for dispute and choice? No debates can arise on political issues without overt conflicts on real and potential policy issues. In their absence, the notion of 'choices' is void. Similarly, there can be no real Europe-wide competition for government offices. Neither can there be any assurance of transparency or accountability.

The case of the revision of the TWFD in the aftermath of the adoption of the TEU at Maastricht is particularly interesting not only for the reasons referred to concerning Article 151. In fact the TEU and thus also the EU as such had been challenged by negative public opinion surveys and the referendum in Denmark (Papadimitriou 1999: 134). These events called for some politically corrective measures. Yet, even though the De Clercq report (1993) came up with a number of conducive proposals and the revision of the TWF presented a good, if not the best, opportunity for incorporating the requisite political communication measures, no enlargement of the scope of the directive was considered in this regard. Notwithstanding the challenges or the policy demands placed by disaffected citizens, no feed-back response was produced by the EU system either via broadening the scope of this policy or otherwise.

This then highlights the total reluctance to create a common European sphere of public communication. It thus became increasingly clearer that the EU was both unwilling to create a space for its polity and unable to democratise its institutions. Democratic politics and the EU started to figure as contradictory terms. Therefore, the real question is whether this is an issue at all. Under the mantle of democracy, hegemonic forces rule, and they feel that they can dispense with political communication or frameworks for public dialogue. "Discussion becomes meaningless where one's partner has already decided on his position before the discussion has begun... As a result the intellectual foundations of liberalism and parliamentarism have been shaken" (Mazower 1998: 17).

European citizens would have to wait until the following decade for the next revision of the Directive. To the extent that reluctance to re-orient communications policy continues, European citizens have every right to feel betrayed in their expectations. The prospects were then not bright and this malaise was set to stay just as long as the control of the policy-making agenda in the communications sector was allowed to be held exclusively in the hands of market forces, while the body politic and its representatives were being ignored.

Chapter 4

COMMUNICATIONS POLICY AND 'COMMUNICATION RIGHTS' IN THE ERA OF INTERACTIVE TELEVISION

The EU has now entered the third decade of its involvement in communications policy. The socio-political, economic and technological environment within which the Community must now produce or revise its communication policies have changed considerably since it first intervened in this field. Some of the central features of the present environment are:

(a) the severe and increasing decline in the popularity of the EU, which itself reflects trends towards disintegration rather than unification;

(b) the advanced levels of alienation of citizens from significant public affairs and their public concerns and priorities, which itself is the result of depoliticization and of the effacing or the reduction of political communication.

(c) the near total commercialisation of television broadcasting, especially in its transfrontier aspects;

(d) the rise of the Internet and of interactive communications systems that technologically decentralize and democratise communicative action notably for individual users;

(e) the immense proliferation of channels of the supply of information, which segmentalises markets for viewerships and which, thereby, increasingly counteracts the implementation of economies of scale.

This particular situation raises the prospect that television may lose its tight commercial grip as a source of revenue. Conversely, there are increased prospects that this medium may be validated again as a forum for political communication.

In the previous chapter I examined the first revision of the TWF, of the 1990s, with a particular focus on whether the Community did re-orient its original, strategic, 'Internal Market' framework in response to the adoption of the proclamation of European citizenship by the TEU and changes in the TEC. The combination of these factors facilitated the consideration of citizens' needs in political communication from 1993 onwards. Even though the EU then had the opportunity to do so, it did not alter the aberrant and biasing framework of the Internal Market. As a result the audiovisual sector and communications policy remained deeply trapped in this framework.

EU institutions, notably the Commission and the EP, are currently once again in the process of revising the Television Without Frontiers Directive (TWFD) for the second time. This process began in 2002, following the Commission's review of the impact of TWFD in the market, especially in light of dramatic, technological innovations and market adjustments to digitisation and to convergence. This new revision is still an ongoing process and its eventual conclusion cannot be anticipated. One may ask, what are the key aspects of this ongoing process with a regard to the possibility of new political communication objectives materialising in this revision?

Just as with the incentive of European citizenship and of Article 151 of the TEC in the previous revision, there are currently new challenges and new opportunities. Indeed, there are some compelling reasons for correcting the original directive, which led to communications being abused uniquely as a profit-based market. More specifically, I argue that that the above factors, (a), (b) and (d), provide the basis for an alternative communications policy at the EU level.

The incentives are there (Internet and interactive media) and so are the needs and political imperatives. But are there any signs of a shift in attitudes towards a political communications policy or perhaps even towards a participatory framework? This could be expressed in the ongoing process for the revision of the TWF Directive from the perspective of viewers' and users' interests as citizens. A positive consideration of citizens' interests should comprise a new and democratically, radical, policy approach to *communication rights,* as distinct from mere *information rights* (which implies mainly passive information management of past eras), and it should signal a conceptual and actual leap ahead.

Synergies between Mass and Interactive Media

The advent of broadband and on-line networks, in combination with the wide diffusion of new media such as the Internet, are generating a significant, structural transformation in the media landscape. 'Point-to-multipoint' and 'one-way mass media', such as television in its traditional form, are rapidly becoming outdated. Significantly, the potential of interactivity afforded by new information and communication technologies, is structurally transforming the relation between senders and receivers. This reshuffling is particularly affecting television, notably its commercial role, as the extraordinary proliferation of content supply segmentalises audiences and inhibits economies of scale. In this transformation of the economic role of television, there may lay a hope for its emancipation from the yoke of commercialisation and for the reclamation of this medium by polity, society and culture. Despite these changes, television still remains the most watched and popular medium worldwide, and therefore it possesses a particular, political centrality and importance.

Television is also changing functionally, and it can be used in a more dialogical, participatory fashion, both directly and indirectly. While remaining a centralising medium of visibility it can also become reciprocal, encompassing and inclusive. By allowing interaction and collaboration or even 'co-authorship' between its own producers and viewers, converging media and interactive TV, for the first time in history, allow *communications rights* and *interests* to materialize fully on a large scale. Viewers, in their capacity as citizens, thus have at their disposal new possibilities for civic exchanges and initiatives.

There are a number of benefits that may accrue from a policy-induced synergy between television and the Internet, provided that this policy is oriented towards political communication. First, the agenda of televised issues can come from more varied sources and thereby be more pluralist. This can invigorate the medium, both by enriching contents and also in terms of a new *modus operandi*. Secondly, the synergetic combination of these two types of media can safeguard an essential role of a public, electronic sphere, which presupposes universal access and common central visibility. Thirdly, the development of a common, transnational, European, public space, could create a new impetus towards a European integration involving the people and coming from them. Advanced television holds still more potential for participatory communication, if technological options are fully exploited, and if media owners' reactions and fears curbed and viewers' inertia are also overcome through bold public policies. Fourthly, the use of interactive television – through synergies with other media for political communication – could remedy the EU's political crisis and the alienation of EU citizens. Abstract and exclusive politics could be thus democratised. If the common, European, media deficit is a constitutive element of the EU's democratic deficit, as it is argued here, then the creation of a space for political communication can contribute to the solution. But are EU politicians and policy makers up to the task?

Structural Shifts in Euro-politics and in Communication Policies

The political and policy question most central in this conjuncture of revision of the TWF Directive is whether media policy will be treated, at last, as an opportunity for the re-distribution of communicative and political power. Whether opportunities will be granted for participation so as to emancipate citizens as user-viewers this time, or whether once again, communications policy – element (A) of my triangle – will treat this sector as a branch of industrial policy, is no longer an open question. Everything points to the latter.

As things stand, European citizens are afflicted by ignorance of their common, public affairs and are obliged to be silent about their common interests in the main, widely-available, electronic, public space, that of television. The example of the Constitutional Convention of the EU is a case in point. European citizens largely ignore it, yet they were not given the opportunity or the means to learn about it by a Union that, nevertheless, proclaimed European citizenship. Nor had they any chance to discuss it publicly through pertinent media in order to exchange views and to form opinions. Euro-barometer surveys have exposed worrisome facts and trends of that growing ignorance (Summer 2004) (Peel 2004: 13).

It should have come as no surprise, in the face of the indifference towards EU citizens displayed by the Brussels elite, that the referenda on the Constitutional Convention of May 2005 in France and the Netherlands were negative. So long as citizens are deprived of meaningful information and spaces for their own communicative action, it is logical that they will fight against such authority and doubt even the legitimacy of EU institutions.

Digital convergence, with its potential for interactive, televisual communication, allows the full deployment of communication rights and interests. Thus, it may irrevocably alter power relations in the fields of media, culture and politics. But, how is this social power-shift to be handled fairly and intelligently at the supra-national policy-making level?

The EU itself has developed into quite a different, political hybrid, both in terms of political integration and of decision-making. The expanded Union of 25 member states poses acute, additional challenges for political cohesion, co-ordination and co-existence. The restrictions on communication and audiovisual policy, imposed by the Internal Market framework on the TWF Directive sixteen years ago, are now called into question by the sheer avalanche of technological and socio-political change.

Since Europolitics is generated in Brussels, and since European political affairs concern us equally, it is vital that there be common and interactive, electronic, public spaces, notably, those offered by the main, transnational and commonly, visible medium, television. Common, public affairs are typically in need of visibility and scrutiny through public dialogue. The right to vote without adequate and relevant, political information is meaningless (Garnham 1986:37). As argued also by Meyer

> The fundamental condition and role of communications media is to make appropriate political communication and its scrutiny and evaluation possible. If public communication in a society cannot, in principle, fulfil this condition, then no one can make a serious claim that it is democratic. In any event guarantees of free elections and the elite competition that they enable do not suffice to make good the promise of democracy. (2002: 9-10)

Traditionally the regulation of television has been legitimated (1) on the grounds of the power this medium exercises on viewers, (2) on core democratic requirements such as pluralism and diversity of information sources and (3) on scarcity. The reasons for the first two of these grounds for regulation are more pertinent than ever before, as commercial media seem to be colonising the political while producing *political ignorance* (Meyer 2002). The need for direct regulation "based upon scarcity of distribution channels has been wholly undermined by technological developments" (Cave 1997: 590). Indeed, not only is scarcity no longer a motive for regulation, but, in fact, the contrary is the case in our time. Channel proliferation and the abundance of transmissions media make the 'economy of attention' a lot more difficult to manage.

Opportunities and Challenges

The management of passive attention is gradually being phased out and new modes keep emerging. A rising and expanding *communicative activity* increasingly occupies a time-space previously held by *communicative passivity* and this changes formerly–prevailing, exchange relations. The further liberation of frequency capacity is becoming once again a facilitator for new strategic planning and regulatory shifts. This time, however, developments do not necessarily favour fortune hunters in communications.

The prevalence of star-shaped, network architectures safeguards communication feedback and opens the door to mediated, participatory communication. All these changes mean that technically and economically, we can now head towards establishing and implementing 'communication rights'. So, what is preventing citizens from benefiting from accessibility to interactive television? Economic interests? Fear of public participation? Given such ground-shaking changes in the ICTs, in the media landscape and in political processes within the EU, it is clear that the time is ripe for a politically empowering, communications policy.

Converged Digital Media in the Era of Communications Rights

In view of the revision of the TWF Directive, the Commission conducted three thematic reviews (Commission 2002a). The first of these aimed to assess the impact of the Directive provisions on the promotion and distribution of European-made programming on television. The implementation and the implementability of the TWF's quotas provisions were a contentious issue from the point of view of both operators and producers. The second review focused on technological innovations and market responses to such developments in the audiovisual sector. It sought to establish possible cause-and-effect relations on the techno-economic axis. The third review elaborated on the development of new modes of advertising and the potential of it to be separated from non-commercial content. The interesting point from my perspective is that all of these studies revolved around the developmental needs of market forces, be they operators, advertisers or producers. No study or Commission policy,-discourse document examined the democratising potential of new media or the political, communication space that these are giving rise to, especially in synergy with the public medium of television.

On the basis of these studies the Commission produced the Fourth Report on the Application of the TWF Directive (Commission 2003), which it submitted to the Council and the EP. This was a summary of the reviews on the changing landscape for the European, broadcasting market and a projection of the findings concerning the effectiveness in implementing the provisions of the Directive. The key point made in concluding was that the EC ought to opt for creating an environment favourable to competition[69] and conducive to growth. This point and the attendant objectives move purely and exclusively in the market-driven and market-led conception of the audiovisual sector, yet without any clear goal. Nevertheless, this market-centred Fourth Report was subsequently approved by the Council in June 2003.

On this endorsement, the Commission went on to draft and publish its Communication on the Future of European Regulatory Audiovisual Policy at the end of 2003 (Commission 2003a).[70] The document offers information, moreover, on policy actions undertaken by the EU up to that time and then deploys its rationale on imminent, regulatory steps. Similarly, it describes the long-term *consultation process* that it has launched, which involves interested parties, experts and Commission functionaries

---

[69] This was the point made also in the TTR in 1990, though it was admitted that European producers could not compete on equal terms with their chief rivals.

[70] Communications by the Commission of the EU are formally addressed to the Council, the European Parliament, the European Economic and Social Committee and the Committee of the Regions.

in discussing future, policy options.[71] I shall go into a more detailed analysis of this document, which crystallises key trends in the audiovisual landscape in Europe as well as technology and market developments.

The longest and most important chapter of the document is the third, entitled, Towards new governance for European audiovisual media, and comprises ten sub-sections, each of which focuses on a specific matter. The first elaborates on 'definitions and the central concepts', while the second lays out the 'general rules'. The third section goes on to explain the Commission's rationale on the 'Right to Information'. This reveals an approach in favour of 'information rights', which should be distinguished from the more progressive stance of 'rights to communication'. The fourth section describes the regulatory measures taken both by the EU and at World Trade Organisation (WTO) level for the 'promotion of audiovisual production'.

The theme of 'commercial communications' is the object of the fifth unit. This designation is pertinent here, because, in the previous amendment of the TWF Directive, corresponding provisions for such activities as tele-shopping were inserted. This is followed by an account for the 'protection of minors and public order', while section seven elaborates on the status of the 'right of reply', discussing the possible changes needed in regard to it. The latter two areas belong to civil rights and political, public goods that do not belong in the traditional set of concerns typical of the Internal Market framework. The following section, eight, clarifies some 'institutional aspects', while section nine announces a Recommendation on the protection of minors and human dignity. Recommendations being the weakest and the least implementable instruments, this choice demonstrates the community's 'commitment' to the respect of such provisions and values.

---

[71] The Communication also raises procedural issues, i.e., the launching of a consultation process (with written opinions and public hearings). It provides for focus groups and conferences on scheduled themes through which policy options are aired. The results of the consultation process are discussed with the Contact Committee and the regulatory authorities of member states.

The final section, headed 'Co- and self-regulation', is devoted to delimitating regulatory roles and prerogatives between market agencies (self-regulation) and political regulation (i.e. Community or state). Throughout the document, it is either explicitly stressed or it transpires that Community authorities intend to avoid 'over-regulating' this field, for fear of stifling the (economic) development of the sector. Once again the supreme emphasis on economic objectives looms large. Reading between the lines, this may be implying that the 'industry' requires, or even makes, imperative demands on 'self-regulation', free of any interventions towards proactive, political or socio-cultural goals. The Communication concludes with some self-satisfactory and vague promises, but without any concrete propositions yet for revision. In this way, the document provides a picture of the Commission's current thinking, explicit or implicit, and of its problematic. This, then, is an appropriate guide for identifying the main orientation and the prevalent concerns about what to include, what to exclude and where to place special emphasis in policy-making. Sections 3.1, 3.2 and 3.3 are characteristic of the Commission's 'philosophy'. I shall, therefore, look into these in more detail.

Shifting Structures and New Opportunities for Media Policy

Interestingly enough, the document starts by admitting that "The *Internet*, with the development of graphic browsers on the World Wide Web, has dramatically changed the way people communicate and has opened up new access to audiovisual content" (Commission 2003a: 5). The Council of Ministers also highlighted the implications of the new synergetic means of delivery of audiovisual content, in its conclusions regarding the TWF Directive, in December 2002, (Commission 2003: 1). Thus, Commission policy-drafters were well aware of the increasing importance of interactive and converged media as well as of the implications of their extensive use. Yet, this concurrence of interest in synergies was only restricted to economic aspects. Notwithstanding these remarks, the drafters of the policy document do go on to state that "the main patterns of audiovisual sector: business models, transmission modes, consumer behaviour, consumer electronic goods, etc., have remained largely constant in recent years after undergoing deep changes in the 1990's" (Commission 2003a: 5). Subsequently, they, remark that, with the exception of events affecting the life of *operators*, no dramatic changes in market patterns were expected in the future landscape.

Thus, while a cosmogony of upheavals has taken place, notably in the period of 1999-2002, in the relationship between senders and receivers, or to put it in economic terms, between supply-side and demand-side agencies, these policy initiators see no changes *in relations between the key agencies of this field*, but notice only changes in a single factor: the *operators*. In this light, it is further assessed that more important "developments could result from commercial exploitation of a number of technologies which are already available, but remain largely unused because of lack of clear added value for the consumer or uncertainties concerning the supporting business models" (ibid). The nature of all the concerns expressed pertains to industrial policy affairs.

Low up-take is due also to hesitation and to lack of proactive measures for the benefit of all interested parties. Added value certainly exists, but for viewers as consumers only, not as citizens. Hence, the exploitation of this potential is a matter for a different and certainly a proactive, public policy. It is pointed out that "apart from digital television the main technical innovations which could contribute favourably to the development of the audiovisual sector are: – flat panel displays; – HDTV and – *interactive television*" (ibid: 5, emphasis added). Interactive television transactions are, thus, targeted exclusively as a potential, profit-growth contributor. The permanent and only concern is with the economic role of the media.

Interactive TV practices are already advanced, albeit rather haphazardly, throughout Europe, (Garitaonandia 2004, Colombo 2004,

Kaitatzi-Whitlock 2004).[72] The market limits of this field are identified and the positive political potential is also. However, a proactive policy on the synergy of television and new media, with a view to political communication, is not considered. Commission, when asked, say vaguely that such an option, though not out of the question, may take several years to arise (Ducatel 2005).[73] This 'futuristic' approach is of course incongruent with the pressing political imperatives that arise for the EU from the growing disaffection of its citizens. Democratizing or participatory options for citizens on interactive television are thus beyond current consideration, as far as the field of television is concerned. Citizens' interactive, communicative skills in relation to the most popular medium similarly are not considered. The only centrally visible space for all Europeans, that of television and its central role in public and political affairs, is not an object for policy.

Shapiro argues that if governments are "to accept the individual power that technology makes possible, then we [citizens] need to demonstrate a capacity for balance and responsibility" (1999: 165), while Cave suggests that many of the "proposed digital applications will be dependent on the ability of the viewer to interact directly with the service provider via a return path" (1997: 586). Hence, forging the social elements of interactive practices and acquisition of interactive skills are an issue for policy. If realizable prospects do not materialize on this front, lack of political will and of a corresponding policy should account for them.

Participatory and Interactive Television?

Thus, the handling of the interactive television issue by the EU appears to be narrowly defined and concerned exclusively with its economic

---

[72] See for example several more case studies from the network of researchers of COST A 20 The Impact of the Internet on Mass Media in Europe.

[73] Kenneth Ducatel, member of the Cabinet of Commissioner Viviane Reding, interviewed by the author 28-11-2005.

capitalisation. The Commission continues to regard the audiovisual sector exclusively in terms of an industry just for profit, and in that its key concern is the economic growth of the sector, notably that of operators. When stating the guiding principles of audiovisual policy the Commission document emphasises that "regulatory intervention should... [be] enforced as closely as possible to the operators concerned" (Commission 2003a: 6). The fact, that this expresses a bias in favour of operators, does not appear to be a problem. In addition, the word *operators* often appears to stand for the entire range of professionals implicated in this multifaceted market. This biased approach to a policy area of such centrality to polity and society is rather 'thought provoking'.

The document provides an additional account of the achievements of related policy and regulatory measures and elaborates on the ways that these interact with the TWF Directive. Telecommunications legislation, as revised in 2002, is one of the two regulatory measures which complement the TWF Directive. This "guarantees basic user interests' that might not be guaranteed by market forces, something which belongs to the main objectives of the policy. Interestingly, there is also a reference to 'must carry rules' (ibid: 9).

It is worth remarking that while "must carry rules" are thinkable for telecommunications suppliers, they seem to be entirely taboo when it comes to television. The mere fact of raising this possibility to Commission cabinet member Kenneth Ducatel caused something of a shock. In regard to television, this possibility was inconceivable: "We think that competition is the best mechanism for value allocation in this market" (Ducatel 2005). This stance is diametrically opposed to the same Commission's goals concerning Plan-D:

> The Commission shares the views of Heads of State and Government that these debates should involve "civil society, social partners, national parliaments and political parties" but also believes that there would be an added value in listening to specific

target groups, such as the young people or minority groups. (Commission 2005a: 3)

The problem for such policy-designers is that with a 'hands off' approach to television such goals are just rhetoric. So again one is faced with the problem of incompatible objectives and a dual language.

The Directive on electronic commerce, which is also called the policy on 'information society services', is the second complementary regulatory measure.[74] As is explicitly spelt out, the concern with these two policies was for regulation to remain minimal and, in fact, *"aiming at deregulation"* (Commission 2003a: 9-10, emphasis added). Although these policies are meant to complement one another, they appear, however, to function in a parallel kind of fashion, as there are no provisions for synergies between television and the Internet. Since these media are treated separately, benefits cannot readily accrue from their synergy. It is, namely, explicitly stressed that "Community law at present distinguishes between 'television broadcasting services', subject to the 'TWF' Directive, and 'information society services', subject to the 'e-Commerce' Directive" (Commission 2003a: 14). The decision to continue treating these closely-knit and converging sectors 'separately' without any further qualifications appears paradoxical. As is explained, the former is more detailed than the latter, due to the "paramount importance and the unparalleled impact of television broadcasting on our societies through the effect it has on the way people form their opinions" (ibid).

In assessing the impact of all previous policies on the system of European media and its market, the Communication drafters never identify any problem or failure. Quite the contrary, they assume and reflect an air of complacency. Yet policy drafters report on the low penetration of information, society services, adding that these have not reached the level of impact that television broadcasting still maintains. This is put down simply to the slow uptake of the broadband networks and services, although policy intervention could have boosted a faster

---

[74] The e-commerce Directive was adopted in June 2000 (2000/31/EC, 2000/06/08).

uptake. Moreover, no explanation is ventured as to the relationship of EU telecommunications policy and this outcome. Thus, EU policy and its impact on society are not correlated. As things stand, according to recent Eurostat data, Internet penetration in the EU concerns 44% of the population of the 25 member states.[75]

In proactive policy terms, the Commission disregards the challenge of *de facto* synergies between the Internet and broadcasting. The two most prevalent features of new synergetic communications' technology, that of television with its mass and central visibility and of interactivity, are thus deprived to public sphere objectives. The naturally participatory and dialogical components of the new 'information society' are sidelined in regard of political ends. Such a crucial neglect or a 'decision not to decide' on such a policy-option must then have very good reasons for it.

Yet, this does not mean that the Commission fails to appreciate the stakes involved in interactivity – quite the contrary. But evading the challenge to politically engage with the nexus of emerging, conflicting interests amounts to inaction. This is a complex new area fraught with conflicts of interests, but even if hesitation is understandable it cannot account for lasting policy inaction.

What transpires is a decision to avoid policy-making so as to avoid putting the issues in question on the political agenda completely. Decision-making in the EU, never very fast or effective, thus classically tends towards non-policy-making, when it comes to thorny issues, thus allowing industry players to decide on all issues.[76]

---

[75] Significant, demographic biases exist in the spread of access to the Internet in terms of country, sex, education, socio-economic group (Eurostat 2004). But the prevention of such biases is also a policy objective in a democracy. See also Kaitatzi-Whitlock 2002 / 2003 'Six Arguments Against the Notion of cyberdemocracy'.

[76] This was the case with digital TV standards, which were relegated to the DVB group. See Chapter 6, also David & Shurmer 1996 and Cave 1997.

The Tacit Privatization of Policy-making Prerogatives

A number of academic analysts have remarked on the fact that EU policy is market-driven, and this takes various degrees and shapes depending on the policy field. In the field of television, this problem is by now totally out of proportion. Media economist Martin Cave remarks that the Community's handing over of standardisation prerogatives to the DVB group is one illustration of a new approach to standards setting which "represents a *privatization* of the traditional standards setting processes involving public sector bodies such as CENELEC" (Cave 1996: 593, emphasis added).[77] Similarly, David and Shurmer (1996) warn of the "dangers (that) lie in the possibility that these profit-driven ventures 'bypass' not only institutional procedures that delay the production of standards, but, in doing so they omit important public interests safeguards built into the formal process".

The logic of leaving the terrain open to market forces in order for them to shape developments and to determine the course of action, which is detectable here too, demonstrates the continuation of handing over political authority to market operators. Going back to the original schema of the interlinked elements (A) communications policy-making (B) political communication and (C) democratic politics, is pertinent here.

It is evident that as long as element (A) is, directly or indirectly, under the control of media operators and market forces, there can hardly exist any chance for a European, political communication or for a European, democratic politics to emerge. Emerging conditions and rules will then be shaped in the absence of the public at large, and beyond the control of their political representatives. Once the dominant market players have set the premises and established the going norms, then the Commission may come along afterwards to try *post facto*, to ensure 'fair play'. But, this *a posteriori* attempt neither regulates, nor balances out interests, nor secures the common interest, and rarely has any effect. Any empowering,

---

[77] See Chapter 6, and Cave, 1997.

synergetic functions that could accrue to end-users and interacting, TV viewers are thus cancelled out.

Citizens' and viewers' groups that anticipate prompt Community action in this area find such a stance frustrating: "Evidently the technological tool of the Internet can alter the isolation of the television viewers, who long to become active" (Hennebert 2003: 75).[78] Media activists are asking for 'communication rights', which are now technically available; the Commission, however, argues that "in relation to the TWF Directive, the e-commerce Directive clarifies some legal concepts and harmonises certain aspects enabling the information society services to benefit fully from Internal Market principles" (Commission 2003a: 14-15). The ubiquitous Internal Market thus shows itself to be insensitive to socially important needs.

Frustrating Citizens' Policy Expectations

The policy document makes frequent reference to the 'interested parties', yet no explanation is given as to how they are defined and how their representatives are selected.[79] Who is to be invited to the consultation process, and who qualifies as an *interested party* in the parlance of the Commission? (Commission 2003a) Given the Commission's *separation* between television and information, society services, TV viewers are not conceived of as users. The term *users* occurs just once in the entire document. Significantly, in this single occurrence it refers to selecting optional, advertising spots and to electronic shopping. Conversely, the

---

[78] Translation from the French by the author. Similar trends to those expressed by Hennebert are obtaining in the USA. Kellner accounts that "National surveys of viewer preferences for cable programs also indicate that public access is a high priority for many viewers". Thus he advocates that "there is definitely a receptive and growing audience for public access television, and the possibility of making alternative television programs by progressives should be a much higher priority for radical media politics" Kellner, 1990: 224).

[79] The document comprises a section on definitions and basic concepts. Yet, rather than definitions there we find a summary of the key goals of the original TWF Directive.

concept of 'viewers' interests' does not figure at all in the discourse of the Commission.

Citizens' groups and activists are not given due consideration, even though they pursue dialogue on these issues. As is pointed out by Hennebert (2003: 53): "without a guaranteed dialogue, how can the viewers make their weight felt against the interests of economic and the political lobbies?" But even if we suppose that representatives of such civil society organisations participate in the consultation process and the decision-making processes, what would their input be worth? They are interested in counterbalancing "the interests of economic lobbies". As we have seen, however, the Commission intends to regulate "as close as possible to the operators".

The Commission's policy stance could not have been more partisan. TV viewer activists position themselves favourably and positively towards technological changes and the social restructuring that these changes entail. As is argued by Hennebert again, "first of all we must favour the advent of the tools and the structures which permit the public to enter into a contact with the channels and the regulatory institutions" (Hennebert (2003: 52). As a matter of fact, their policy preferences and demands do not feature in the available policy documents. Hence their requests do not reach the agenda. Viewers, as citizens, are not seen, let alone respected, as stake-holders. They always figure as consumers. Meanwhile, the term 'operator' looms large in most policy drafts.

Just as in the case of the first revision, one of the issues facing policy drafters was whether or not to enlarge the scope of the TWF Directive. There seems to have been reluctance – or a definite resistance – to this. But even without enlarging the scope of policy, there could still be room to positively exploit interactive and synergetic possibilities. It has been observed, for instance, that 'the right of reply' is hardly exercised at all (Kaitatzi-Whitlock 1999). Thanks to their immediacy and pervasiveness, new interactive and synergetic tools can greatly facilitate the exercise of this right. This is all the more important if one considers that this provision can employ citizens' accessibility to television screens.

Given media convergence, this measure could, in fact, have been part of the previous revision of the TWF Directive in 1997. Disaffected citizens could be given concrete application guidelines for filing complaints electronically, for immediate correction. Through interactivity, responses by insulted members of the public can be instant, efficient and well-designed. Indeed with new constructive 'must carry rules', apart from accessibility for grievances only, interactive facilities could be granted for other contributions such as ideas, proposals, or participation in public debates. This would require a major re-orientation in communications policy-making, which is at present being resisted.

As stressed by the Commission, the media have enormous power to "form users' opinions". The monitoring of the conditions under which opinion polls are performed by various 'operators', could then and should be the subject of a very necessary and desirable regulation. Without transparency or accountability, 'results' may be ambiguous, or even tendentious and misleading. So far, operators have been left to their own devices on this. However feasible or beneficial these suggestions might be, the Commission's fixed intention was not to 'over-regulate' in order not to stifle the economic *development of the industry.* Again, here we observe the damage occasioned by the exclusively economistic conception of the policy.

The Commission Communication informs us that certain interested parties have voiced their desire for a significant broadening of the scope of the Directive in the next revision, without, however, providing details. In this respect, the drafters of the document admit that "a thorough revision of the Directive might be necessary to take account of technological developments and changes in the structure of the audiovisual market" (Commission 2003a: 14). At the end of November 2005, the submission of the Commission draft policy proposals was still imminent (Ducatel 28/11/2005, Sifounakis 29/11/2005).[80] So, to date, the Commission has not put forward any distinctly novel ideas about how

---

[80] The Commission's Response to the EP position was adopted on December 13 and subsequently was in preliminary draft form promoted to the EP.

to exploit the unique synergetic nexus between TV and the Internet for socially and politically beneficial objectives. Instead, vague promises are made that the Commission will

> reflect with the help of experts (in focus groups) whether any changes to content regulation for different distribution channels for audiovisual content would be necessary to take account of media convergence at a technical level and any divergence of national regulation which affects the establishment and the functioning of the common market. (Commission 2003a: 14)

But even in this hypothetical case, the policy mandate shall be based on the present framework: "Any intervention would have to ensure proportionate application of content rules and the coherent application of relevant policies..." such as "competition, commercial communications, consumer protection and the internal market strategy for the services sector (Commission 2003a: 14).

'Interactive' Advertising without Communication Rights

Already in 1999, the Commission, in its "Communication on principles and guidelines for the Community's audiovisual policy in the digital age", emphasised the importance "not to restrict the development of advertising techniques but to ensure that basic principles... continue to apply" (Commission 1999). Given the preferred Internal Market frame-work and the commitment to the interests of 'operators', it is hardly surprising that the disregarding and deferring attitude of the Commission does not apply to 'interactive advertising'. Once again we discern a clear case of a positive discrimination in favour of the already-strongest market players, and to the detriment of the public interest. In a recent, interpretative Communication (23.04.2004), the Commission makes a point of explaining the exceptional, policy provisions for this commercial innovation. This instructs us that interactive advertising allows viewers to supply information directly to the broadcaster via a return path or to interactively explore a chosen environment for as long as they wish (Commission 2004).[81]

This then is a specimen of what is meant by 'co- and self-regulation'. The exceptionally fast accommodation of commercial interests in regard to interactive advertising reveals that the Commission appreciates profit-making opportunities deriving from synergetic functions and can see what is at stake. They, like the lobbyists of the ACT, acknowledge the dynamic opportunities, both present and future. So, what conclusions can be drawn from this privileging of commercial interactive functions over non-commercial ones?

We can perhaps only judge this when the final policy arrives. Meanwhile, critics might claim that the intention is to allocate these new resources exclusively to private and commercial exploitation by media interests. At all events, *timing* is a hugely crucial factor in policy-making and is used strategically for privileging and prioritising. The Commission *will* come up with a policy proposal for non-commercial uses of interactivity, but this has so far not been ascertained. In either eventuality, the likelihood that citizens will be excluded from this re-allocation of *power* is very high. In case anybody might have doubts about future policy orientations, it is stressed that, when the time comes for Community action, this will be based on the framework of the Internal Market. This means that it will definitely maintain its dominant market-led position. So, whatever the political developments may be the ubiquitous Internal Market framework will always be the 'appropriate legal basis'.

The Commission's Communication on the future of the European Regulatory Audiovisual Policy was submitted in 2004, (Commission 2004). It comprised its recommendations for the revision of the TWF Directive, which generally procured a 'muddling through' (Lindblom 1959) policy stance: the new TWF to emerge should take onboard the

---

[81] Readers of the document are referred to the EGTA (European Group for Television Advertising) code of conduct and the ITC guidance notes.

technological and economic transformations challenging the *status quo* of European Audiovisual space and the television market place.[82] These include the emergence of new forms of consumption as consumers engage with alternative forms of communication and interactive services. Such reforms may have a dramatic impact on traditional forms of advertising as niche audiences develop and television ceases to be a mass medium but one of a range of information services (Iosifidis et al. 2005: 99).

Policies against the Current for Interactive Publicness

The Weber Report of the EP, which also comprises a Resolution, develops its array of special sensitivities in regard of the media sector. Significantly, this particular report is dedicated once again to the defence of the quotas articles of the TWF Directive. On more general issues and in Paragraph 19 the Report underlines the following:

> that universal public access to quality and diversified content is becoming ever more crucial in this context of technological change and increased concentration in an increasingly competitive and globalised environment; considers that public broadcasting services are essential to forming opinion in a democratic manner and permitting people to experience and familiarise themselves with cultural diversity, and that such services must have equal opportunities of priority access to the market, including in the new media. (EP 2005 - "Weber Report")

Yet from what can be seen in the draft directive submitted in December 2005 by the Commission, these points that the EP stressed did not translate into any specific provisions or pertinent articles. As a result the original Directive is not going to be broadened in scope in that

---

[82] See also Iosifidis et al. 2005: 99.

direction. Interestingly though, the Commission's Proposal for amending the TWF Directive (Council 1989), in the first paragraph of the preamble, legitimates its propositions on the fact that

> new technologies in the transmission of audiovisual media services call for adaptation of the regulatory framework to take account of the impact of structural change and technological developments on business models, especially the financing of commercial broadcasting, and to ensure optimal conditions of competitiveness for Europe's information technologies and its media industries and services. (Commission 2004/5)

This preamble in fact sets the tone for the proposed policy. As is evident, this rationale elaborates on such purely economic concerns as business models, the financing of digital enterprises and competitiveness. As anticipated in the analysis on preceding documents, the Commission leadership is exclusively concerned with industrial, policy objectives. Conceptually, the only mode of perceiving broadcast contents is as pieces of information received by private individuals as rights-holders of freedom of information. Nowhere is there any rationale as to the positive and engaging public and political role that especially interactive broadcasting can play.

In fact all the proposed measures relate to furthering, extending and diversifying the possibilities of commercial activities, notably of course *advertising* the types of which have increased enormously since the original directive of 1989. In this vein, eleven new definitions on an equal amount of new or redefined concepts are provided.

These concern: (a) audiovisual *media services,* which refers to the renaming of the previously central term of the directive: broadcasting. So, henceforth there will not be any broadcasting. It will be 'audiovisual media services'. The renaming of course aims at extending the pervasive commercialising logic to all current and future to become 'audiovisual media services'; (b) in line with the first change, the notion of broadcaster is replaced by the corresponding 'media service provider'; (c) 'television broadcasting', which henceforth is referred to as *linear audiovisual media service*; (d) broadcaster of linear broadcast services; (e) 'non-linear service', which refers to a service where the user decides upon the moment of consuming a transmitted service, that is a generic category of on-demand services; (f) 'audiovisual commercial communication': this is commercial propaganda for product promotion being upgraded semantically; (g) 'television advertising' as a separate notion from advertising on other new electronic carriers; (h) 'surreptitious advertising', which refers to commercial propaganda that appears 'imperceptible' as such to viewers, in short, grey advertising; (i) 'sponsorship': this is the term for the financing for promotional purposes of programmes by private or public entities coming from outside the sector of 'audiovisual media services'; (j) 'tele-shopping'; (k) 'product placement'. Product placement was a controversial matter in this revision, since to some, it is a form of surreptitious advertising. According to the commission's definition, this means "any form of audiovisual commercial communication consisting of the inclusion of or reference to a product, or device or the trade mark thereof so that it is featured within audiovisual media services, normally in return for payment of for similar (sic) consideration" (ibid: 10).

The ensemble of these definitions and all the associate semantic interventions in fact reflect the entire breadth of concerns of this policy process. Hence, no broadening of the scope is in view, other than for private exploitation. The policy's central focus and its steady orientation are firmly fixed towards the permanent imprisoning of the medium of television in serving exclusively commodifying and commercial goals. This evolution does not simply constitute a *'regression to the status quo'*, but a galloping regression to feudal enclosures. Hence, "the consequences are a return to prepolitical human existence, to the end of democracy, and to its epitaph: the private (Venturelli 1996: 121).

Through its spokeswoman Françoise le Bail, the Commission of the EU, in May 2005, acknowledged a European *information deficit*: "We accept that it is a 'no' vote…There is almost certainly an *information deficit* [83] and efforts will have to be made to explain things more clearly to citizens…" (*Guardian* May 31st 2005). The analysis of this policy suggests that, contrary to such pledges, the EU, in its communications policy-making, blatantly disregards the options offered by the radically changing media environment to cure this information and communication deficit.

By their very nature advanced and innovative media empower and emancipate users on the horizontal level. Concurrently, this potential is very much needed for the creation of horizontal ties between the members of the various European peoples and *demoi* which as we have seen is a structural precondition for a higher social legitimation (Chryssochoou 2005: 86). Yet EU politicians obstinately ignore this potential in their pan-European, communications policies. Yet even if politicians are fixed only on commercial interests, this relevant counterfactual is unstoppable. The control revolution (Shapiro 1999) is itself advancing in an uncontrollable way thanks to steps taken by individuals and members of the community. Active information users and communications-rights practitioners will have to become, on their own initiative, albeit haphazardly or defiant. They will simply have to circumvent the fast obsolescing and autistic system of EU politics. These emerging conditions broaden the scope for participation; they open the gates for putting users and citizens on the policy map in a distinctly different, but political way. Individual citizens are significant stake-holders and an emerging agency. Ultimately, neither media entrepreneurs nor media policy-makers can ignore this factor. But Eurocrats have.

The political challenge was for a proactive policy attitude, but EU policy-makers continue on the path of de-regulation and privatization, exclusively with a view to commercial targets. Thus, this potential is not taken up by Eurocrats and EU politicians for facilitating communitarian objectives and political aims. This policy analysis establishes that, currently, EU policy-drafters avoid taking any measures to safeguard European citizens' 'communication rights'. They do not initiate and

---

[83] In Chapter 8, I elaborate further on the issue of citizens' ignorance and its causes.

safeguard publicly-accessible political communication despite the ample possibilities for this. The critical question that arises is: what could today justify excluding citizens' 'communication rights' and the exclusive prioritising of private commercial interests? There are important political benefits to be reaped from developing policies drawing on the synergy between television and the Internet which are significant for *all interested parties*.

In this chapter I have assessed the actual difficulties faced by the institutions of the EU, in conceiving and realising a citizen-friendly policy that would establish and defend communication rights and interests of all Europeans. This counterfactual strategy is realistic. Community policy-makers, however, demonstrate not only ambivalence but a positive reluctance to connect 'communications rights' to the only pan-European, popular medium of television.

No doubt the usual 'select' forces, who are reluctant for developments to turn in any direction other than the one prescribed by them, have once again influenced the agenda unilaterally. The typical obstacle to a re-orientation of EU, communications policy, the EU's unshakable, indeed structurally neo-liberal and economistic, Internal Market framework, as usual, comes to their assistance. Not surprisingly then, the reference to the term 'operators' in these policy documents is so frequent that it is impossible not to observe a bias in favour of these actors. By the same token it is impossible not to observe the gross negligence of the interests of a huge variety of other stake-holders, most notably those of citizens. EU policies indeed advance quickly, when they serve the interests of those privileged actors, always in the name of the 'competitiveness of the economy'.

A policy instrument that could greatly enhance the quality of politics, political relations and European public affairs thus remains a counterfactual. In the past, a standard concern with policy analysis was whether it was proactive or reactive. In the era of *co- and self-regulation*, the key question is whether public policies make it to the fore at all. In any case, it is clear that the choices of the EU in the new millennium work in favour of the privatization of communications policy-making.

Chapter 5

PLURALISM AND CONCENTRATION OF MEDIA OWNERSHIP

The media play a constitutive role in society and in social conflict; they are vehicles of decision-making and are concurrently defined by it. A thriving pluralism is dependent on a viable media sector, presupposing financial independence; this, however, is by no means sufficient: media regulation is a *sine qua non* for a diversely-sourced, media sector and for fending off unilateral and abusive control by state or market.[84] This chapter examines a policy process, during which attempts to regulate both the structure and conduct of EC audiovisual activities, notably through restrictions on concentration of media ownership, have failed. The attempts to safeguard pluralism and diversity of programming, which became more focused after the adoption of the TWF Directive of 1989, have been going on for over six years, during which 'merger mania' has grown unabated.

A precise correspondence between the territory of a lawful activity and its regulation is indispensable. This condition does not obtain in the audiovisual sector where there is a partial discrepancy between sites of operation and of regulation. While broadcasting is transfrontier, its regulation, as regards pluralism, is relegated to the member states of the Community. When the transmitting state applies different and less protective regulation on pluralism, the receiving state and their citizens are *de jure* placed in a defensive and a disadvantaged position. This not only creates a divergent audiovisual environment in which conflicts are likely to occur but also one which *a priori* puts democratic rights in question. Once

---

[84] For further discussion of the sufficient conditions for pluriform and diverse media content see Peacock (1989), Cave (1989), and Murdock (1984).

transfrontier television transmission is both *de facto* and *de jure* an EC-wide practice, the issue of pluralism and of diversity of programming becomes an EC as well as a national problem, and should, therefore, become an object of EC policy-making.

The attempt to produce a policy on pluralism coincided firstly with the revision of the TWF Directive and secondly with the GATS controversy (see Chapter 7) and thirdly, with the policy on conditional digital pay-TV services. Consequently, it is characterised by the same dynamics and prevalent trends also observed in those concurrently running policies. The pluralism issue raised a highly agonistic controversy, which unfolded in the EP, on communication-policy conferences and in the consultation process.

The battle to induce a Community policy for pluralism and for curbing concentration of media ownership was, in fact, a battle on re-gaining the political control of communications policy, (element 'A' of Chapter 1), after this had been lost with the adoption of the TWF within the Internal Market framework. As a corollary, this battle was also about safeguarding, primarily, a space for political communication (element 'B'), in order to maintain and to develop political relations and democratic politics in the EU (element 'C').

The main proponents of media-specific, all-encompassing Community regulation on pluralism were the EP and the Economic and Social Committee (ECOSOC). The debate and the implicit conflict of interests concerned the distribution of power between, those claiming private control and unconditional profit-seeking via communications and those claiming communications for politics and defending the public: in other words, the conflict was between marketeers on the one hand and civil society and the body politic interest on the other.

This chapter explores the succession of events and elucidates why the real confrontation between these positions was never allowed to be decided politically, and why an elaborate, politically supported and consistent effort by the EP to safeguard pluralism was first rejected and ignored, and later 'redefined'. I also discuss the impossibility of fitting the political and cultural issue of pluralism onto the economistic Procrustean bed of the Internal Market. The TWF Directive of 1989 expressly aspires to prevent 'any acts which...may promote the creation of dominant positions which would lead to restrictions on pluralism and freedom of information and of the information sector as a whole' (EEC/552/89, preamble) in a free economy. This entails medium-scale and diversely owned and sourced channels, which militate against conglomerations and the rationalisation of mega-units. In practice, pluralism requires a diverse market with internal checks and balances to maintain both the internal and the external pluralism models in a complementary fashion. Concurrently, The European Council declarations of 1988 and 1989 pointed out the importance of *cultural diversity*.

The Commission's approach to this issue presents successive twists and changes. 'Turning unduly timid' during 1992-1994, and in spite of Article 6 (ex Article F) and Article 151 of the TEC, it defined pluralism as being outside its sphere of competence. It then restricted the scope of its potential intervention to a competition and 'freedom of establishment' approach, according to which firms enjoy 'freedom of access' to alien markets, thereby effacing once again the democratic and political role of the media. Concurrently, it invited the interested parties to a 'serial' consultation process – the outcome of which it subsequently patently ignored. Thus, rather than safeguarding pluralism by a timely regulation of both market structure and *a priori* conduct, through the adoption of additional 'must carry rules', the Community has so far managed to provide us with policies of *de facto* deregulation.[85]

Inaction on such political communication values as pluralism meanwhile gave precious time to powerful operators who could, in the meantime, thus create irreversible concentrations in the media sector. The chapter concludes that the main problems for regulation are attributable

---

[85] In the 'supra-national' setting there are no adequate political and structural means available to both liberalise and regulate. In September 1995, Commissioner Mario Monti once again identified the positive need for action on this issue, and a new policy proposal was announced again in July 1996, but to no avail.

to the EC's 'impotence' in dealing with such problems in the given political economy. Its lack of institutional and political development makes it unable to withstand the pressures of global competition and global capital integration.

The Concept of Media Pluralism

Media pluralism is a qualification of the freedom of information. It encompasses diversity of programming, the balanced representation of views and the constant goal that the maximum number of voices be heard over a wide political and cultural spectrum. It is affected by and has an impact on information sources, editorial and management policies, ownership patterns and such economic indices as viability, externalities and profits. It answers to distributional questions, such as how much, and what kind of freedom of information should be allowed, and to whom? At what cost to the public interest and to other values? How far can the egalitarianism inherent in pluralism be allowed to be compromised by economic imperatives?

Pluralism is not an end in itself. It is a precondition of a democratic political communication. It provides for the unhindered circulation of diverse or even oppositional ideas and of the exchanges of such ideas in democratic processes of making choices and decisions.

> Democracy thrives on controversy and requires participation in social processes; it presupposes that people are motivated enough to want to get involved in public life. Democracy thus requires a degree of 'civic virtue' and a lively public sphere in which discussion, debate and participation combine in collective decision-making. (Kellner 1990: 95)

Media pluralism could be said to be the equitable management of the principle of freedom of information. An integrated, media pluralism would seek to correct imbalances generated by either structural constraints or agency factors and should also look into the interplay between these factors.[86] The management of the freedom of information may lead to unilaterally favouring corporate interests or, if it is pluralistic, to the protection of the public interest. The commodification and the commercialisation of broadcasting inevitably lead to the former state of affairs. Nevertheless, a tight regulation of the media might strike a balance between these options, as in the UK 'duopoly' (in a national setting) as long as that lasted.

Opponents of this view argued that freedom of information can be assured through channel proliferation, and that unrestricted media ownership, which entails concentration, is imperative for Europe to gain a larger share of the global information sector (Gyllenhammar 1994).[87] It was also argued that by "global standards European media companies tend to be small and fragmented. Without new markets and wider investment opportunities, these companies would not be able to face up to American and Japanese competition" (EP 1994a (Rawlings): 355). Opponents held also that pluralism is an 'exclusively' national issue, thereby splitting the management of freedom of information between the national and supra-national levels. By refusing to view the EC as a unity, this position counteracts the extension and safeguarding of a democratic role for the media throughout the Community. The possibility that receiving member states may *a posteriori* ban transmissions which infringe their national pluralism regulations is to convert a general issue into a local one. This means making light of a fundamental question of principle. National governments cannot be expected to enter into 'transfrontier wars' each time transborder broadcasts violate local pluralism laws. Legal action on a case-by-case basis can be no remedy for this, as it reduces a question of democratic principle to one of *post facto* legalistic dispute.

---

[86] See also Murdock 1982: 125.

[87] Per Gylenhammar, Swedish industrialist. This was an excerpt from his speech at the European Audiovisual Conference of 1994.

The EC Competition Framework

The TEC does not address the political or cultural functions of services and the media specifically, even though these functions are strongly invoked on several occasions in EC documents, notably the 1984 TWF Green Paper, whose most important objective was to legitimise a commodifying and liberalising EC intervention in the cultural domain (GPTWF: 1-10). Articles 81-89 (ex. 85-94) of the TEC lay out the EC's fundamental philosophy, which aims to enhance competition and forbid market distortions. But mergers creating competition anomalies may be justified and desirable on other grounds (as in the case of United International Pictures). The exemptions indicated in 81(3) may allow mergers and conglomerations in the media industry for the sake of innovation and the high technology transfers involved.[88]

The Council Regulation of 1989 on the control of concentrations between undertakings aimed to control concentrations (in general) and their effect on the competition structure. This was in fact the only instrument applicable to transfrontier concentrations, and its monitoring was the exclusive responsibility of the Commission. This entailed that member states could not apply their own relevant legislation to concentrations with a Community dimension (Council 1989a). They might, however, seek to protect other values than those pursued by the regulation, such as interests of public security, plurality of the media and prudential rules (Druesne & Kremlis 1990: 80). This is the grey area that

---

[88] Article 81 (ex-85 §3) of the TEC stipulates the cases that are exempted from these general prohibitions and the terms under which this is possible. Provisions may be inapplicable in the case of

- *any agreement or category of agreements between undertakings;*

- *any decision or category of decisions by association of undertakings;*

- *any concerted practice or category of concerted practices which contributes to improving the production or distribution of goods or to promoting technical or economic progress, while allowing consumers a fair share of the resulting benefit, and which does not a) impose on the undertaking concerned restrictions which are not indispensable to the attainment of these objectives; b) afford such undertakings the possibility of eliminating competition in respect of a substantial part of the products in question.*

allows receiving member-states *a posteriori* to ban infringing transfrontier emissions from other member-states.

Absurdly enough, receiving member-states and individual citizens are expected to initiate legal actions to protect their universal democratic rights. From the perspective of the need for a pan-European, political-communication framework this was preposterous. The ECJ would be expected to decide on a case by case basis if such banning is admissible in Community law (Van Loon 1992: 43). In the Gouda judgement, the ECJ held that pluralism may be considered a legitimate aim of regulation in view of the TEC. Even so, the principle of proportionality was also mobilised and the regulations in question were considered as 'unnecessary obstacles' to the transmission of foreign programmes and to advertising (Hoffmann-Riem 1992: 159).

For the assessment of concentrations, the Council Regulation had introduced two parameters: (1) geographical area of the activity and (2) a quantitative threshold. A merger is considered to have a European dimension when a) the combined world turnover of the firms involved surpasses the threshold of five billion ECU, or b) when the total turnover of at least two of the firms involved individually surpasses 250 million ECU except when each firm achieves more than two thirds of its turnover in one member state.

The geographical coverage is problematic in the case of satellite services, as firms may control larger areas than what is 'technically' provable. The parameter of the quantitative threshold has been criticised as extremely high but Commissioner Leon Brittan denied reports about lowering it to 3 MECU (*European Report*, 14.09.1991). Although the stipulated thresholds are high, multimedia types of mergers and strategic alliances could easily surpass them even in the early phase of the 'European audiovisual space' subsequent to the adoption of the transfrontier Directive.[89] In any case assessment is extremely difficult,

---

[89] "...it has already become clear that certain types of media concentration are able to meet these high thresholds', claims Van Loon (1992: 37, note 1), referring to Case No IV/M110 –ABC / Generale des Eaux / Canal+ / WH Smith TV (ECJ 1991e). This case was notified to the Commission on 07.08.1991. Since the parties did not achieve more

since vertical and cross-ownership as well as multimedia diversification strategies incapacitate the assessment of concentration on the basis of a one product market. In effect then, this regulation provided no restrictions on monopoly trends in the media sector. Indeed, in 1990, the Commission admitted that the application of Community competition law, "in particular Articles 81 and 82 of the Treaty, [cannot] cover all situations in which a threat to pluralism is posed, notably in the case of multimedia ownership. Likewise, the Regulation on mergers, adopted on 21 December 1989, covers *only* large mergers which affect competition on the market in question" (Commission 1990: 21). Meanwhile, according to the Commission, the rate of mergers and concentrations was faster in the media sector than in the rest of the economy (Commission 1992b: 27). As pointed out by Rawlings, by "global standards European media companies tend to be small and fragmented" (EP 1994a (Rawlings): 355). They therefore 'needed' new markets and wider investment opportunities "to face up to American and Japanese competition" (ibid). Under this ideology of *gigantism* for companies and of global competition a number of spectacular mergers became known.

(1) United International Pictures (UIP), a distribution group that comprises Hollywood majors Universal, Paramount and MGM, and which operates globally, was granted exemption from the competition Article 81 by the DG IV of the Commission on 12 July 1989 – which, however, took effect in July 1988 – despite the fact that this group undoubtedly held a dominant position in EC, audiovisual, stock-programming distribution.[90]

---

than two-thirds of their aggregate Community-wide turnover in one and the same M-S, it was deemed that "the operation has a Community dimension within the meaning of Article 1(2) of the Merger regulation" (C.EC 10.09.91: 2, see also OJ C 244/5, 19.9.91, 'Non-opposition of notified concentration'), and therefore enshrined as legal in this Franco-American takeover of WH Smiths' TV interests.

[90] About preferential treatment to UIP by DG IV and about other cases of dominant positions, see the Think Tank Report (Vasconcelos 1994) and Pressley's article "UIP Expects EU to Renew Competition-Law Exemption", (*Wall Street Journal*, 1.07.94).

(2) A 'Eurocartel' of major media companies', such as Kirch, CLT, Fininvest, Telepiu, Banque Internationale du Luxembourg (BIL) and Compagnie Internationale de Télécommunication (CIT) dominated a large part of the EAS, but seems also prone to constant restructuring and concentrating changes:

> *L'alliance entre Leo Kirch et Silvio Berlusconi forme 'un réseau international difficilement controlable... Silvio Berlusconi servirait-il de prête-nom à Leo Kirch dans DSF (ex-Telefünf), et Leo Kirch, en échange, servirait-il le prête-nom de Silvio Berlusconi dans Telepiu? En clair, Leo Kirch, ami du chancelier Kohl, et Silvio Berlusconi auraient-ils ainsi contourné les lois contre la concentration audiovisuelle, chacun dans son pays?* (Rouard 1994)

(3) A cooperative attempt was made between the EC and the Digital Video Broadcasting (DVB) group, which represents the market forces to regulate transmission standards for advanced television. This culminated in the 1995 standards Directive 'granting' monopoly control for the encoding, conditional access (CA) system of the currently, fastest-growing, media-market segment of pay-per-view (PPV) services, to the backers of the SimulCrypt system, controlled by Rupert Murdoch (BSkyB) and Rousselet (Canal+). Before this 'regulation' there was a *de facto* monopoly of the same companies on the CA system, the gateway to 'owning' the viewer. [91]

(4) In April 1996, the president of Petrofina (the largest Belgian oil company), who is also the owner of the Group Bruxelles Lambert, which is the largest shareholder of CLT, entered into a merger agreement with Bertelsmann, the largest publisher worldwide (*Vima* 1996).

(5) Bertelsmann and Kirch attempted a mega-merger with Deutsche Telecom, which was eventually stalled by the competition DG IV in 1994 for contravening the provisions of the regulation on mergers.

(6) WH Smith was acquired by a Franco-American group in 1991.

---

[91] See Chapter 6 for a full discussion.

(7) In July 1996 BSkyB, the multi-channel satellite broadcaster 40% owned by Rupert Murdoch's News International, which was also the co-owner and co-controller of the SimulCrypt CA system, established a partnership with the Leo Kirch Gruppe, one of Germany's largest media conglomerates. The partnership is known as DF-1 and has launched 17 channels in Germany, the first to be digitally transmitted (*Times*, 9.7.96).

(8) CLT, the first commercial TV channel and one of Europe's largest media companies, owns interests in ten television networks and 13 radio stations in eight different countries, including Germany's biggest commercial network RTL and Britain's fifth terrestrial channel. CLT merged with *Ufa*, the television and film subsidiary of Bertelsmann, another German giant of world dimensions. The merged companies, called CLT-Ufa, are based in Luxembourg and are involved in numerous joint ventures (Stüdemann 1996: 19). As was argued by Stüdemann, this was "basically about clearing up commercial television in Germany. There used to be three main players: Bertelsmann, Kirch and CLT. With the merger Bertelsmann narrowed that down to two which has made life easier" (ibid). This *mergermania* reflects then the measure of pluralism allowed. The two players left in the German speaking region were considered an acceptable level of diversity. A true market place of ideas, of political dialogue and of chances for developing political discussion...

Early Warnings against Media Concentration

The EP had focused its attention on pluralism before the merger mania gained the formidable momentum of the 1990s, fostered by the prevailing liberalisations. In its resolutions following the TWF Green Paper (GPTWF), but also in its amendments on the TWF draft Directive, the EP drew attention to the dangers of media concentration. It advocated the deterrence of private monopolies in the audiovisual sector and called for the guaranteeing of cultural diversity. This stance was entirely in line with its conception of the role of the media in European integration as paramount: "The Community must put up a determined struggle against the pathological tendencies to destroy fair competition and real variety. If the market is to be dominated by a few media companies, we risk losing freedom of choice" (EP, 27.4.1988). Moreover, the EP's 1990 resolution on pluralism called specifically for action and for the initiation of EC-wide policies against media concentration: "But restrictions on concentration are essential in the media sector, not only for economic reasons but also, and above all, as a means of guaranteeing a variety of information and freedom of the press" (EP, 15.02.1990). The Commission, subsequent to this EP resolution, made its 'concerned' reference to the kind of policy that was needed with respect to concentrations and pluralism in the media, in 1990:

> The establishment of the European audiovisual space does not derive merely from the wish to promote the audio-visual industry but also from the importance attached by the Community to the requirements of a democratic society, such as, notably, the respect for pluralism in the media and for freedom of expression. The Community's audiovisual policy seeks therefore, also, to ensure that the audiovisual sector is not developed at the expense of pluralism but, on the contrary, that it helps strengthen it by encouraging, in particular, the diversity of the programmes offered to the public. (Commission 1990: 21)

So, at this stage, one observes a coincidence of views between the EP and the Commission on the importance of *pluralism for democracy*. Significantly, the Commission communication asserts that Articles 81-89 of the TEC are inadequate to cover all cases that might threaten pluralism, particularly those deriving from multimedia ownership (ibid: 21). This admitted gap could then be corrected only with a due policy on pluralism, as a step towards guaranteeing a minimum of political communication in the EU.

A new EP resolution was adopted in 1992 that encompassed detailed structural and conduct criteria for regulation. In their path-breaking report, MEPs Dieter Schinzel and Ben Fayot clarified why (general) competition law can be no substitute for media law or for a media-specific law on concentration: "...concentrations in the media sector which threaten diversity of opinion do not necessarily also involve distortions of competition, just as, conversely the conditions of freedom of competition are no automatic guarantee for diversity of opinion" (EP 1992).

The Fayot & Schinzel report, which radicalised the debate and broadened the scope of this issue, was endorsed by the EP in September 1992, when a promising resolution was adopted. It included measures to curtail the powers of 'media moguls' not only in terms of ownership, but also in terms of management and conduct. Questions of journalistic and editorial integrity (ibid, §24) were addressed in the proposal of a European Media Code for journalists' and publishers' organisations (ibid, §23) including a charter for European non-profitmaking broadcasters.

The Green Paper on Pluralism and Media Concentration

In order to assess the need for action, in 1990 the Commission committed itself to study the options for an appropriate Directive 'on the account of the importance it attaches to the objective of media pluralism' (Commission 2003a: 21). This 'study' came in response to repeated EP requests to regulate these aspects, particularly as these were condensed in the resolutions of 1990 and of 1992 and took the form of the Green Paper on Pluralism and Media Concentration (Commission 1992b: 12). Paradoxically, however, and contrary to explicit Commission statements in favour of pluralism and diversity, this Green Paper identified no objective with respect to media pluralism, as such, at EC level. The attack on pluralism was direct: "safeguarding pluralism of the media is neither a Community objective nor is it in the Community's jurisdiction" as laid down by the TEC and the TEU (ibid: 59). So, a 'content pluralism issue' was identified but it was relegated to the member states, in spite of adoption of Article 151 in the TEC. Thus, not just a definitive change but a veritable turning upside-down of the Commission's position occurred between 1990 and 1992 (ibid: 58-60).

Two novel elements emerged instead. First, the Commission made a U-turn regarding the principle of pluralism and its significance for the *democratic constitution* of the Community. This was a diplomatic manoeuvre reflecting policy preferences which sought both to further deregulate the enlarged EC market, and to keep it unregulated. Consequently, the Commission had to renege on its earlier promises for the defence of pluralism. This move exposed the controversy that arose between the Commission and the EP concerning the way to handle this problem.

The Commission's view of pluralism as a derogation of freedom of information was severely criticised by several commentators. EP rapporteur (Committee on legal and citizens' rights) Kurt Malangre, drawing on an analysis by Konrad and Albrecht Hesse, notably argued that such definition misses the dual character of the *fundamental right* to express opinions as a subjective *civil right*, as embodied in Article 10 of the European Convention on Human Rights (ECHR). Malangre highlighted that pluralism is a "constitutive element of the objective democratic legal order" (Malangre 1993: 6).

This crucial clarification elucidated in a crystal clear way that here we are not dealing with the restriction of the *freedom of expression of media operators*, but with the restriction of their activity, when such activity restricts the individual *freedom of expression of citizens,* that is, when the activity of these operators endangers or influences the media in their role as opinion formers. This is an ultimately political function. It is one that constitutes or de-constructs the most central aspect of political communication. When such unregulated activity may precondition public, political opinion, this activity by such operators expropriates the very function of the media in their service of the public sphere.

Malangre also stressed that, although the GP distinguishes between internal and external pluralism, it fails to consider this significant distinction when assessing the extent of concentration and the options for action. This remark once again reveals that the EC's handling of this issue separates paragraphs one and two of Article 10 (ECHR). This bias served to legitimise the EC's feat of its intervention in the communications policy area in 1984, in order to entirely commodify and to liberalise this sector. Yet, under the Community's splitting approach, paragraph two remains conditional on segmentalised, national regulation and on a putatively positive judgement by the ECJ.

In addition to this, the GP confusingly conceptualises the optimum number of distribution operators as 'pluralism'. But plurality or even plethora of distribution channels, however small their audience-share, does not in itself constitute pluralism. Pluralism refers to diversely originated and scheduled content. 100 channels delivering a similar menu in different packages do not lead to 'pluralism'. The Commission, then, conflated or even 'replaced' *quantitative plurality* with pluralism.

The GP set out to explore two distinct categories of questions. The first asked whether there is a need for action at Community level or not (no action, Option I). The next categories arise only after the exclusion of option I, that is, only when a need for Community action is positively established. These questions addressed the kind of instrument to be adopted and its content: sub-option (I) a regulation for harmonisation; sub-option (II) a recommendation for transparency; sub-option (III) a Directive or regulation with or without a European Media Council. Instead, the three options as suggested by the GP were: (I) taking no action, (II) a recommendation to enhance transparency, (III) the harmonisation of national restrictions on media ownership by (a) a Council Directive, (b) a Council regulation, or (c) a Directive or a regulation together with an independent committee (ibid: 9). These conflate a series of successive options, which are therefore incomparable. According to Commission statements, the objective of the consultation process following the Green Paper was first, to assess the need for Community action relating to pluralism. Secondly, it was to consider the kind of action that might be desirable and/or feasible in terms of Community objectives and needs.

The framework given was the Internal Market and the GP's 'idiosyncratic' definition of the concept of pluralism, which ignored the conception of pluralism applying in the constitutions of most member states. The GP's definition, furthermore, disregarded internal pluralism as exercised by psbs, which were, and still continue to be, the only media that consistently address viewers as (national, not European) citizens.[92] The perspective and the thesis of this book is that it is indispensable to acknowledge and to provide equally for both the national and the European citizenship. In this respect, it is important to stress that national psbs address viewers as national citizens exclusively.

Key characteristics of most European psbs are: universality of access irrespective of geographical location or socio-economic group, fair and impartial representation, a diversity of programming to cater for a variety of needs, including the needs of unprofitable minorities, and an emphasis on education, information and entertainment. Psbs is a broadly European concept. The need to fend off state or any other abusive control or paternalism of psbs does not entail that this (in the final instance politically accountable) system should be replaced by a feudalising, privatized and commercial media model. The former addresses the viewer as a citizen, while the latter aims at, and is constrained by, profit maximisation (Garnham 1990). Because of this crucial difference in role, and in spite of psb profile changes in an environment of competition, psbs must be examined with political and cultural rather than market criteria.

At the Amsterdam Treaty of the EU in 1997, a special protocol of exemption was adopted to secure the position of the psbs as a distinct part of the European political communication and political culture. MEP Carole Tongue in co-operation with a broad spectrum of political forces forged this special status for public broadcasting in an international

---

[92]. For a discussion of distinctions between the two systems and minimum prerequisites for what is termed 'consumer choice', see Peacock (1989) and Cave (1989).

'constitutional legal text' (Sarikakis 2004: 102). Welcome though such a measure of securing the key bastion of political communication in European states is, it should be admitted that it too represents only a '*regression to the status quo*'.

The Treaty of Amsterdam aimed to secure that psbs continue to exist in the face of invasive moves by the media moguls who consider that licence fees or state aids constitute violations of competition rules. The protective exemption that the psbs were granted is important for their survival as politically accountable media – in the national framework – usually of superior, quality standards than the commercial channels. But from the perspective of what is needed for the entire EU, psbs are hardly the solution for the new European regime. In short, psbs are important but not adequate for the pan-European dimension of political communication. In this regard it is interesting to recall that that the Green Paper added that in case of harmonisation of national, anti-concentration legislation, psbs should also come under that regulation, thus compounding the damage from an insufficient political analysis.

The Commission declared that it was open to other options and called interested parties to reply to a seven-point questionnaire. There are, however, no other obvious options between taking action and not taking action. What shaped the real policy *options* and opened the dead-end course on this issue was (a) the preferred framework of the Internal Market, which put the media on a par with any other economic activity and sector, (b) the economistic analysis of the Green Paper and (c) the split and biased definition of pluralism, linked to numbers of players in the market. Inconsistencies, bias and omissions reveal that the 'no action' option, which utterly misconstrued the role of media in power relations, was never excluded. By placing the issue solely within the Internal Market framework and by launching a destructively narrow definition, the key term of the Green Paper prepared the field for either dropping pluralism from the agenda or neutralising it.

An Impossible Framework

The plethora of contradictions and biases could not be concealed. The 1989 Regulation on concentrations prohibits member states from dealing with concentration cases with a Community dimension. The TWF Directive provided for the principle of channel control by the transmitting state. Meanwhile, national governments were supposed to 'maintain' their cultural and pluralism prerogatives. The politically tragicomic implication was that the job of the EC was to commodify, liberalise and deregulate (through the TWF), while that of the member states, if and whenever they could, would be to regulate. So the question of competences and sovereignty surfaces again. So, the contrast of unsustainable roles between the national and the supra-national levels could hardly be starker. The Commission did not deny the political role of the media. It rather stated that it could not deal with that sort of 'problem', which was thus, thanks to a convenient invocation of the then new principle of subsidiarity, devolved to the member states. Thus, that 'problem' of the need for political communication was restricted to the national territory and handed over to national governments by the TEC, thereby to be incapacitated. In this way, it prompted for a fragmented and inconclusive as much as a *post facto* approach.

This approach removed from the EC agenda problems of agency subordination to structural constraints (editorial policies conditioned by the controller). But as the 2004-2005 Greek 'basic shareholder' case has shown clearly (Kaitatzi-Whitlock 2004b), whenever member states' governments attempt to establish national policies for safeguarding minimum measures of transparency and/or pluralism or for the most elementary regulation on the conduct of operators,[93] the Commission

---

[93] The specific pathology of the Greek case is that media owners, notably TV channel operators, forge 'special liaisons' with politicians in government. Media barons, particularly those who are diversified owners of other industrial enterprises as well, thus use their media power and their ability for 'management of the image' of political personalities and parties as leverage against government contracts. This of course obtains also in places like the UK, Germany or France. But this became a 'Greek case' at

intervenes to penalise them. The Greek government has been threatened with injunctions at the ECJ but also with the freezing of its share of structural funds unless it revises not only its broadcasting legislation but also the Greek Constitution!

This arrangement, however, conceals real interests and potential issues of the receiving member-states and of European citizens more broadly. This is precisely the locus of transformation of the reduction of an issue of general interest. A public–communications, media policy is transformed into a narrow, industrial policy. Market access and freedom to supply services take precedence over impartiality (crucial in cases of contested issues), and locally meaningful and diverse content. But this is then also the point of turning away from democratic solutions in media policy (Ward 2004, Sarikakis 2004).

The Commission's assessment that the safeguarding of media pluralism was a national concern was quite conveniently predicated on the principle of subsidiarity (Commission 1992: IV). There is indeed a widespread view that cultural issues should be dealt with by member states, primarily, but not exclusively. This accentuates problems of the 'elasticity' of definitions of such central terms as, subsidiarity, pluralism and freedom of expression. How can the 'right of reply' be a Community objective (according to the relevant TWF Directive Article) and pluralism not be? What is the difference between the two? Quite simply, safeguarding pluralism endangers big economic and political interests, and it is expensive to keep up. As was very aptly put by MEP Ben Fayot *"Il y a dans le domaine des medias beaucoup d'hypocrisie. Tout le monde veut le pluralisme le plus pur et c'est très bien, mais peu de gens acceptent que l'Europe s'en donne les moyens"* (EP 1994a).

Subsidiarity provided for legislation at national and sub-national levels for issues that pertain there. It cannot be taken as a hiding post for non-decision and non-resolving Community-dimension problems. Most clearly, these problems pertain to both levels, but originate at the supra-

---

the EU level as soon as both the Greek Constitution and the Greek broadcasting law attempted to curb the awesome power of these media barons.

national level. Article 2 of the TWF Directive establishes the control of channels by the originating-state, rather than the receiving-state or the two in combination, embodying thus the principle of mutual recognition (the 'Cassis de Dijon' principle) in the cultural field. This is the sweeping rule of the Internal Market. By applying the mutual recognition principle, the Community put the audiovisual sector on a par with any other good or service, despite rhetoric to the contrary. This is the root of all problems, and this is certainly also what hinders a Europe-wide, political-communication policy.

The problem facing both national governments and the EC is that national measures are ineffective in dealing with the concentration of power (both economic and cultural/political) given the transfrontier and international scale of media undertakings (Papathanossopoulos 2002: 25-26).[94] According to the GP, this was not a serious problem (in 1992), as only a few undertakings had what it defined as a European dimension. Quite contrary to the EP's evaluation, the GP held that obstacles to the Internal Market were 'potential'; it is noteworthy that this Commission evaluation was changed in the 1994 interim report (Commission 1994d) where worries were expressed about 'lack of legal security' (ibid). Moreover, the GP held that any potential measures should seek to defend the functioning of the Internal Market rather than pluralism (Commission 1992b: 91-98).

In any case, it is inconceivable that media regulation be considered an exclusively national affair any more without creating major inconsistencies and policy anachronisms. This would indeed ignore the creation of the EAS. It would ignore the fact that transfrontier channels are received in countries outside those where they originate. It would refute the entire EC media policy and its underpinning rationale, including the battle for cultural exemptions and cultural specificity at the GATS negotiations of the Uruguay Round.[95] There is a flagrant contradiction between the

---

[94] "The globalization of financial markets makes it increasingly difficult for nation-states to preserve autonomy of action" (Mazower 1998: 405).

[95] See Chapter 7 for an explicit account of this.

objective of the EAS for production, and the GATS liberalisations (which cover the audiovisual sector). Due to price competition, it is impossible for small- and medium–sized, European producers to compete with very cheaply imported US programming, (irresistible to, and conditional for channel competitiveness). On the other hand, stock programming is the main-stay of channels that supposedly 'cross-subsidize' current affairs programming in generalist channels. Price competition and an inundation of low-grade and cheaply imported programming is then corrosive, not only in economic terms (EAS), but also in cultural political terms, particularly for the smaller linguistic areas. This relation is accentuated by the tendency for thematic channels, which monopolise the 'cash cow' sections (entertainment) of the content schedules of the audiovisual sector.

Procedurally, it is significant to highlight that rather than assigning this issue to the DG X (responsible for media and culture), it was assigned to DG XV, which deals with the Internal Market and does not 'understand' cultural issues. The DG XV exercises exclusive surveillance over the Internal Market, and the placement of such a cultural issue within its framework demonstrated the effacing of political communication outlets and the cultural characteristics of the audiovisual altogether, or to permanently preserve the dichotomy between the 'supra-national' and the national prerogatives, which the GP analysis introduced. Consequently, the GP's approach to pluralism via its potential impact on the internal market constitutes an essential deviation from the actual problems facing the member states and their citizens. The GP, nevertheless, stated that the Community must at least ensure that its activities do not adversely affect pluralism (Commission 1992b: 7) and acknowledged that pluralism and competition are different and complementary criteria, and that for pluralism, control has to be tighter than for competition (ibid: 81-82).

Reactions to the Green Paper: The Consultation Process

During the first April Hearing of 1993, 40 interest organizations formed two oppositional groups expressing proprietary and non-proprietary interests. These failed to agree on a common policy. The former, in the minority, rejected EC action altogether (Option I). The second majoritarian group (professionals, industry interest groups, civil society) demanded immediate action, specifying option IIIc, some proposing more comprehensive measures in defence of pluralism (Commission 1993). The April Hearing highlighted an acute intra-sectoral conflict and clarified how action, its timing or inaction could be biasing or damaging to particular interests. Economically, concentration of ownership of this industry entailed fewer and worse jobs for media professionals, through redundancies and labour casualisation. From the perspective of political communication, it entailed less or no diversity of opinion and the risk of increasing agenda-setting manipulations.

There is a vital link between the fight for pluralism in the EC and the battle against the GATT/GATS liberalisation of the audiovisual sector at a global level. This link explains why professionals, appealing for urgent action, opposed both media concentration and multilateral liberalisation. The exact obverse applied for operators. The objectives pursued in these distinct policy efforts were complementary. The groups that fought for the audiovisual exemptions from the multilateral liberalisation agreement also fought for pluralism in the media. Conversely, the ACT owners, who opposed restrictions on ownership, favoured multilateral liberalisations and sided up with the 'external enemy', in that case the MPEAA and the USDT in this tug of war. Simply, diversely-sourced programming costs considerably more than competitively-priced (and dumped) US imports. The connection of interests between the ACT and the MPEAA is then strong as these interests are mutually reinforcing. This leaves the general European interest and the EAS totally exposed.[96]

This is the point where European media policy collapsed, degenerating into a club-interest, industrial-policy issue. The oscillations of EC media-policy are shown up whether we look synchronically at what different DGs promoted or at what the Commission has proposed diachronically over the decades. Restructuring in the audiovisual market occurred to the detriment of all and to the benefit of the select few.

The Commission stressed that pluralism was only a *potential problem*, as no cases of its violation had thus far been reported. So, 'technically', BSkyB, was not a European-scale or a concentration-of-control problem (Commission 1992b: 35). Evidence suggested the contrary. News International controlled five national newspapers reaching 35% of the readers, when its owner and controlling shareholder of BSkyB started transmitting five channels from the Astra satellite outside the UK. Interestingly enough, the 1990 British Broadcasting Act created a loophole to suit Rupert Murdoch by excluding channels using foreign satellites (Barnett 1993: 115-117) which is considered a UK, legal anomaly (Garnham & Porter 1994, Tongue 1994). Thus a haven created by the UK, deploying privileged pan-European activities, was tolerated due to a lack of EC-wide regulation. Other cases referred to the circumvention of Swedish, pluralism legislation by transmitting from UK territory and to cases of licensing 'wars' between German Länder with differing licensing criteria. Several comments focused on timing issues, some fearing precipitate and others delayed moves. Numerous participants suggested that internal pluralism be appreciated and made to apply (Commission 1993). It is noteworthy that internal pluralism is a function of 'must carry rules'.

Despite a clear 'mandate' from the consultation procedure, a further consultation was called for, so a second, complementary, questionnaire

---

[96] This pattern of relationships is observed again in the relationship between the ACT and European hardware producers as evidenced in the EC HDTV fiasco. See Kaitatzi-Whitlock 1994a and 1998.

was delivered. This focused on the interplay between new technology and media concentration, on the end of scarcity, and on market segmentalisation due to digital compression. It also launched the concept of 'real audience' as a control criterion.

The Response of the European Parliament

In its response to the Green Paper, the EP Resolution of 20.01.1994 called on the Community to accede to the ECHR and, thereby, undertake political obligations to protect freedom of expression and diversity of opinion.[97] The EP, thus, advocated the EC-wide institution of positive freedoms (EP 1994a, §1). This highlights the absence of an EC, constitutional obligation to guarantee fundamental individual and collective rights of its citizens. This lack entailed that from a strictly legal standpoint, through interpreting available provisions such as Article 151 of the TEC (culture/audiovisual) restrictively, and given political discord (veto), pluralism could easily be 'organised out' of EC objectives and decision-making indefinitely.

The EP resolution called on the Commission to propose a Directive regulating both the ownership structure and the content of this cultural industry at a pan-European level. It is the thesis of this book that this is the only path to incorporate the two levels (national and supra-national) and the two natures (political/cultural and economic) of communication. The EP considered media pluralism as "an essential element in the construction of the European Union in accordance with the requirements of democracy" (EP 1994a, §N).

Very aptly, the EP held that legislation on media concentration "must take into account not only the economic but to an equal degree the cultural dimension..." (ibid, §L). It also asked that a separate Directive on the impact of multimedia development on pluralism be launched.

---

[97] According to Vincent Porter, it is the UK and Denmark that oppose the EU becoming a signatory to the ECHR (interview with the author 26.06.1996).

Stressing the employment potential of a sound media policy, the EP called for a framework Directive and option IIIc. It stipulated detailed criteria for the entire media sector: (a) that not only ownership, but also programme supply sources, be vetted against diversity criteria, (b) that the criteria of disqualified groups/persons as owners of media corporations apply, (c) that the editorial autonomy from advertising, purchasing practices be considered, (d) that strict competition rules apply to links between programme suppliers, producers and broadcasters, and (e) that the criteria of 'controlling owner' and 'audience share' attracted by a single channel apply and additionally, that absolute transparency of ownership and transactions apply, opposing any rules of confidentiality for commercial reasons.

In the EP's view, non-profit making, media organisations that can prove that they are operated independently from government control and are safeguarding internal pluralism should be exempted from such regulation. This view was fully shared also by the ECOSOC. The EP's approach to subsidiarity considered the rights of local communities to cultural self-determination and allows for positive national measures. Moreover, consistent with its pan-European approach, the EP advocated the creation of a European Media Council (EMC) to observe developments and ensure transparency and implementation and to propose divestitures of over-concentrated, market segments. It called for a Directive proposal incorporating its 1992 resolution and proposed an action programme to promote pluralism and diversity of opinion. Despite internal divergences of opinion, the EP, as the public interest representative *par excellence,* has demonstrated a long and determined commitment to this issue. In short, the EP provided he most coherent and the most complete proposal of a viable policy for political communication of a democratic polity. But the EC denied it.

The ECOSOC in Concert with the EP

The ECOSOC came out strongly in favour of pluralism, considering that it should receive more attention than the competition issue. It endorsed the EP's central points of the September 1992 Resolution, such as its concern at the increasing concentration in advertising and its corrosive impact on programming and on competition. It advocated for the European, media charter for non-profit making channels and the Media Code on professional ethics and editorial independence. It urged for complete transparency on ownership, financial transactions, local and worldwide holdings and concealed, third-party holdings in media of any range (ibid). It endorsed Option IIIc (ESC 1993: 1-8).

The ECOSOC asserted that a media policy which "entails the creation of opinion-forming cartels" threatened European development and advocated the safeguarding of fundamental rights by obliging media entities to "respect the principle of free expression of opinion for all social groups". With hindsight, after the rebuffing developments of 1994/1995, the ECOSOC could not have proven more right. It emphasised the 'need for securing pluralism inside publishing houses and broadcasting stations [and]... to secure editorial independence'. The ECOSOC reproached the Commission for reneging on its earlier warnings and argued that ownership restrictions were not incompatible with Community. Directives cannot just liberalise, it said, characterising the GP's approach as an *oversimplification*. Finally, it clearly showed why national measures were inadequate *per se*, so the ECOSOC was also vindicated on this point. It was evident that the basic *policy framework* in fact favoured the expansion of "international, media corporations whose interests and programme policies are not guided by pluralist ideals". In short, the ECOSOC expounded and argued most convincingly that 'there is now sufficient evidence to show that far from increasing pluralism, commercially-oriented, broadcasting policy simply leads to more of the same, i.e. merely the plural rather than pluralism' (ibid).

Stakeholders' and Interest Groups' Responses

Private and commercial media proprietors were among the most well-represented in the consultation process. Broadly speaking, media proprietors' federations, newspapers (ENPA-CAEJ),[98] periodicals (FAEP), the European Publishers Council (EPC) and the Association of Commercial Television (ACT) constitute the single most important force which obstinately opposed any EC action. The 'no action' lobby basically consisted of the 'club' of big proprietors. However, it was made to appear bigger than its actual size. Most proprietors made use of both their individual and multiple, collective rights to submit opinions. Fininvest, for example, consulted three times, once individually, once through the Federazione Radio Televisioni (FRT) and once through the ACT. Bigger players participated through still more outlets. Murdoch's views were launched through News International plc, through BSkyB, through ACT and through ENPA-CAEJ contributions. As was succinctly put by Lhoest, "simply whoever has the most media space will undoubtedly be the most persuasive in this debate" (1983: 11). Not surprisingly, most proprietors agreed with the GP's narrowly economistic scope. In addition, contrary to relevant calls by the EP, the ACT insisted that any potential harmonisation should also cover the psb channels.

Yet, interestingly, not all proprietors were happy with the *status quo*. Quite a few felt threatened and pleaded for a level playing-field: for anti-trust, and transparency measures. Pearson plc, a holding company of BSkyB and the publisher of the Financial Times, for example, called for an EC *action "now"*(my emphasis), "As the pace of change quickens the regulatory environment... is characterised by increasing uncertainty and inconsistency" it argued (Commission 1993g, *Commentaires* Vol. II, item 8:

---

[98] It is noteworthy that ENPA/CAEJ, started to invoke media pluralism vigorously a year later. This came in its consultation regarding the revision of the TWF Directive. Namely, the proposed increases for television advertising in the revised Directive threatened even further the survival of the daily press. Pluralism issues clearly arise whenever the press is not sourced and owned or cross-owned by the same groups (See also infra 179).

3). On its part ITV also attacked BSkyB, which circumvented British law by registering as a non-domestic broadcaster, but holding UK programming rights. Favouritism towards BSkyB and abuse of competition at the EC level was also denounced by the British TV operator Channel Four, EGF and the International Federation of Journalists (IFJ). ITV argued that there was justification for a "legislative intervention *as soon as possible,* in order to eliminate existing anomalies and prevent any future ones from arising" (ibid, item 5, emphasis added). Editoriale L'Espresso, a multimedia company of Milan, concurred "Il devient clair que cette action (communautaire) doit être commencée le plus tôt possible" (ibid, item 1: 11), because disparities between national laws "pénalisent les pays dans lesquelles les régimes juridiques concernant la propriété des medias sont plus rigides" (ibid: 4).

The confrontation between proprietors is extremely interesting. It showed that the EC communications policy served the interests of a select club of operators, in general setting ordinary people against proprietors and the big barons against the small proprietors. Secondly, the fear of extinction (via mergers or acquisitions) by these smaller media firms showed the risk of concurrently eliminating even the quantitative type of pluralism.

Two more fears were revealed. Firstly, that legal inconsistencies would cripple robust, medium-sized companies, because of the privileges that the select 'media barons' got from these anomalies, and that the promotion of an industrial policy of 'selecting winners' and 'Euro-champions' would threaten their very existence. Secondly, that entire national media sectors and their associated political-communication environments would be incapacitated, since Euro-champions could hardly evolve from all fifteen member states!

The European Broadcasting Union and Independent Producers

Largely concurring with the EP and the ECOSOC, the European Broadcasting Union (EBU) pointed out that national measures were inadequate, since a small number of media groups had quickly acquired strong positions. It favoured transparency, but questioned the 'real audience' criterion for control (Commission 1993g *Commentaires*, Vol I, item 12). The EBU argued for safeguarding the freedom of imparting information, and the democratic process of opinion forming (ibid: 6). In contrast to calls by the ACT, the EBU demanded that psbs not be subject to harmonisation measures, because its members practice internal pluralism. The need to distinguish between and adopt both internal and external pluralism was advocated also by journalists and independent radio representatives.

The Comité des Industries Cinématographiques et Audiovisuelles des Communautés Europeénnes et de l'Europe Extracommunautaire (CICCE) is in a way the counterpart of the omnipotent Motion Picture Association of America (MPAA). Its lobbying power, however, is not nearly as strong, as the CICCE represents a fragmented collective of hundreds of creative artists. There is then an important comparative difference between the CICCE and their American counterpart the MPEAA, which got all the requisite diplomatic leverage and attention that it needed.[99] It argued that the GP failed to address the relationship between producers and broadcasters (Commission 1993g, *Commentaires*, Vol I, item 12) and warned that financial control by broadcasters would ultimately be translated into control and rationalisation of creative production, which *per se* was incompatible with pluralism. This point well illustrates the relationship between structural constraints and agency subordination (Murdock 1982). '*(L]a coexistance de "portes francs" et des pays à "hautes normes" comporte le risque de "dumping culturel"*' (ibid: 2). The CICCE

---

[99] As discussed in chapter 7, both the State Department and the US Department of Trade provided dynamic and sustained support and leverage to MPEAA in diplomacy and in international trade battles.

lamented the extremely limiting approach of the GP framework and demanded (a) an integral definition, (b) urgent action and (c) a code of behaviour for producers and broadcasters safeguarding their independence.

Artists, Media Professionals and Employees

Media professionals' organisations notably the European section of the IFJ, the European Committee of Trade Unions in Arts, Mass Media and Entertainment (EGAKU) and the European Graphists Federation (EGF) called for urgent EC action. EGF identified "an urgent need for political action at Community level, to safeguard pluralism, information, and cultural identity in the long term, as bases of democracy" (Commission 1993g, *Commentaires*, Vol III, item 1, 1993: 5). The EGF in fact postulated that the dangers to pluralism originated precisely from the very site assigned to confront the problem, that is, the Internal Market (ibid: 8). This was an upfront accusation against the Commission. It advised the Commission to find a 'suitable political and legal means', suggesting then applying Article F, §2 of the TEU. It favoured option IIIc suggesting EU-wide restrictions on shareholdings. The CICCE submitted a long list of media concentrations with a Community dimension, including the axis of the Leo Kirch Group, Berlusconi and Spanish TV interests (ibid: 30-43).

The IFJ proposed an alternative definition of pluralism (proposed by W. Hoffmann-Riem, and supported by, among others, MEP Kurt Malangre), the freedom of citizens to information rather than the unlimited freedom of communicators. It argued that the crucial thing was who controls channels and for what purpose, and what the information source and content structure is. It, too, disputed the view that the Commission lacked the legal instruments to intervene. The GP framework seems to disorient the issue from the actual problems facing the EC, suggested IFJ, which also provided that "there is virtually no large media company in Europe which does not own shares and whose shares are not owned by another media company" (ibid: 9) thus corroding diversity of opinion. The IFJ called for urgent action and option IIIc.

Advertisers and Consumers

The European Association of Advertising Agencies (EAAA) claimed that market access and media availability are "twin requirements for the proper functioning of the Single Market" (Commission 1993g *Commentaires*, Vol I, item 2). Surprisingly perhaps, the EAAA concurred with the majority group on the imperative dual necessity to regulate both structure and agency factors. Thus the EAAA comments stressed particularly that, even when ownership is not concentrated, the selling arrangements are often concentrated through sales agents or "regies" who can abuse their selling power" (ibid). As a consequence of this practice, competition prerequisites were needed. These required: "transparency, ownership and selling regulation such as the banning of the practice of conditional selling" (ibid). The European Advertising Tripartite (EAT) did not forward positions on media ownership. Nonetheless, it commented that "the advertising industry needs a truly diversified media to convey its message to a variety of consumers in a variety of environments" (ibid, item 4).

Viewers' organisations were absent from the consultation (Commission 1994d: 45-46). The Bureau Européen des Unions des Consommateurs (BEUC), a generic consumers' federation, though invited, was unable to formulate an opinion. (BEUC, interview with the author, 02-12-94) Citizens, who, as audience, are finally the most interested parties were thus effectively absent from the consultation process. Thus, their real or potential interests, not even articulated, can be easily ignored in decision-making. Of 70 organisations consulted more than two thirds answered positively on the need for EC action specifying the most suitable instrument and content. At least half of them qualified the need for action as 'urgent' (Commission 1993g *Commentaires*, Vols I, II & III). But instead of a policy proposal DG XV submitted an Interim Report Communication.

Endless and Flagrant Contradictions: The Interim Report

The Commission will shortly "take a position on the different options regarding the need and the appropriate level of intervention... in particular to avoid the risk of further fragmentation of the Internal Market with the emergence of national regulations" announced the *Action Plan on Europe's Way to Information Society* in July 1994 (APEWIS: 7). Nevertheless, the DG XV, in its subsequent Interim Report, proposed the launching of yet another round of consultations, which "should be useful to confirm or reject the need for a Community initiative" in view of the new technologies (ibid: 40). Since the first and second consultations had had the same objectives, it seemed likely that re-launching consultations would end up in another mere ritual.

Yet, the Interim Report drafters of the DG XV identified a definite need for Community action but in a totally opposite direction. Considering the objectives of the Internal Market, 'Urgently' needed direct investments were "discouraged because of legal uncertainty and lack of harmonisation of ownership rules", while certain undercapitalised, media enterprises did not attract investments. Meanwhile "European operators invested in non-European markets" (ibid: 17).[100] Thus, the reported cause of operators opting for extra-European, strategic alliances was the absence of a genuine Internal Market for media. Logically then in order to prevent the strengthening of this trend, the Commission ought to propose a due policy.

Moreover, while big players worked against regulation, the DG XV blamed the absence of regulation for their investing outside Europe, which amounts to a paradox. Concurrently, the Commission did not propose any corrective regulation, which amounts to a double paradox.

---

[100] For a list of European media investors abroad see Chapter 5 and TTR 1984: 17.

The logic of the market dictates that certain undercapitalised, media sectors will never attract entrepreneurial investments, and this creates a gap in pluralism. However, the EC wanted to ignore this failure. All but a very small section of the media owners agreed that existing regulation is inadequate to ensure pluralism. But the Community had decided to remain loyal to those select and powerful few.

The Interim Report, moreover, neglected concerns about the timing of the policy. This was a flagrant omission, since first, the Green Paper had included this aspect in its questionnaire, secondly, a majority of the interlocutors qualified their appreciation of the need for action as 'urgent' or 'immediate', or as 'act now', and thirdly, the timing issue was disputed in the 1993 hearing. In the interim Report, those against regulation were incorrectly reported as supporting transparency measures, those favouring action as opposing transparency. The empirical data suggest the opposite. Big proprietary, corporate interests opposed both anti-concentration *and* transparency measures, while pro-action groups thought transparency measures in themselves inadequate but indispensable for the operation of the proposed option IIIc. (Commission 1993g *Commentaires*, Vols. I, II & III).

The EP Plenary Session Debate of October 1994

In October 1994 the EP categorically condemned the Commission's inertia as *contemptuous* towards itself and called for urgent action once again (EP 1994c). Commissioner Vanni d'Archirafi received questions from an outraged EP plenary, but answered incoherently: an initiative "might" prove necessary, he said. Contradicting himself, he continued: "taking no action" had been rejected.[101] Put in affirmative terms, action was endorsed by the great majority. This then made redundant any launching of new consultation rounds. The plain, logical issue that arose for Mr D'Archirafi

---

[101] *"L'azione 1 prevista nel libro verde, che consisteva nel non prendere alcuna iniziativa, e ormai chiaramente scartata"* (ibid: 102-103).

was that a Community initiative 'might' not 'prove necessary', because it had already done so in the previous consultation round. The ostensible aim of the new consultation round was the content of the 'action' as the Commission did not dispose of enough data thereof; while the majority of the contributors were blamed for this (ibid: 102-103). But the only contributors who ignored question four (on the content of a possible instrument) were really those opposing action. This negation showed contempt for the European, political forces and citizens. Launching the new consultation round meant 'playing' with time. Gaining time through deferring decision-making is a classical ploy for procrastinating policy demands. This of course made crucial business sense for players of global calibre, whose concentrated ownership power was both indisputable and growing rapidly.

Unending Consultations

In the beginning of 1995, the DG XV's new Commissioner, Mario Monti, launched a third questionnaire for yet another consultation process. Although the "no action" option had clearly and admittedly been rejected, this questionnaire also referred obstinately to a "possible" instrument. But to make the contempt against the participants in the consultation process quite explicit the Commission stated: "the fact of answering questions concerning the content of a possible initiative does not imply acceptance of the need for action (sic)" (Commission 1995 – *Questionnaire* No. III). This revealed a clear confusion and definite insecurity on the part of the Commission. The questionnaire stressed 'real audience' and 'channel control' as criteria for pluralism, as the completion of the internal market was the chosen, justifying framework.

In September 1995, Commissioner Monti, speaking before the EP, in the presence of Marcelino Oreja and Karel Van Miert, Commissioners of culture and competition respectively, recognised on the part of the Commission the importance of pluralism in the media, thus re-launching the debate: "When the disparity between national regulations is harmful to the single nature of the market and to freedoms within the border-free area, then, there is a Community problem which must be addressed by Community jurisdiction" (*Agence Europe*, 28.09.95). Meanwhile valuable time granted was impacting favourably on the side of concentrating moguls. After several years of EP and Commission policy elaborations, the objective of safeguarding pluralism was fully frustrated. The reason commonly accepted by most interviewees "for the non-policy on media concentration and pluralism, was the enormous pressure from private interests that were against any policy..." (Sarikakis 2004: 154-155). Thus, by shifting the terms of the policy, the Commission buried the politically crucial problem of lacking pluralism.[102]

Persistent Incongruities between Policy Preferences and Outcomes

Although the consultation process favoured an integral definition of pluralism and established the need for urgent action against media concentration to prevent monopoly control on opinion forming and market domination, an EC-wide structural and agency regulation was frustrated. The Community did not act positively despite long-standing and multiple calls by the single elected 'supra-national' institution of the Community, the EP. An approach fraught with inconsistencies featuring an endless stop-go-stop *modus operandi* was displayed by the Commission; the other 'supra-national' Community institution. These facts which exposed such a deeply problematic 'supra-nationalism' reinforced the view of the Community as an intergovernmental but democratically contestable hybrid regime. Moreover, this provided a regime determined obstinately

---

[102] The fact that the Commission went on to elaborate on the concepts of 'real audience' and of 'channel control' is an indication of this. Unless these 'new' criteria would be adopted as supplementary to content pluralism and ownership restrictions, further media deregulation was only a matter of time. Meanwhile the notorious non-decision-making practice resulted in further disintegration and further concentration as is concurred by the latest EP Weber Report (EP 2005).

to solidify and further build up its democratic deficit rather than the contrary.

Possibilities for using different, more holistic, legal bases in confronting pluralism issues do exist and have been suggested. Yet the Commission opted to ignore such legal bases.[103] The linking of pluralism and media concentration with the Internal Market restricted the scope of regulation and constitutes a regressive development, heralding not only the neutralisation of 'pluralism' but also the further deferral of a common, anti-trust legislation in the media, since governments will not easily agree to abandon pluralism altogether.

Schematically put: the EP put policy A on the agenda. The Commission responded by (1) defining this policy as being largely beyond its competence, (2) launching a consultation ritual and (3) promoting policy B which was, in effect, the opposite of policy A. So the Commission first rejected the issue, secondly redefined it to suit the Internal Market, and thirdly, procrastinated through repetitive, ritual consultations. So far the Commission has: (a) caused a deterioration of pluralism as defined by public interest representatives, (b) disadvantaged small- and medium-sized enterprises, and cultural/linguistic areas, (c) actively favoured concentration and anti-competitive trends by granting strategically precious time to already dominant players, resulting in irreversible market distortions, (d) refocused the debate in the direction of deregulation and further loss of regional control by foregrounding Internal Market objectives and emphasising market access in fields of local discretion and cultural specificity, and (e) pitted Community institutions against each other. The DG XV course of action, moreover, ignored other concurrent EC media policies, thereby augmenting confusion, as well as compartmentalised and mutually exclusive approaches. The overall

---

[103] Ben Fayot, MEP and rapporteur for the pluralism issue at the EP, concured with this appreciation. Moreover, he stated that the Commission had committed itself politically for tabling a worthwhile, pluralism-regulation proposal in 1992 (interview with the author, 28.8.1994). The implication was that this was reneged on later on in 1994. This must be also connected with the fact that, in the autumn of 1994, the then Commission was on its way out and was therefore not in a strong position.

outcome was to favour a 'European breed' of fragmented liberalisation that discriminates against the strictly–regulated, national, media markets and the general interest.

Media pluralism and freedom of information are endangered on the economic, the cultural/political and the national levels. When a small member state loses a plural, media-ownership structure, sacrificed in the name of creating 'Euro-champions for global games', there is no scope for the exercise of national, pluralistic measures, since the plural, locally-owned media-structure will have been destroyed. The invocation of a lack in EC competence, despite Article 151 of the TEC and the fact that the EC had been dealing extensively with audiovisual policies for over ten years by then, revealed lack of common political will for a political unification and a space for political communication. In fact, political will appeared and disappeared interchangeably, depending on whether the issue was for or against regulation or for or against the private interests of the 'select barons'. This chameleonic stance in fact reveals the lack of statesmanship at the 'supra-national' level. Indeed, their inability for forging any proactive policies in the public interest proved their veritable, political impotence.

Thus, there were two interlinked reasons for this non-decision-making. Firstly, the EC continued to maintain a weak, intergovernmental, decision-making structure. This was set against the overwhelming power of market interests on the one hand and hegemonic, national governments with discriminatory transcontinental goals and alliances on the other. These forces relentlessly located demands for deregulation, exemptions of global concentrations and mergers, and even the de-linking of the EC from such central functions as the control of competition (*To Vima*, 2.6.1996).[104] Secondly, the pressure for operations beyond the European boundaries

---

[104] In the spring of 1996, the later disgraced German Chancellor Helmut Kohl called even for the 'privatization' of Commission DG IV functions, that is, the functions of overseeing EC competition (ibid). This was related to disagreeable stoppages of mergers by Commissioner Karel van Miert, such as that between Kirch, Bertelsmann and Deutsche Telekom.

required the commercialisation of the entire cultural sector, which would undermine locally relevant and pluralistic freedom of information.

The power-game was threefold: (1) for political control versus unilateral, economic control in policy-making; (2) for the political role and control of the media and for the attribution of a common space for political communication of a pan-European dimension; and (3) institutional, between the elected and non-elected power centres in the EC. Structural, policy-structure and policy failures account for this state of affairs. Developments so far vindicate Keohane and Hoffmann's assessment that certain "governments sought to use Europe to promote deregulation" (1991: 21). The inability to legislate is attributed to the EC's weak institutional framework, to the divergent goals of the European economies, as seen within the context of the *global political economy*, and the constraints that the latter places on the process of regional integration. Hence, the EC not only presents the famous, democratic-accountability deficit but suffers from a problem of 'non-government', eventually afflicting both the national and the supra-national levels. Evidently, the control of broadcasting and the regulation of the system as a whole was impossible, "when operating against the economic and journalistic interests of the broadcasters" (Hoffmann-Riem 1992: 163).

Ten years after the bitter conclusion of this non-policy case, it is perhaps useful to end this study on the political economy of EU, communications media with a fresh EP note. It is not astonishing to observe that even in its current (2005) discourse, the EP returns to these same, flagrant aberrations. In its response to the communication by the Commission in regard of the ongoing revision of the TWF Directive, the EP, in its habitual style, generated fresh calls and worries over these politically-insoluble problems.

Notably, in paragraph 42 of the Weber Report, the EP admits that it is "alarmed at the tendency towards (vertical and horizontal) concentration of the media in Europe, which poses a *threat to democracy*" (EP 2005: §42 emphasis added). But what is democracy? How many decades can it keep being threatened and yet survive? The EP is also alarmed at the risk of such concentration to "cultural diversity" and that it "could accentuate tendencies towards the extreme commercialisation of the audiovisual sector and the *hegemony* (sic) of certain national products over those with narrower linguistic areas and smaller production;" (ibid, emphasis added). On these grounds, the EP "invites the Commission to take into account previously existing studies on media concentration and media ownership, particularly in view of the recent enlargement" (ibid).

The EP, moreover, stresses that "particular care should be paid, in the interest of guaranteeing pluralism of opinion and variety of broadcasting services, to ensuring, when drafting rules on the switch to digital mode at Community or national level" (ibid: §43). Then it exhorts again, in its habitual hortatory yet ineffective style, that the majority of newly-opened–up, digital, broadcasting services "do not come into the possession or under the determining influence of large, capital-rich, multinational media groups – particularly those with interests outside the EU" (EP 2005 – Weber Report: §43). So the EU 'policy ritual' goes on: on the one hand the EP keeps calling for radical action, and on the other hand the Commission and the Council feign deafness and impotence.

Thus, as in 1985 the EP, guardian of the democratic values and the symbolic political pillars of the EU, in 2005 again declared its dismay at both the prevailing media hegemony and the emerging hegemony of digital communication space again and again. It appears as unable to take a different course of action today, just as also in 1995 it failed to have the policy on pluralism and media concentration adopted.

Chapter 6

THE PRIVATIZATION OF CONDITIONAL ACCESS IN THE EU

This chapter looks at the EU policy which led to the allocation of control of Conditional Access (CA) services,[105] to the SimulCrypt System. The SimulCrypt CA system is a proprietary system owned by a global media conglomerate. Hence, this policy touches on a nexus of key issues. It concerns the reallocation of significant power in directly economic terms, but also, and most importantly, the usurping of considerable strategic power in social, political and institutional terms. Both intergovernmental, public-policy institutions at the supra-national level and market forces were implicated and mobilised in this process. I shall, therefore, look into the inputs and the efforts of both of these policy actors. I shall investigate how market forces dealt with this issue internally, first without the interference of public policy-makers, after being given the explicit mandate by the EU Council to self-regulate. I shall then examine the corresponding public-policy intervention which was induced when 'self-regulation' was effectively frustrated. This is embodied in the preparation and the final adoption of the Directive of 1995 on the use of standards for the transmission of television signals (Council 1995) particularly Articles 3 and 4.

This Directive, which also repealed the previous 'interventionist' HD-MAC Directive, overturned overarching values and technology strategies

---

[105] CA services are privately purchasable audiovisual and data services in a variety of modes. Pay-per-view, video on demand (VOD) and subscription television are the most common forms on offer to interested consumers by broadcasters, television service providers and by telecommunications suppliers. Alternative terms used for CA services are encoded/decoded, scrambled and encrypted.

which had prevailed in EU policy-making in the 1980s (Kaitatzi-Whitlock 1998). The changed 'European' doctrinal co-ordinates which brought about this important reorientation towards so-called, 'globally coherent' EU policies risked leading to an irreversible 'feudalisation' and de-Europeanization of information and communication systems.

The Problem

The first and most crucial change that was brought about by the advent of the new media was the need for an economically vigorous viewing public, a public which would be able to pay in order to watch (Sabah 1985). Encryption systems rely on the ability to encode and decode information for the purpose of commercial exploitation. For the same purpose the control of information destination-flows, as well as other prerequisites, should obtain. Encryption systems establish artificial gateways for the access of information at two key points along the information supply chain. The first gateway is at the sender level and concerns immediate, information, service provision. I shall call this the 'upper gateway'. It permits information suppliers to encode and pass on their services down to the second passage and then to viewers. The second gateway, I shall call it the 'lower gateway', can only be accessed by the paying viewers, via an electronic, decoding device (set-top box) placed on the television receiver. The definition, which views the conditional access system as an "effective and secure subscriber authorisation mechanism so that only those viewers who have paid for a programme or service are able to receive it" (ITC 1995), is rather restrictive; because, starting from the lower gateway, it depicts one set of the involved relations only.

Pay services come into existence precisely by erecting an essential, social division between those who can afford it and those who cannot. It might seem at first glance that policies regarding pay services concern only the first social group, the paying group. This may be misleading. Such policies impact directly, both culturally and materially, also on those social groups who cannot afford, and will not demand, pay services. This is because a critical mass of audience is needed for the survival of conventional, universally-received services. Similarly, a critical mass of meaningful and diverse programming is indispensable. There is fierce competition to control these very resources. Viewing time and attention being very scarce resources, the fiercest competition occurs over them. The buying up of copyrights in bulk is quite prevalent in recent, market dealings, while subscriber viewers usually become a captive audience for the pay-TV system that happens to control a market.

If absolute freedom of information is to be aimed at, any conditional gateways either for the supply or the reception of information should be abolished. In this case of course we would not be talking about commodified information (a commercial good) but about information as a public and universal good. What arises from this as a challenge for policy-makers is to be able to strike a balance between the conflicts of interests at the interface between the value of diverse information and the economic viability of information-providing enterprises.

To exploit the commodity of information in an equitable and fair manner, unhindered access to the artificial upper gateway by any information supplier is indispensable. Thus, if access safeguards are restricted only at the receiver end, the lower gateway of the set top box, and even if these are in the form of open or additional interface decoders, this does not guarantee fair access to the supply of information through the upper gateway. Neither does it guarantee freedom of choice or *pluralistic information* effectively because the encoding gateway may be or become *de jure* or *de facto* open only to one supplier (monopolistic), or to a cartel or oligopoly of suppliers. At best, it provided an ostensible or a theoretical pluralism to viewers.

This commercial practicality demonstrates the inadequacy of theories of 'consumer sovereignty' that place all responsibility on the choices of the end-consumer and disregard the pre-selection phases that take place in the chain of production and distribution of information. A unique, open and a fairly and commonly–managed, CA system would safeguard the fair and equitable access to the upper gateway for audience shares by all interested, information suppliers.

A unique but proprietary CA system, by contrast, entails the operation of a single monopoly controller at the upper gateway. Fair and equitable access to this gateway may be affected or manipulated, for example in terms of 'preferred' genre or type of programming, peak-hour-service, priority supply and tariffing. The upper gateway owner thus acquires unwarranted and disproportionate controlling and censoring power over the supply of information which, although commodified, does not cease to be culturally and socio-politically significant. If, on top of everything else, the proprietary, upper gateway controller happens also to be a competing broadcaster and service supplier (and so we have vertical integration, as in this case) then one competitor is granted a 'feudal' type of privilege over the other market players. The structural framework of free and fair competition is thereby destroyed.[106]

This establishes relations of a new inequality and of dependence between competing service providers.[107] This undoubtedly works against the 'applicants' of transmission service and in favour of the controller of the upper gateway and service provider. The establishment of a proprietary and unique, CA system, as opposed to an open–interface, CA system, establishes relations of supplier and customer between formerly equal competitors for the same type of service. This is an intervention of a directly structural nature which counteracts fair and free competition. In effect we are witnessing the creation, through EC policy intervention or through non-policy-making, of vertical integration in this market.

Most crucially, since this gateway does not transport ordinary economic resources but it lets in and shuts out streams of information, knowledge or entertainment, it can concurrently discriminate against

---

[106] See also Styliadou (1997: 50) discussing, in principle, a similar situation of uncompetitive behaviour between vertically–integrated, market players being concurrently competitors in one product market and suppliers of service to that same market.

[107] This set-up in the ordinary types of industrial sectors evolved, traditionally, through the process of picking winners and of creating economic 'champions.'

certain news or views, while favouring others. As a consequence, the structural interventions which counteract fair and free competition are deeply worrying, because they are biasing and undemocratic. Such phenomena are even more worrisome if they are policy-induced. Since we are talking about a market of ideas in the communication and audiovisual fields, the significance of the upper gateway is indeed strategic. In such a market of ideas diversity and free circulation of ideas are a *sine qua non*. Diversity may be divided into diversity as access and diversity as supply: "Diversity as supply offers opportunities for more or less professional senders (producers, artists etc.) and receivers (reviewers etc.) to exercise their professional competence..." (Hilve et al. 1996: 4, after McQuail).

So 'Europe's way to the information society' has taken off by creating vertical integration and erecting inequality between the various categories of information suppliers and receivers in the knowledge economy. In a climate of competition for the control of viewers (the truly scarce resource), for hours per head, for paying viewers and for the limited, financial resources investable in the media sector, the general interest is under severe threat. Locally and nationally–relevant, public service and quality channels, diversity of access and supply are all in jeopardy. These dangers are far more acute in member states which have smaller audiovisual markets population-wise and worse still in those which are linguistically limited (Greece, Finland) as broadcasters have much less leeway to compete and to cross-subsidise their national services, quality programming.

Neutrality, Privatization and Global Coherence

The strategic frameworks of the EU, in broader economic terms but in the information and technology sectors in particular, explicitly intensified their shift towards deregulation, privatization and global competition in the early 1990s. This applied to all sectors of the economy (and society), even sectors where EU markets, by definition, cannot compete globally.

Such are the culturally and politically strategic sectors of communications and of the audiovisual in particular.

The specific strategy elaborations which made up the structural framework within which the CA policy was fostered included: first the *Action Plan on Europe's Way to an Information Society* (APEWIS), secondly, the twin Resolutions of 1993 and 1994 regarding the EU's revamped technology policy, and thirdly, the practical, market initiatives and developments, notably the rise of the ELG-DVB group of market players and the global dictates for EU policies such as those expressed at the G7 meeting of February 1995. The ensemble of these elements incarnated the 'global coherence' and the 'market-led' economic developments that are envisaged in the adapted, EC strategy documents of the 1990s. The implicit normative and imperative politico-economic and institutional choices which were evident in these three documents forged the transmutations which were needed for market globalisation.

The combination of all these elements suggests an explicit endorsement by the EC of the American, market-led approach. The decision, however, to grant prerogatives selectively to the DVB unjustifiably privileged this group over other incumbent (or even potential) participants with legitimate economic and civil rights at stake. The EC vested the DVB group with disproportionate prerogatives on issues directly linked with the public interest, thereby subjecting constitutional and media policy to industrial policy and to the commodification and commercialisation of the media sector. Nevertheless, the ideology of the technological determinism which prevailed was congruent with the EC brand of economism. This economism, however, as yet obstinately refuses to 'spill over' into political and social integration, and instead lends itself to uncontrolled global capital integration.

The Action Plan on Europe's Way to an Information Society

APEWIS was adopted concurrently with the Framework Resolution, and fully echoes its global-market orientation and technological determinism[108]: "A digital revolution is triggering structural changes comparable to last century's industrial revolution with the corresponding high economic stakes. This process cannot be stopped and will lead eventually to a knowledge-based economy" (APEWIS: 1b).

Apart from legitimising the 'omnipotent logic' of this technological determinism, APEWIS went further. It provided that "Public authorities will have to set new 'rules of the game'" and that "the deployment and financing of an information infrastructure will be the primarily responsibility of the private sector" (ibid). The acceleration of the liberalisation process loomed large in APEWIS, and so did the role of the DVB group, particularly with regard to standardisations. The spirit of 'global coherence' and co-operation with global partners, such as the United States and Japan, which was reflected in the two technology policy resolutions, were also salient in APEWIS. In short APEWIS delineated responsibilities and competencies on two crucial axes: the public policy versus private policy axis and the national versus the EC/global axis. This amounts to a virtual *neo-liberal manifesto*, albeit 'hidden' in an information–technology, policy framework which essentially aimed at curtailing political control in policy-making in favour of market control, and thereby debilitating politics itself.

The Information Technology Policy Resolutions

The community's new, strategic and policy-structural co-ordinates were set out in the Council Resolution on technology policy (Council 1993).

---

[108] The European Council unanimously adopted the recommendations of the "Bangemann high level Group" on 25.06.94. Bangemann was Commissioner of DGXIII for telecommunications and technology policy.

This aspired to establish 'timely mechanisms' and implementation measures for the new digital era and urged for a "flexible and workable regulatory framework" for the needs of the market in the light of current technological developments and market imperatives. Europe, it was stated, needed an approach of 'global coherence' to the development of technology and standards for new digital systems in order to 'bring it into line' with prevailing market and technological circumstances (ibid: 1-2). The same resolution urged that the Commission consider early agreement on forging common, digital–television, transmission standards and the "possible need" to "establish a European *non-proprietary encryption-conditional access system* serving a number of competing providers" (ibid, emphasis added).[109]

Indeed, following this decisive shift of perspective the Commission promptly submitted its draft Framework Resolution for a community Policy on Digital Video Broadcasting (Commission 1993i), eventually adopted in July 1994.[110] The Council concurrently forged a new 'flexibility', which overshadowed the emphasis that the Commission had previously put on the need for an 'orderly regime'. Thus, while the 1993 precursor resolution marked the shift of perspective and of emphasis towards neutrality and globalisation, the Framework Resolution entrenched the deregulatory flexibility dictated by dominant players among the speedily rising digital market forces.

The Framework Resolution invited DVB market forces to join in the processes of policy formulation and standardisation. It was thus argued that the preferred way to achieve the objective of harmonious market development "would be by means of a consensus process involving all relevant economic agents including broadcasting organisations." It was additionally stressed that the Council "looks forward, with great interest, to any voluntary agreements which may be made by such agents in this

---

[109] It is interesting to observe then that the adoption of an encryption system ranked high on the agenda in 1993-1994 and to compare it to a previously-frustrated attempt to impose the HD-MAC-attached EuropCrypt system (discussed below).

[110] See the 'Delors' White Paper, op. cit.

regard under the auspices of the European Digital Video Broadcasting Project" (Council 1994a: 4).

The Council, nevertheless, also stated that, if the DVB failed to self-regulate or if fair and open competition, consumer protection and the public interest required it, the Council would prompt to regulate this issue. This allegedly obliged it, in the absence of adequate consensus and should the necessity of guaranteeing fair and open competition require it, to take regulatory measures (Council 1994a: 3-4; LeClercq 1994: 4). This innovative practice brought in the idea of a *government on stand-by*. The attribution of this significant role to the DVB, by EC institutions, corresponds entirely with the autonomous assumption of such a politico-economic momentum, role and prerogatives by the DVB forces themselves.

The other transcendental 'nuance' of the Framework Resolution concerned the new 'global' strategy of co-operation and the deploying of a "dialogue with third parties including the United States of America and Japan" (Council 1994a: 4). The underlying rationale was that, since digital technology is a global phenomenon, a high compatibility between the world's regions was a desirable objective (ibid: 3). Thus, the idea was that European policy-makers should aim at reaching common, world-wide, TV standards and systems. In addition, this was the *commercially correct* policy to adopt as blessed by the heads of the G7: "The Presidency's conclusions at the G7 Conference on the Information Society... highlighted the need for a regulatory framework ensuring open access networks and respect for (sic) competition rules" (Council 1995, Directive preamble). What requires special attention, then, are the concurrent invocations of an 'orderly regime' and of 'competition rules'. This type of policy is most hazardous, since it can rhetorically claim to be managing this power resource while merely rhetorically invoking 'free competition'.

The Broad Consortium of Market Forces: the DVB Group

The emergence of the European Launching Group for Digital Video Broadcasting (ELG-DVB, or the DVB group) was sparked by the revolutionary invention of digital bandwidth compression. This heralded the end of scarcity and the qualitative enhancement of digital transmissions and thereby obliged European entrepreneurs to face the challenge of introducing an all-digital technology and of phasing out analogue systems. It thus fostered the DVB group of market forces.[111] As of 1991, information-service entrepreneurs joined forces. A rapid growth in membership resulted initially in the formal organisation of the original ELG initiative takers and subsequently the development by the DVB of unified all-digital, TV systems (DVB Sept. 1995).[112] The formation of this consortium was the incarnation of a "virtual convergence of interests in action" (Flynn 1993).[113] The DVB undertook the standardisation (negotiations and testing) of all major technologies used in digital transmission, notably the MPEG-2 system. Similarly, it orchestrated the necessary initiatives for ETSI[114] approval of the new standards and forwarded them to the EC Commission. This thrust in setting new standards and in launching new products and services characterised the determination of the DVB market forces to self- regulate.

---

[111] Influential in this was the 1994 Federal Communication Commission's call for an open bid for a digital, terrestrial TV system in the US *(Economist,* 29.5.93).

[112] Satellite operators and broadcasters anticipated standardisation of the channel coding and modulation technologies in the MPEG-2 standard. Thereby, they also anticipated gains in the cost and the availability of equipment (Healy 1993). MPEG-2 set the standard for the compression of digital signals, which was the most complicated and the most expensive component of any digital broadcasting system *(The Economist,* May 29, 1993: 74).

[113] They adopted a Memorandum of Understanding, which set out the rules of a collective action, thus entering into a new territory of market organisation which confirmed the necessity of commercial competitors to gauge common needs and advance common agendas (DVB, 1995: 4).

[114] European Telecommunications Standards Institute.

With the prospect of global competition for the aspirant Euro-champions, the *laissez-faire* approach that was promulgated actively forged private, multinational, mega-monopolies that were politically threatening. However, in a Union whose very existence is legitimised on the goal of balanced regional integration, the process of random and strictly economic globalisation and of an unaccounted for – for example, in the national parliaments – globalisation of its economic policy-making, betrayed a huge deficit of control by its political institutions. In fact, this was a clear case of *democratic deficit*. Contradictions and uncontrolled developments of this sort pointed to the fact that EU institutions could not face up to these external challenges in the way that unitary governments can. This led to questionable developments: the overriding of the national policies of member states and the one-sided consideration of the imperatives of industrial elites such as the Union Nationale des Industries de la Communauté Européenne (UNICE).

Quasi-public Policies

It is quite remarkable that the EC Commission had attempted to regulate the CA system also in the past (1990-1991), yet unsuccessfully. Significantly, that attempt was made in connection with the EC's intent strategy to control global, high–definition, television-transmission standards and associated markets through the HD-MAC project. At that time the proponents of the European HDTV project, notably Philips, Thomson and the DG XIII of the Commission, had endeavoured to establish a unique CA system, called EuroCrypt, incorporated in the HD-MAC Directive of 1991.

Thus, in the *dirigiste* days when the Community was still pursuing its grand HDTV strategy, Philips had been pressing for EuroCrypt to be made the sole, satellite-encryption standard. The then–commissioner Pandolfi had not mentioned this issue at the Luxembourg Council meeting and thus it had remained unclear whether it was going to be included in the Directive. That ambiguity prevailed, because "there [was] some doubt legally over whether it would be possible for the Commission to stipulate which encryption systems can be used" (*Cable & Satellite Europe*, July 1991: 16). Such cases of impromptu policies also demonstrate a trend towards unaccountability and depoliticization.

Having failed to incorporate *EuroCrypt* in the Directive of 1991, the same proponents attempted to include the EuroCrypt CA system in the proposed Memorandum of Understanding (MOU) that was to be signed by involved market and political forces following the adoption of the same HDTV Directive in May 1991. But even then this attempt was eventually frustrated. The MOU was never signed because business leaders, notably the ACT, either gave it up or fought directly against it (Kaitatzi-Whitlock 1996 & 1998). Apart from the hesitancy of the Commission regarding legal competence, what was invoked as a counter-argument against the potential introduction of EuroCrypt at that time was the heavy cost of a possible CA system to the receiver (*Cable & Satellite Europe*, August 1991: 42). In fact, the cost-efficiency and market-viability problem proves to be a valid point even in the 1995 policy and in subsequent, market applications. In the face of the 'risk' that a unique CA system be granted in connection with the MAC transmission system, which was promoted at the time, oppositional market forces took charge: "The matter has been taken seriously enough by BSkyB for it to put forward a proposal that a new interface connector be introduced which would facilitate *use of different decoders*" (*Cable & Satellite Europe*, July 1991: 16, emphasis added).

So, at that time BSkyB defended several, alternative, CA systems not only in order to secure its right to access encrypted markets, but also, strategically, in order to scupper the HD-MAC transmission system. Significantly, the dominant forces of the ACT (notably BSkyB) had managed at that time to exclude the Commission's option from the EC agenda (*Cable & Satellite Europe*, August 1991: 42). The wheel came full circle when the same market forces (the ACT) and indeed the same conglomerate (BSkyB), having won their victory over the MAC system, imposed also their own unique, and proprietary at that, CA system. Oddly enough, the cost argument at that time had worked in their favour and, indeed, in favour of establishing their monopoly control.

After the 1993 strategic and doctrinal shifts, the familiar type of EC ambiguity regarding legislative prerogatives, whenever a contested issue surfaced, was overcome, as if by magic, in the 1993-95 policies. This happened by first, bringing in the market forces in the decision-making of this affair and having them shape the *agenda* and endorse the developments; secondly, by emphatically stressing the voluntary nature of such an agreement within the DVB. This time round, and once *policy prerogatives* were *devolved* to market agents, there were no objections voiced as to the legality of such radical redistribution of public and national resources at the intergovernmental EC level. Nor did anyone bring up the concept of *subsidiarity* in order for national political forces to have a stronger say in this crucial issue of general interest.

The motives that made BSkyB oppose a unique CA system in 1990-91, but made it desire and energetically pursue its imposition in 1995, are quite transparent. The unique CA system of 1991 (attached to MAC) would have excluded or conflicted with the old PAL and SECAM technologies. And BSkyB was a PAL-affiliated enterprise. By contrast, the unique and proprietary CA system of 1995 (of BSkyB, Filmnet and Canal+) discriminated against all other market players apart from SimulCrypt owners, thereby welding the monocracy of these media entrepreneurs. The strategies and tactics of the SimulCrypt proprietors make perfect business sense. What was baffling was the behaviour of the 'European' public policy agency. This could only be explained by looking at the political economy of this sector, which was increasingly becoming more and more de-Europeanised.

'Self-Regulation'

Despite the fact that the DVB had already established itself as an essential technology policy-agent by 1993, in practice, even though fully endorsed by EC institutions, fair, transparent and effective self-regulation proved unobtainable by it. Antagonisms and conflicting market stakes led to *predatory practices* among DVB members and soon divided the newly-aligned market forces. DVB indecision was clearly manifested in respect of the thorny issue of a single CA system and concerned notably the DVB's inability to approve a single, commonly-accepted system of CA and of a code of conduct at the sender level (upper gateway). It appeared initially that the DVB could not deal promptly enough with this 'minimal and flexible' regulatory issue. After a year-long effort, the DVB Steering Committee eventually ran into a terminal deadlock over forging and endorsing a unique and commonly-accepted CA system.

The tug of war was about the encoding/decoding system of signal control at the sender level. On the one side, there were those in favour of the common interface which would enable any broadcaster to access that system on equal grounds. On the other side, stood Canal+ and BSkyB, which proposed their own proprietary SimulCrypt system based on a 'first (and strongest), come first served' principle for the possession of proprietary monopoly rights. More specifically, the SimulCrypt strategy relied on different, proprietary, CA systems for each zone, controlled by the major pay-TV providers (LeClercq & Flynn 1994).

In practice, the SimulCrypt system would allow its proprietors to be 1) monopoly owners, 2) sole controllers, and 3) sole, *de facto* regulators of market conditions, such as tariffing, programming structures and menus, promotional policies etc. Acceptance of such a strategy would mean the enshrining of outright, predatory strategies on the grounds of property rights and initial investment, in contravention of competition rules and free-market practice. This would entail a colossal concentration of power.

According to some analysts, the advantages in this CA system lay in that it would require "a single set-top box and a single smart card" and that the very "dominance of a single proprietary standard would simplify access to customers at the cost of substantial power ceded to SimulCrypt firms" (Collins & Murroni 1996: 39). By contrast, the same authors argued the MultiCrypt system would be more expensive while not promising a sure prospect of financial returns to its sponsors: "Who would spend the ECU 500 million required to commission MultiCrypt without being able to capture proprietary revenue from its deployment?" (ibid: 39-40). Indeed, this was part of the same rationale that the proponents of SimulCrypt themselves promoted in pursuing their EC- monopoly control of this market. Nevertheless, this very rationale was somewhat reluctantly at a later stage adopted by certain MEPs.

In order to pre-empt criticism, SimulCrypt proponents had expressed eagerness to "ensure equitable access" by proposing a "code of conduct" to rival pay-TV operators (LeClercq 1994: 4). However, the DVB Steering Committee later rejected the code of conduct put forward by SimulCrypt proponents for not being open on commercial issues (LeClercq & Flynn 1994: 7).

DVB opponents of a proprietary smart-card interface, notably the EBU (a member of the DVB Steering Board), made counter-proposals and fought politically for the establishment of the common and open CA interface system. The DVB Steering Committee failed, however, to decide in favour of one of the two competing systems. In the face of this impasse and the ongoing polarisation, in the meeting of May 1994, the DVB Steering Board approved both these antagonistic systems, that is, both MultiCrypt, offering an open interface for digital decoders, and SimulCrypt, the proprietary, smart-card interface of Canal+ and BSkyB. Thus, the eventual resolution of this deadlock was deferred to the subsequent Steering Board meeting of August 1994, but even then it was in vain. In view of the lacking consensus, the DVB had in the end to endorse both CA systems.

Problems within the DVB group were inevitable, as stakes and conflicts of interest were enormous. The methodology applied by SimulCrypt proponents (controlling the majority of the Steering Board) were criticised by market analysts and interested parties, as constituting a covert manoeuvre which relied on a questionnaire of disputable validity. It was held that respondents to this questionnaire, among the DVB members, *were duped* in order to elicit support for the SimulCrypt system as well as for the associated code of conduct that went with it. Thus, the early fears of certain DVB members that the sole motivation for Canal+'s membership in the DVB was to block agreements that threatened its pay-TV monopoly (Flynn 1993: 2) were amply vindicated.

Having failed to secure the open interface system within the forum of the "self-regulating market" forces, and in order to render the inclusion of the common interface in digital decoders mandatory in the Directive, SimulCrypt opponents fell back on public-policy agency, political means and lobbying. This was encouraged by statements by official bodies. The DTI[115] Council stressed, for example, that, if agreement on a voluntary basis, did not materialise, then the EC would take action (Council 1993). Competition Commissioner, Karel Van Miert stated:

> The Commission's aim is to keep the market open and to prevent the erection of barriers to new market entrants... to this end, suppliers of coding technologies and decoders must be prevented from using restrictive practices in order to restrain access to competing television systems. (Leclercq & Flynn 1994: 7)

MultiCrypt proponents anticipated confidently that while "the DVB's input to the Commission would be to back both MultiCrypt and SimulCrypt" as alternative systems, "MEPs and ministers would tend to back only the MultiCrypt proposal" (Leclercq & Flynn 1994: 7). Quite the contrary. These policy expectations were frustrated. Thus, official EC messages had confused MultiCrypt proponents and tricked them into believing in such a development and into nurturing a naive optimism about the prospects of MultiCrypt. Hopes based on such an industry analysis proved over-optimistic and, finally, unrealistic. Both the EP and

---

[115] Trade and Industry ministers' Council.

the Commission proposed neither the "dual system" nor the mandatory inclusion of the common interface, but indirectly approved the rival SimulCrypt system. At that stage, that was regarded as maximalist, notably on account of "technical absence of the common interface system".

Mismanagement of the regulation tasks that were undertaken by DVB and loss of policy-making time was now caused by the inability of market forces to efficiently, voluntarily and consensually reach an agreement. Thus, digital–TV, market forces failed to deliver their sought-after and promised "self-regulation". In view of the DVB deadlock, the Council urged the Commission and the member states to assume the resolution of this issue (Council 1994; *I&T Magazine,* Summer 1994: 4), thereby re-locating the agenda for conclusive decision-making on this issue to public, policy-making institutions.

EU 'Commitments' to the Public Interest

On the basis of extensive consultation with economic actors,[116] in November 1993 the Commission proposed its new draft Directive on the use of standards for transmission of TV signals (Commission 1993). This complied fully with the changed political and economic conditions in the European, television, technology-policy sphere. It incarnated the industry's imperative for a "minimum and flexible regulation", which aimed to clear "unnecessary restrictions" on operators and to avoid extra costs on consumption. As required by the resolution of 1993, it was allegedly geared also towards digital developments and challenges (ibid: 5). Issues surrounding the type and the nature of the conditional access system became immediately the most controversial of this policy.[117]

---

[116] A formal consultation with economic actors was held on 13th July 1993.

[117] These were tackled in Article 4 of the draft Directive, which gradually grew in size, commensurate to its importance, to become as big as all the other parts of the Directive combined.

Notwithstanding the call by the Council resolutions of 1993, which had originally set (the observable part of) this *agenda*, this first Commission draft entirely ignored, firstly, the requirement for a common and non-proprietary CA system[118], and secondly, the issue of access control at the encoding level (higher gateway).

This self-chosen "discretion" of the Commission may be explained (and justified) by the fact that the DVB group was mandated (by the Council) to resolve such a controversial issue by themselves. So a possible "determining" tackling of the CA issue by the Commission could have pre-empted DVB group decisions,[119] and could, therefore, be seen as unduly 'interventionist'. To be fair, the Council had only asked the Commission to consider "the *possible* need for a European non-proprietary encryption-conditional access system serving a number of competing providers in flexibly putative terms" (Council 1993: 1, emphasis added). Consequently, the Commission was facilitated by the Council in dismissing this consideration. The Commission, which should have been unprejudiced, in this case pre-empted the option for a non-proprietary system in its draft.[120]

Thus, a non-proprietary CA system was both put on the agenda by the Council and simultaneously excluded from it. This was realised by the Commission. In policy-making terms, this approach shows how concurrently–running, policy processes (which may, furthermore, be pursuing divergent or conflicting objectives) in different systems (market and public system) of policy production are impossible without one of the systems being trapped or subjugated to the other. The dual approach of

---

[118] The Commission's draft ignored even the fact that such a common interface of diverse encryption systems had gained broad support inside the DVB (Renaud, Nov. 1993, ATM 11).

[119] Having first mandated the DVB group to resolve this contentious issue internally, it would have appeared rather incongruent for the Commission to pre-empt or predetermine the kind and type of the CA system in the political policy-making process.

[120] The Commission invited the DVB group to develop an industry position on CA for digital TV systems particularly in connection with this Directive (See Schoof & Watson Brown 1995: 335).

parallel market and political efforts is confusing and opens up grey areas in the policy process and of course in the outcomes.

The Commission's by-passing of this consideration, which could and perhaps should have forestalled DVB indecision on the non-proprietary nature of the system, resulted eventually in the establishment of a proprietary CA system. This happened precisely by omitting to explicitly secure the possibility of a non-proprietary, conditional, encoding, access system in its draft Directive. So, this possibility was "organised out"[121] at a primary, policy-making level, and remained forever what it was at the outset of the policy: a rhetorical and putative option. The possibility of a proprietary CA system was, however, established at the primary, policy-making level. So, although the policy started out with reassuring references to a non-proprietary, CA system, it steadily veered towards a proprietary system. This permits one to surmise that the development of a proprietary system may have constituted part of a hidden agenda.

A rather usual policy pattern emerges here, in which Council decisions and common positions, precisely because ministers are politically accountable at the national level, tend to be democratically more open, more radical, and more carefully and diplomatically phrased. Then, when issues are taken care of at the subsequent Commission level, and since it is not a directly-accountable institution to any electorate, issues are trimmed and adjusted so as to accommodate industrial imperatives. The importance of the control of access was further reduced by limiting the handling of this key issue at the reception end of the chain.[122]

As discussed above, the DVB failed to deliver the voluntary agreement on the CA system issue despite a year-long attempt to do so. So, the new

---

[121] This suggests then the intentional production of a non-policy-making case. For a discussion of non-policy-making, non-decision-making theory and conceptualisations see Lukes 1974; Bachrach & Baratz 1962, 1963 and 1970; Kaitatzi-Whitlock 1996.

[122] "Any television set... shall be fitted with at least one standardised open interface socket permitting simple connection of additional decoders or peripherals," (Council 1995, Article 4: 52-53). Despite the operation of prior controlling knots in the chain this meant that the token of "control of access" was trickled down onto consumer-electronics manufacturers.

Council Resolution of 1994 urged for measures by EC institutions to resolve this impasse politically. Consequently, "further examination by member states and by the Commission is necessary to determine... additional measures required in order to achieve the [EC] objectives" (ibid, Council 1994a: 4).[123] A new regulatory input was then required by all pertinent EC institutions in order to settle this problem.[124]

Given the centrality of the conditional-access system, and given also the concurrent sensitivity of the EP to the pluralism and concentration-of-ownership issue, one would anticipate that the EP would clarify its position by taking an unequivocal decision on an issue of such structural importance to citizens and to the media order as a whole. The first EP opinion on the proposed Directive, however, which emerged on 19.04.1994, bypassed the essential question of the type and the nature of the contestable CA system. Oddly enough, it did not favour the establishment of the common, open, MultiCrypt system which would have guaranteed supply diversity and fair competition at the encoding level (upper gateway) (Article 3bis).

Thus, the EP appeared once again to have either misjudged the affair or to have shied away from the essential issue. So, despite the fears explicitly expressed by DVB proponents of MultiCrypt, in order to put

---

[123] This Council assessment was concurred with by Commissioner Martin Bangemann: "further progress was now required to achieve an overall consensus between the various members of the ELG-DVB" (Flynn 1993: 2).

[124] Although "the industry consultation process on conditional access under the auspices of the Digital Video Broadcasting Group has allowed progress to be made... it is not yet concluded" (Council 1994). Meanwhile, in view of the DVB's failure to provide an acceptable settlement to all market players, but also in view of the evidently hesitant, not to say restricting Commission draft, fears were voiced by threatened industry players that major, pay-TV operators could abuse their dominant positions, if a CA system were only optionally linked with receiver equipment, as was the case with the Commission's draft. It was argued that "Leaving the interface out could be a condition of purchase or subsidy which might not be covered by these licensing provisions" (LeClercq 1994: 4). Thus, it was suggested that so long as inclusion of a decoding interface remained optional, proprietary, CA-systems operators could make deals with TV-set manufacturers to include interfaces exclusively compatible with their system, (de facto standard setting). The same result could obtain via vertical integration between operator and manufacturer. This seemed all the more likely in the general climate of 'mergermania' of the period.

pressure on the EP to adopt a strong corrective, the EP hesitated and focused instead on the procedural issues and on imperative safeguards.

Consequently, at the first reading of the draft, the EP effectively missed the opportunity to make the non-proprietary system mandatory and thereby to structurally promote content diversity as supply and as access. This was surprising as the EP had persistently sought to secure diversity in its policy endeavour over the pluralism and concentration-of-ownership campaign.[125] This amounted to a veritable paradox. In perplexing contradiction to itself, then, the EP allowed the major, pay-TV players to continue with SimulCrypt, "unhindered by a threat that they could have competition from other operators addressing the same set top box population" (Renaud 1994: 4). By the same token, the segment of the viewers who would buy those set-top-boxes would be converted into a "captive commodity market" of the first investor in that technology.

Whatever the reasons, the EP thus fatalistically accepted the outcome of this uneven power game between the competing forces within the DVB. It provided that, when licensing manufacturers of CA systems, this ought to happen "on fair, reasonable and non-discriminatory terms"; that is, in such a way as not to inhibit the inclusion of either another conditional system or a common interface in the receiver, provided that relevant security conditions relating to the CA system are met (ibid, Article 3bis).[126]

Following the DVB's eventual failure to agree on a single voluntary system, the second EP reading of the draft proposal made further imperative amendments on the controversial issue of conditional access.

---

[125] For a specific discussion of this see Chapter 5.

[126] 'All consumer equipment... shall possess capability to allow descrambling of such signals', manufacturers should include conditional access systems "on fair, reasonable and non- discriminatory terms" (Commission 1994a). It is noteworthy that at the time of adoption of the EP amendments (19.04.1994) the internal DVB consultation was still in process and a final conclusive decision was still anticipated. Thus, as with the Commission, the EP, in making its amendments, carefully avoided interfering in DVB decision-making and restricted itself to enhancing the terms of competition at the receiver end (the lower gateway). One EP amendment stipulated for example that interfaces in TV-set equipment become mandatory.

These were made on June 13 1995 and partially addressed the problem of fair and free competition between broadcasters. Such amendments were taken with the support of the absolute majority of its members, as stipulated by Article 251 (on co-decision procedure) of the Treaty of the European Community, on the proposals of rapporteur G. Caudron. This indicated the emergence of a new convergence or at least a *modus vivendi* between the views of the Commission, the EP and the majority of the DVB partners. Thus, structurally, a new, private-monopoly system was established and fully enshrined by the EP, albeit along with imperative regulatory guarantees.

In summary, neither the EP nor the Commission were prepared to impose mandatory inclusion of a common interface in conditional access systems. Fear of opposing or challenging the wishes of dominant investors was reflected in their justification. The rationale given by MEPs for not counteracting the establishment of a proprietary, CA system consisted of three arguments: first, that the majority position of the DVB Board insisted on the voluntary nature of the introduction of the common interface; secondly, that the interests of the first investors, who wished investments in a base of digital decoders should be protected as considerable marketing efforts would be required to establish such a base of decoders; and thirdly, that, supposedly, the common-interface system was not yet technically available and could not, therefore, be included in the first generation of digital decoders (Eberle, 12.10.1995, interview with the author).[127] This should be seen in conjunction with the clear political/industrial urgency to introduce digital TV services and the hurry to market decoders without further delay.

DVB Steering Board, however, aiming to ensure the possibility for the alternative, open-access system, announced in March 1995 that the Common interface was in fact technically developed, but that it "should remain optional" (DVB 7.3.95: 1) in any case. This DVB statement

---

[127] The sources for these evaluations come from interviews with Dr. Jur. Michael Wagner, EBU legal advisor and Dr. Professor Carl-Eugen Eberle, ZDF – Legal and Public affairs. Interviews with the author conducted at Delphi, Greece, 12.10.95.

showed that the three arguments of the privatization rationale amounted really to one imperative: the will of the strongest market forces to secure their investments. It also vindicated those who doubted the seriousness of such arguments stating that "the *politicians were duped*" (Morgan 1995, emphasis added).

The DVB opposition failed to secure the mandatory inclusion of the MultiCrypt system either within the market forum or via the EC policy process. Both these systems (self-regulation and public policy regulation) failed to establish a satisfactory or an acceptable regime for the competing interests. The adoption of legal safeguards was the only success of MultiCrypt proponents; these were indeed stronger than the self-commitments that were offered to the DVB in 1994 by SimulCrypt proponents in their original Code of Conduct maintained EBU legal Committee advisor, Michael Wagner (interview, 12.10.1995).[128]

Notwithstanding the proprietary system, it was assessed that the array of EP amendments which were eventually incorporated in Article 4 of the final Directive conferred satisfactory elements of fairness, transparency and dispute resolution to this aspect of the policy (ibid, 12.10.95). So, MultiCrypt proponents were moderately content and nurtured hopes that the common interface system had a fair chance to develop in the medium term. Meanwhile, in the short term all interested broadcasters had to utilise the proprietary, conditional-access system (Eberle, 12.10.1995). In fact violations would be dealt with (administratively or legally) a *posteriori*,

---

[128] EP amendments provided: 1) that consumer equipment for de-scrambling digital, television signals must display signals transmitted in the clear; 2) that CA, service providers offer all broadcasters, on a fair, non-discriminatory basis, technical services enabling the broadcasters' digitally transmitted services to be received by viewers by means of decoders; 3) that separate accounts be kept for CA businesses; 4) that holders of industrial property rights to CA systems be prevented from prohibiting, deterring or discouraging manufacturers from including a common interface allowing connections with several other access systems; and 5) that an appropriate dispute resolution mechanism should be set up to deal with potential conflicts between manufacturers and property-rights holders of CA systems.

by which time the damage to a competitor in securing a market share should have been irresistible.[129]

Such rules do not touch the crux in this market: the private monopoly control of significant flows of information. Given the comparative advantages of the first investor, hopes for a future change looked quite unrealistic. The collapse of ITV digital in 2002, in the UK, in fact proved the veritably monopolistic set up of this market. A first-mover, Murdoch outmanoeuvred all his competitors. As is pointed out by Papa-thanassopoulos, Rupert Murdoch's method of expansion is simple. He expands by entering first in new markets while closing off market entrance to his competitors. (2005:129).[130] This he does by manipulating political decision-making as well as by sheer market power. Yet all this initiative by the EC took off ostensibly in the name of competition. EC commitments to the public interest thus proved shaky. By contrast, the dominant DVB forces eventually imposed their line, stepping closer to *laissez faire* and away from the consensual and voluntary agreement on standards originally laid out by the EC and the broader spectrum of market forces.

The Outcome: Media Lords Made in the EC

Eventually, the new climate of agreement between leading market actors (the DVB) and political actors (EP, Commission) enabled the European

---

[129] The failure to agree to just one system is likely to be only partially offset by these amendments. In particular, the ability to resolve disputes speedily will prove to be the crucial point..." (Collins & Murroni 1996: 40).

[130] As is pointed out by Papathanasopoulos, Rupert Murdoch's method of expansion is simple. He expands by entering first in new markets and by closing off market entrance to his competitors. This strategy was successfully applied, certainly in the case of ITV, but also in other national and linguistic markets. For instance, he came out as the winner from the digital-TV war in Italy after the merger between the two competing companies Stream and Telepiu. (ibid :129).

Council to adopt unanimously the amended Directive on 24 July 1995.[131] It is nowhere explicitly evident in the Directive that the proprietary, CA system is privileged or not. Yet, the main contribution of the new Directive on the use of standards was to enshrine the proprietary, conditional-access gateway. Moreover, a separate text approved by the Council ministers was attached to the Directive but was not published in the official journal. This appendix, arguably, set out a gentlemen's agreement on political support for the SimulCrypt system.

In view of the market potential that was created by the digital upheaval both in quantitative but also in qualitative terms, thematic subscription services, as opposed to universal access services, loomed large. This undoubtedly vindicated the formerly-anti-MAC forces, which 'coincidentally' are the leading forces of ACT. These same forces are also the leading investors in co-productions in Hollywood and the opponents of any proactive, European policies for the programme production industry (European Audiovisual Conference, July 1994). Even if an optimal regulation were undertaken in due course to protect the rights of others at the member state level, the essential relation of dependence on the proprietor's power would remain.

The aim was "to contribute to the proper functioning of the internal market..." (Council 1995, Directive preamble). But, for an instrument whose most crucial contribution is to entrench a global, private conglomerate into a monopoly control of a strategic gateway, it is hard to claim that this benefits the internal market. The attempt to flexibly harness the economic possibilities of an emergent market, prompted considerably by technological and ideological hype, thus gave birth to an EC-made, vertical concentration in the new media markets. It is interesting to see how this Directive compares with related cases involving

---

[131] Although it was adopted in July 1995, in order to finally formulate and approve the attached memorandum text which was demanded by the UK government, the Directive was officially published in October 1995.

risks of vertical integration and concentration of power as these have been handled by DG IV of the Commission.[132]

Unlike the DG for competition, DG XIII not only allowed vertical integration to obtain, but it favoured it directly by creating secondary law: the Directive on transmission standards. That is, it established a monopoly, service supplier who was concurrently a competitor to their own customers in a successive, market segment. This effectively entails the gross bypassing of EC competition framework. This policy case shows up the familiar gap between the various Commission DGs. But this is not merely a manifestation of the serious difficulties in establishing a working culture of co-ordination within the Commission and between diverging DGs. It points to an intention and a tendency to circumvent politically the remaining EC restrictions on competition via 'supra-national' political levers.

The Impact

Of course players like BSkyB, Filmnet and Canal+ were aiming at gaining full control of the CA system. Apart from securing their market viability, it would allow them to concentrate vertically and to further expand their *global empires*. It is hard, however, to explain or justify the official turning

---

[132] Since Kirch is a leading programme producer, MSG could offer attractive packages of pay-TV programmes more easily than potential competitors. Furthermore, MSG's potentially strong position as operator of digital infrastructure for pay-TV would mean that potential pay-TV suppliers may be underlying services from their main competitor. The Commission considered that this created a serious risk of MSG discriminating in favour of its parents (Styliadou 1997: 56). Here, the Commission competition Directorate General, DG IV, in interpreting Article 81 of the Treaty of the European Community in 1994, on the grounds of potential anti-competitive behaviour and market dominance, blocked the creation of MSG which would have come about through the merger of such companies as Bertelmann AG, Deutsche Telekom and Taurus Beteiligungs GmbH (Commission 1994c). That is, it precluded the possibility, among others, that a company become both a provider of service and a competitor in a secondary market segment down the scale of its vertically-concentrated market, with other competing firms (Styliadou 1997). See also Chapter 5.

of the EU media into a monopolistic, and potentially monopsonistic, market exchange for cheaply-imported and monolithic, cultural products by the EC authorities. Such a handling of the CA-system issue makes no public-policy sense whatsoever.

How could a unique CA system, considered unacceptable on legal, economic and political reasons in 1991, become not only acceptable but imperative in 1995? Why was the failed attempt to adopt an encryption system in 1991 seen as daring interventionism (despite its associate importance for the HD-MAC project)[133] while the same attempt in favour of a private system, was not seen as interventionist in 1995? Can a CA system be given over to private conglomerates of global calibre without forfeiting the EC competition framework?

Did not such a development have a negative impact on the freedom of information for citizens, and endanger broader EC interests? Was the consideration of the damaging effects of this policy irrelevant to EC policy-makers?

Notwithstanding the safeguards that were eventually squeezed in by the EP, against the proposal of the Commission, this policy seriously endangers a number of interests: first, the general interest in the EU, secondly certain national interests, particularly those of the media-wise, weaker and linguistically smaller areas and member states, and thirdly the interests of competing broadcasters of generalist and universally-receivable services, and other competing service suppliers.

Five main interfaces of power relations were affected by the Directive in question: an unequal relation was established between suppliers of

---

[133] Such an option was at that time vehemently rebuffed by ACT and by BSkyB in particular .In addition, since SimulCrypt is linked with PAL plus, transmission technology, contrary to all claims about ostensible 'neutrality' in the policy of standards, the Council Directive of 1995, in fact, blatantly favours PAL broadcasters and Astra satellite operators. This necessarily meant that the much-vaunted argument of neutrality towards other transmission standards did not apply. Besides, the combined effect of the operation of a conglomerated, vertically-integrated audiovisual sector with its practise of programming pre-purchases and sales of rights at global level, threatens the European independent producers with extinction, because they are usually of small and medium size and work in a variety of languages and cultures.

exactly the same type of services, since SimulCrypt owners have a dual role: as controllers/suppliers of the CA–system, transmission services, and as competitors to their customers and fellow suppliers of TV services. These competitors risked losing their freedom of access to: 1) the desired bulk of information to be supplied; 2) the kind of information to be supplied – which is threatened by the combined effect of programme, pre-purchasing practices and of bidding higher prices because of the scale of activity of the privileged conglomerate; 3) the priority of information supplied, in a system where first comers scoop the market, (particularly pertinent for big, Hollywood hits or for big athletic events); 4) the targeting of desired time zones, (schedule structure); 5) the setting of tariffs cost-efficient to their needs and their standards of quality.

An unequal relation was established between encoded thematic channels and generalist, universally accessed channels because the audiences of the latter were eroded. Advertiser-funded, generalist channels face unbearable competition for audiences and thus costs undermine their economic viability. Generalist, public-service broadcasters similarly face the challenge of their financial basis, the licence fee. The economic viability and sustainability of these channels becomes impossible in the long run.

Attractive television programming is a scarce resource. If psbs, for example, lose the most value-added chunks of their schedule, due to the pre-purchase of exclusive copyrights at exorbitant prices by their pay-TV-supplying competitors, and to the latter's domination in niche, thematic, market shares of films and sports, then their schedule loses edge and attractiveness. In television, the competitive battle is firstly to acquire exclusive copyrights and secondly about 'capturing' audiences: "Owning programming is an important competitive strategy for a distribution network. Except in circumstances where program exclusivity is prohibited, if you have a program, your competitor does not – or she acquires it on your terms" (Baldwin et al. 1996: 287-288). Thematic channels can compete from a much stronger, financial position in the bidding for titles and copyrights. Having won this battle, they can wage war against the generalist channels by winning-over paying viewers.

This means, first, that generalist channels lose their financial flexibility and their ability to internally cross-subsidise in programming and to invest capital in expensive, quality programming such as documentaries, current affairs programming with an investigative character, and educational programming. All of these require a sound and steady financial base for reasonably long term programming and scheduling. The first to go, then, are the more costly genres of the generalist channel menus such as researched documentaries and current affairs programmes. This leads to failing quality in programming and to the gradual extinction of diversity: "The people who can afford access to VOD and to subscription television will become new television elite who will decide, with the dollars they spend, the substance of program production," (Baldwin 1996: 144).[134]

Building exclusive and large catalogues of programming (usually by block purchasing) is a successful strategy. Thus, new digital, satellite and thematic, conditionally-accessed services with this programming strategy bring in the largest audiences (political currency) and hence the most advertisers (economic currency). The buying up of a critical mass of transmission rights of the most popular shows at exorbitant prices, often beyond the reach of small broadcasters, may be the *coup de grace* for generalist broadcasters, but is also indispensable for the survival of the conglomerates which control the CA system.

Modern 'Enclosures', the Excluded, and the Public Sphere

All this results in diminished diversity and quality of the generalist and psb channel menus. Both citizens' rights to pluralistically sourced information

---

[134] It is noteworthy in this regard that in the US in order "to assure competing video services a source of programming, the federal law prohibits exclusivity arrangements on the part of vertically integrated programmers and cable operators" (Baldwin et al. 1996: 144).

and certain entrepreneurial economic stakes were attacked. Such less attractive channels risked losing their critical-audience mass altogether. In such a case, their political legitimacy and their financial base (licence fee) would be questioned in due course. For obvious reasons, this is a particularly acute problem for national or sub-national psbs. In this way, the EC policies directly counteracted cultural independence and equality and damaged cultural diversity, pitting member states against each other.[135]

The general interest was damaged, firstly, because of the overall effects on the economic health and transparency of the sector and, secondly, because of the socio-cultural effects in the biasing of the selection and distribution of information contents that this process involves. Certain sections of viewers will not afford or may not wish to subscribe to available, private, thematic, information services. The real and potential interests (Lukes 1974) of these sections of viewers are endangered because of the tangible threat of the qualitative devaluation and/or the extinction of alternative types of channels.

But the general interest was damaged both essentially and in principle, since the conception of 'electronic public sphere' of broadcast media was defeated. By definition, this happens with every privatization, and conditional-access systems are nothing less than the contemporary forms of 'enclosures'.

The most crucial impact of this policy was to further augment the power of the media barons who control SimulCrypt. This becomes clearer if we juxtapose and compare this quick settlement with the EU's overall reluctance and/or impotence to check on the concentration of media ownership and to safeguard diversity and pluralism.

Policy paralysis on the anti-cartel front fits well with the CA issue, which reinforces the formation of cartels. This is simply two-faced. It can

---

[135] Since these developments, there were some significant changes on the status of the psbs in the EU. The Treaty of Amsterdam has adopted the protocol endorsing the special political and cultural role of the psbs, but even so the essential and functional safeguarding of their role requires concrete action, notably regulation of the entire market structure for communications, than a constitutional status.

be asked what difference there is between the issue of pluralism and concentration of ownership and the issue of conditionally accessing the gateway for television services. Both deal with the audiovisual sector. Both concern and affect the same viewer populations and the same entrepreneurs. Yet, in the second case, there was a *prompt policy settlement*, while in the first, policy-making was negated. The difference between them is that one would have combated concentration and monopoly control of the media sector while the other helped erect one.

The dealings on the CA issue indicate that the Community chose the short term and the exclusively market-led model.[136] But put in Baldwin's words: "today, financial markets have little tolerance for delayed gratification" (Baldwin et al. 1996: 162). The effort to create a regional economy of broadcast programming, electronic advertising, and new technology manufacturing itself enormously stimulates the forces of even broader trans-nationalisation. Consequently, control over broadcast planning and programmes rests increasingly not only outside any single country, but also outside any region. This process signals a fundamental shift towards "a globally oriented, multinational broadcast enterprise that is beholden to no government or policy authority. The forces of commercialisation and privatization are everywhere and nowhere, and therefore they are increasingly beyond check" (Willard & Tracey 1990: 15). This is most certainly an accurate assessment, but this cannot absolve political agency from its responsibility. Neither should it be seen as a description of a reality which grants alibis for positively abdicating their political role via inaction or via handing over of policy prerogatives to private, unaccountable forces.

---

[136] According to press reports in 1997, market viability and cost efficiency in regimes of raw competition and confusing deregulation were unpredictable even for the most privileged players, thereby jeopardising broader interests. In spite of the major facilitation that the establishment of the proprietary SimulCrypt CA system had afforded its owners, serious problems of market pull, viability and cost-efficiency surfaced for Kirch and BSkyB in Germany, who failed to achieve the necessary critical mass of consumer demand and later collapsed. A similar collapse, that of ITV Digital, occurred in the UK in 2002, when, after making many serious miscalculations, it was outmanoeuvred by BSkyB and the BBC acting in concert. (Randall 2002).

In analysing the joint EC and market forces' policy-process which fostered the Directive on transmission standards and led to the establishment of a proprietary, monopoly, gateway control of the pay-TV services, I have argued that the CA system, its nature and its management lie at the heart of the broad developments in the European communications policy and at the heart of the aspired to 'information society'. This chapter questions the restricting conception that conditional access is an important matter only for "the providers and consumers of pay television services and for the rights holders of programmes" (Council 1994). The handling of the CA system involves a profound structural shift that concerns all EU citizens. In spite of the fact that the Council accepted all the modest amendments proposed by the EP,[137] the end result was the effective adoption of a proprietary, CA system in the interests of Rupert Murdoch and Andre Rousselet. This inevitably entailed the control of this market by these members of the select, club group. The violation of imperative safeguards by the "EC-made owners" and effective controllers of this system, who are concurrently fellow competitors to their customers, can only be judged, settled and penalised a *posteriori*. This fact *per se* points to changes in the structure of power relations between the competing forces in the same market, thereby introducing a new element of inequality.

The interesting element with the policy on the CA system for pay-TV services is that, in spite of the fact that it evidently concerns some very central public policy aspects and issues of democratic organisation, it is the first, media-policy case that has been treated as a typical case of industrial policy by all EC institutions including the European Parliament. In this sense, this policy marks a catalytic/critical turning point in the European conception of the role of the media and of the type of information society that was anticipated for the future.

---

[137] The Commission, in its opinion of 6 July 1995, acknowledged that these alterations conferred new consensus elements of fairness, transparency and dispute-resolution to the previous industry consensus on CA (Wagner 1995).

This was facilitated *inter alia* by the way that communication policy-making is fragmented beyond control at the EC level. Diverse bits of media policies are spread between different DGs in the Commission. Moreover, separate procedural criteria apply for the different aspects of media policy. In the case of communication–media, industrial policy the fast lane, that is majority voting, of EC decision procedures applies. Just as in the media pluralism and concentration of ownership case, BSkyB and Canal+ came out the clear winners over other ACT members supplying the same type of services, over non-encoded, generally receivable, generalist channels, over the prospects of the European, independent production and finally over the public interest at large.

In policy-making terms, what is observable here is that the political decision-making mode was further incapacitated: at the national level because of its inappropriateness for such broad international issues; at the intergovernmental, 'supra-national' level because of ambiguity, disagreement, and/or plain lack of political will. These can all be accounted for by the prevalent climate of deregulation and the belief in the need for 'global coherence'! It is not at all remarkable, then, that the 'supra-national', regional, policy actor in the 1990s started 'legislating' and 'acting' by private proxy and by invoking the G7 Group's conference (February 1995) and the G7 group's policy discourse. But the G7 are not the Community.

Chapter 7

GLOBAL LIBERALISATION VERSUS REGIONAL INTEGRATION

In order to elucidate the main developments in the European Union, some of which at first glance may appear 'incomprehensible', in this chapter, I turn to examine the global context within which all these shifts of strategy and policy, transformations and regressions took place. The macroscopic perspective in terms of both time scale and space requires the investigation of the global dimension over the post-war period. The other necessary perspective is that of the global political economy, with a specific emphasis on the role of information industries, knowledge markets and trade in symbolic goods.

In the post-war period the world went through a techno-economic paradigm shift whereby the knowledge-intensive tertiary sector of services became the most crucial developmental sector of the economy. The driving forces in economic growth and expansion are productive and exchange activities that deal with information (systems and contents), knowledge, research and development for the production and the sale of innovation, communications systems and the trade in symbolic goods more generally. This largely 'immaterial' economy is typically not confined by the constraints of geography and space as was the case with the primary and the secondary sectors of economy. Indeed this economy of symbolic goods is 'naturally' transfrontier and global (Kallinikos 2001, Kaitatzi-Whitlock 2003).

The fact that the economy has become knowledge-intensive rather than labour-intensive is at the root of global trends in trade and transnational political integration. So, we cannot comprehend or interpret developments at the regional, continental level of the EU unless we not only take a broader, universal look at the events that advanced the phenomenon of globalisation but also consider the impact of this phenomenon on national or regional political decision-making.

In this chapter I examine the international institutional frameworks, principles and 'rules' that were in place and the battles that led to changing them. I then describe the emerging new rules and the driving forces that were involved in designing and imposing these rules on the rest of the world. I then look at the battle between the US and EU at the level of GATT (General Agreement of Trade and Tariffs)/WTO (World Trade Organisation) on an issue of communications policy. The policy area of this conflict is that of communication contents and programming, but the aim clearly belongs to political economy: how to capture a foreign market in its entirety. The means to do this was the framework of GATT, the mechanism by which global trade is liberalised. Interestingly enough, in the course of this battle this mechanism itself was in a process of transition and transformation in order to meet the challenges of transforming trade rules and relations more effectively. These multiple and parallel developments are exemplified in the analysis of the case study in question. The battle between the US and the EU at the GATT/WTO level is concurrently a significant if not definitive test of the strengths and the limits of the European project of regional economic-political integration. It is most significant that this test should be unravelled on the most influential type of policy issue, that of communications and the identity-bound domain of culture.

In concluding I examine the challenges facing the political order and polities more generally of a regional political actor, of the *sui generis* nature of the EC/EU, to determine their collective affairs and ultimately their collective fate in the middle of this race for globalisation. The depicted relations crystallize firstly the imbalance of power between economic and political agency and secondly the imbalance of power between the hegemonic political forces of the globe versus the weaker polities of which the EU emerges as an example. Furthermore, the global controversies in question also reflect the marginalisation even of organised citizens' agency in affairs of these order. This however, is not a lesser problem of democratic legitimation.

Global agencies such as the ITU, OECD and the GATT/WTO were and still are in the vanguard of capitalism, creating the conceptual frameworks through which we articulate and understand our lives in all their multifarious forms. They set the norms through which we understand and negotiate contemporary reality. These organisations shape and impose the new rules of the global game. The prime principles of this new game are market liberalisation, privatization deregulation, the 'rights of access' of foreign multinational companies (MNCs) in formerly closed national economies, competition and competitiveness. Even such an important power as the EU cannot withstand this pressure.

The Era of Satellites and of Global Telecommunications Networks

The basis for politics and economy particularly from the early twentieth century was that of the nation state. Sovereignty was the fundamental and absolute principle that underpinned this state of affairs. In the post-war era, due to changes in the economy, the nation state faced explosive pressures for opening up geographical, technical and cultural/political barriers. The developments generated by the techno-economic paradigm shift cannot fit in the national context. These developments claim the global terrain.

The Cold War generated the project for the domination of space in order to control the enemy from above. One spin-off from the space race was the satellite. In 1960 the first communications satellite was launched and started orbiting the earth. The advent of satellites was a landmark in telecommunications history that was soon to prove catalytic in the constellation of international legal institutions, economic exchanges and relations. The political, economic and cultural impact of geostationary satellites was enormous: three satellite positions suffice to cover the entire globe in terms of communications messages (Kaitatzi-Whitlock 2003).

This was a much needed generator for the re-constitution of capitalist economies beyond the boundaries of closed national economies and represented a threat to all states and political forces that were not within the capitalist orb or were on the verge of nationhood.

It is a historic irony that the year of the first satellite, 1960, also marked the culmination of anti-colonial, national liberation movements. Political and cultural self-determination were high on the agenda of many peoples around the globe, and many new states were taking their places in the United Nations.

In this context it was feared that satellite communications would become a new instrument of subjugation and neo-colonialism. In response to such legitimate fears, the 1977 world administrative conference (WARC) of the International Telecommunications Union (ITU) allocated geostationary satellite positions to all members of the UN on a national basis. In parallel with these movements, members of the Non-Aligned Movement in cooperation with UNESCO pioneered the global policy for a New World Information and Communication Order (NWICO). The NWICO project represented the most coherent, concerted and well-organised effort, mainly by poor developing countries, to anticipate the inexorable changes of the then dawning knowledge-based economic development and to be part of it in a balanced and fair way. It was an example of a very advanced, timely and proactive global strategy to fend off possible neo-colonialist incursions. Having just acquired their national independence, the majority of the developing countries envisaged an information society within the confines of the nation state and the national economies.

The Information Vector in Global Antagonisms

Since the NWICO encompassed the interests of most of the developing nations, this policy was endorsed by the great majority of the UN member states. For precisely the same reasons, NWICO was bitterly fought against by the economically powerful, information-rich countries of the UN, notably the members of the G7. It is worth remembering that leading G7 members had already defined their economies as information economies after the last World War (Bell 1973) with an eye on their stakes in the global arena. They were already moving beyond the confines of the nation state and seeking to impose new rules for this new game on their own terms.

Thus the information economy became the site of a battle between developed and developing countries. Apart from the possession of various kinds of know-how and strategic knowledge about information technology systems, the main line of division between the two camps was the locus of its development: where it would operate and under whose control. The global domain was feasible and coveted by the information-rich members of the G7, the national territory was legally protected internationally by the charter of the UN and was defended with zeal by the multitude of information-poor developing countries.

The NWICO was endorsed politically and in principle by the UN. But it was essentially defeated because economically it was disarmed and drained of any actual means of support for development. Know-how, patents, and copyrights, constituting property rights of very high added value were used by their proprietors to dominate the world – not to share. Globally-oriented entrepreneurs sought to use their uniquely valuable assets as levers for their expansion and domination. But how could they go about it if the prevailing international legal system, at the time, was against them? The World Summit on Information Society (WSIS) (2003-2005) certainly 'revisited' some of the original goals of NWICO. But as was evidenced in the last Tunis Summit of WSIS, its processes are entirely controlled by the most powerful MNCs, of course under the auspices of ITU and UNESCO. Researchers such as Padovani and Nordenstreng (2005) question the possible connection between these two distinct processes. There is every reason to doubt the existence of any such continuity or link.

In view of the tremendous difficulties involved in providing universal, international law on satellite regulation, UN Radio and Visual Services' Division Director, Jean D'Arcy had predicted (back in the 1960s) that a *regional option*, rather than a global one, might be the only feasible initial approach to such an impasse (Barker 1988). The divestiture of the AT&T by the Supreme Court of the USA, the privatization of British Telecom and the liberalisation of the telecommunications market in the UK, and the European project as launched by the Green Paper on TWF and pursued with the TWF Directive are certainly some cases in point. They represent regional block solutions to the long-standing international legal and political problems related to satellite emissions. These moves were designed precisely to open the way to the rapid global expansion required by leading business interests.

The concurrence of these crucial events in the world political economy was not accidental. First, there was not only the deregulation and break-up of AT&T, following a US Supreme Court Ruling, which set an obliging precedent for international deregulation but also an array of deregulatory steps taken by the Federal Communications Commission (FCC) in American broadcasting (Zeri 1990). Secondly, the OECD countries adopted the principle of a transborder, free flow of data and information in pursuit of global transactions in the services sector and economic strategies. Thirdly, there was the privatization and liberalisation of telecommunications services in the UK and their knock-on effect on the Single European Market and on other European governments' policies; (the first and third factors should be seen in combination with the looming convergence and eventual integration between broadcasting and narrowcasting transmission media). Fourthly, the European Advertising Tripartite (EAT) and the International Association of Advertisers (IAA) made the insistent demands to open up the new *Eldorado* of televised advertising. Fifthly, there was the preparation for the launching of national and transnational cooperation satellite projects and channels (either bilateral i.e. the Arianne project, or Community in nature) not entirely financeable publicly and hence open to volunteering transnational businesses and to advertising. Finally, it is significant to point out that Green Paper TWF was drafted by the DG for the Internal Market (now DG XV) under Lord Cockfield, a free market advocate and former member of Margaret Thatcher's cabinet (Collins 1994). European and global business forces, furthermore, relentlessly and systematically pushed for the 'subjection' of this cultural sector to commercial goals, via liberalisation.

To put communications and satellite technology matters in the hands of non-governmental agencies was, moreover, a long-standing goal. As is pointed out in the Green Paper on TWF "the so-called super beams, which are consistent with the free flow of information and are able to harness the special technical possibilities of satellite television for serving large cross-frontier areas failed to gain acceptance... at WARC 1977" (GPTWF: 14). This 'failure' was precisely the result of the insistence of the majority of UN member states to stick to national service areas and thereby to defend national state sovereignty. It is thus illuminating to compare this view with that of the EC Commission which went on to reason that national control is sought by those countries "even though from both frequency-allocation and a financing point of view, direct satellites are particularly economic and suitable for broadcasting over wide [rather than national] areas." (ibid).

From 1960 until the commencement of the Uruguay Round (UR) in 1986, the US, assisted by other western nations, actively promoted the free flow of information in such international forums as in the Helsinki CSCE Conference and the Council of Europe. Information-rich countries manipulated this principle with the utmost dexterity for economic goals (Taishoff 1987: XI). In particular OECD countries raised the communications sector "to the status of high politics" (Dyson & Humphries 1990: 236) and actively promoted the process of its restructuring. They thus entered the race to elicit the greatest and earliest competitive advantage. A major shift in the distribution of economic and political power was thus begun.

The American-inspired idea of extending the multilateral liberalising trade framework to services was predicated on their comparative advantage in these growth sectors (Peterson 1988: 6).[138] The forceful, decades-long US endeavour to liberalise services was eventually successful in the 1980s. In 1985, the US position that GATT free trade rules should apply to services was incorporated into the OECD Declaration on Transborder Data Flows (Tunstall & Palmer 1990: 61). This breakthrough paved the way for subsequent moves in an ever-expanding process of liberalisation.

Adding to this climate was the fact that the Commission's 1984 Green Paper on TWF, which was drafted under the leadership of the most neo-liberal forces of the Community, argued directly against 'state control' (in information-receiving states). It stressed that "all the Community members states refused to approve the United Nations Resolution of 10 December 1982" (GPTWF: 27). This was particularly important because its annex "Guiding principles for the use of artificial satellites for international direct television broadcasting" includes amongst other things "the requirement that states must seek prior agreement of countries in which broadcasts might possibly be received before broadcasting any television programmes direct. Requirements of this nature clash with the basic principles of the European democracies" (ibid).

This would have been prohibitive for the prospects of transborder information flows and certainly for the trade in such symbolic services as audio and moving images. The classical liberal principle of freedom of expression was thus converted conveniently into a principle for the free and unhindered flow of transborder trade in information. Thus we observe again how a civil right assumes a commercial guise and is used successfully for the liberalisation and the deregulation of international trade. According to Shallini Venturelli,

---

[138] On international trade theory and liberalisation momentum in services, see J. Peterson 1988, P.A. Messerlin 1993, and S. Woolcock 1993.

The current historical trend, therefore, is for artificial entities to somehow absorb more and more of the status of the individual human citizen and therefore more and more of the private rights originally intended by the Enlightenment founders of modern democratic thought for the emancipation of humans from oppression, tyranny, ignorance, and injustice." (1996 : 122)

These elements then illustrate the broader background context and elucidate certain key decisions, aspects and the leading strategies. They, for example, explain why there was such urgency for pushing forward the transfrontier television policy at this particular time. The concurrence of a number of concerted events and their timing is remarkable. One cannot avoid correlating the policy push for transborder television as the 'flagship of the Internal Market' with the concurrent ascendance of the deregulatory onslaught. This onslaught was set in motion just before with the decision of Judge Harold Green of the US Supreme Court on divesting AT&T.

The battle between the 'nationalists' and the globalists was won *de jure* and *de facto* by the latter, and we are now living in the transfrontier, global, deregulated communications galaxy with 'no sense of place'. Such political, institutional and technological changes articulate quite a different structure of power relations for the production of policy. Indeed, such conditions significantly alter internationally and globally the positions of stake-holders (Raboy 2002, Kallinikos 2001).

The US versus the EU on European Quotas

In line with the goal of liberalising services at the global level, leading international and information-rich states, along with the other diplomatic, legal and political steps that they were pursuing, initiated the Uruguay Round of talks in 1986. Up until 1993, GATT liberalisation provisions on trade applied only to manufactured goods. The objective of these negotiations was to also liberalise trade in agricultural goods and notably trade in services which comprised the growth sectors of the emerging economy of the new techno-economic paradigm.

The leading economies of the world were all in favour of liberalisation as this was indispensable for the global pervasiveness of their national champions. Particularly the triad (USA, Japan and the EC) were in the forefront of these developments. At the same time, however, the USA was suspicious of the fast and steady regional economic integration that was progressing in the EC. This was manifest in the intense challenges to the so-called 'Fortress Europe', which reflected the fear that the EU would become a fairly integrated, independent, increasingly closed and stable state. These challenges were especially intensified at the end of the Eighties and in early Nineties – notably in the run up to the conclusion of the Uruguay Round of the GATT/GATS negotiations for the liberalisation of trade in agricultural goods and services world-wide.

Meanwhile, the entire concept of the new economy was in fact predicated on this liberalisation of global trade in 'symbolic goods'. For the EC, however, pursuing the General Agreement of Trade in Services (GATS) was to undermine the policy of protecting European audiovisual production. This was eventually formulated in the Television Without Frontiers Directive and notably in the infamous television *quotas articles*. Here we can see a patent clash between a goal of a regional cultural political and economic integration *versus* attempts at global liberalisation and global capital integration.

The controversy between the US and the EC on the audiovisual at the GATS challenged the weakest possible link of the EC policy – the legally non-binding quotas articles. European programming quotas aroused discontent and even fury on the part of the Motion Picture Export Association of America (MPEAA) and the US Department of Trade, notwithstanding the fact that audiovisual export flows have been predominantly unidirectional from the US to the EC.

The General Agreement of Trade in Services was concluded on the 15th of December, 1993 and was later ratified in 1994. This formed part of the wider GATT negotiation for liberalising the entire spectrum of international trade. The GATS framework, in principle, covers the audiovisual sector, although, bilaterally, it secured no specific concessions to the USA. This helped to describe the outcome of these negotiations provisionally as a 'stalemate'. Despite relentless American pressure no *market access rights* were conceded by the member states of the EC. Strategically, however, in the medium and long term, the EC had lost the war to defend its distinctive audiovisual culture and succumbed to the supremacy of the USA.

The dispute over audiovisual quotas also pitted two central principles against one another: the principle of state sovereignty and the principle of the free flow of information. Cinematographic films and audiovisual services more generally were the second largest export industry of the US after air transport. Europe was and continued to be by far Hollywood's most lucrative market. Indeed Europe absorbed half of US audiovisual exports – both before the liberalisation of the audiovisual sector (Varis 1984: 143-146) and in the post-1980s multi-channel environment.[139] American media supremacy over its European competitors was consolidated in the cinema (but also in the news agency industries) during the two World Wars that devastated Europe and made the US first a lender and then a leader (Tunstall 1977: 28-32). This trend was reinforced by the application of clever managerial and marketing techniques and benefited also from economies of scale at home. This meant that since production costs were recouped in the domestic market, any extra unit cost would be negligible, while the sale of rights reaped net profits, making the USA the world market leader in most media and information services.

For small countries and linguistic areas, the policies of quotas and direct aid, where applied, fended off this domination and helped bring about a renaissance of national film industries (EIM 1987: 43). But within the momentum gained by the *laissez-faire* ideology, national and regional policies were no longer fashionable or even sustainable. The 'comparative

---

[139] See Chapter 3 on the Think Tank Report.

advantage' theory, surprisingly, convinced many governments that international agreements could not be fair to all interests in all areas.

The film industry in the USA organised itself at the very beginning of the 20th century and was shaped into the MPAA (Motion Picture Association of America). Subsequently, the MPAA for exports was created: the MPEAA (Motion Picture Export Association of America). This powerful lobby managed to get Congress to authorise a Motion Picture Section within the Department of Trade as early as 1926. Thus, it obtained constant and guaranteed high-level diplomatic leverage for its commercial interests (EIM 1987: 42). During the course of the first multilateral Trade Negotiations of 1946 and 1947, the MPAA pushed relentlessly for controls affecting all stages of the film industry – production, sales and distribution (ibid: 44, Ayer 1982: 216).

However, in spite of bellicose bargaining, the GATT agreement provided exceptions for cinematographic works from its rules. Article III (10) and the whole of Article IV of the original GATT agreement were devoted exclusively to cinematographic works (GATT 1986, Filipek 1992: 338-9). Indeed, these guaranteed full exemption and protection for this form of art and industry to develop unhindered within the context of national domestic markets. In this respect it is noteworthy that during the first three post-war decades there were thriving national cinemas in many countries including such small countries as Hungary, Czechoslovakia, Greece and Sweden. Tariffs alone could not protect national film industries from the incursions of Hollywood so the instrument of quotas with no upper limit was devised to secure that protection (Filipek, ibid).

Americans continued to keep this trade area under constant check. In 1961 during the 19th Session of the contracting parties, the US raised the issue of GATT applicability to TV programming although at the time of drafting the original GATT agreement that type of trade was insignificant. This was the prelude to the subsequent long-drawn-out controversy between the EC and the US (Smith 1993: 116-117). The Americans canvassed for a dispute resolution mechanism to look into their claim. The working party which reviewed the American request considered three divergent positions. The US argued that TV programming is a product in the material sense of it, for example like a car is a product as opposed to a service. According to this logic, GATT general rules should, therefore, apply. A second view held that TV programming is like cinema and that Article 4 exceptions should apply *mutatis mutandis*. A third view questioned GATT's competence to deal with television altogether. As a result of this divergence of views, no consensus could be reached and consequently the issue was left dormant. Two more attempts were made by the US in 1962 and 1964 intended, as ever, to elicit a 'reasonable access' recommendation, but to no avail (Filipek 1992: 341-42).

European Quotas and Article 4 of the TWF Directive

Article 4 became the most controversial article of the Transfrontier Directive. It established programming quotas on European TV services although its terms were most ambiguous. Divergent views concerning quotas were exposed between member states and by broadcasters (EIM 1987: 111). Positions on the internal front regarding quotas were roughly polarised. There were also those who were neutral or equivocal; that is, while they objected to quotas originally, they later changed their views. Prior to the adoption of the directive, the EBU had stressed that the absolute majority of its members opposed protectionist measures as not suitable to stimulate cultural production (EIM 1987: 111). In the controversy that arose within the GATT context, however, the EBU broadly supported the pro-quota EC policy. Quotas, which were inserted in the Directive under pressure from the ECOSOC, the EP and certain member states such as France, aimed to foster and develop the European audiovisual industry and its world-wide competitiveness (ESC 1985: 13-14). The French government further sought to impose an obligation on the channels for production investment quotas rather than a screening-only quota but this failed to get any support (Stuart 1989: 6-7, *Broadcast*, 10.10.1991: 42). Production quotas would have meant that each new channel would have to produce its own programme hence contributing to the fostering of local cultural forces and the solidifying of European audiovisual space. This policy, however, was opposed by the broadcasters' lobby ACT.[140]

EC television channels broadcast about 250,000 programme hours in 1987. This amount was expected to increase exponentially in the 1990s due to channel proliferation and scheduling expansion. Yet, as I have commented elsewhere, a proper economic and market analysis must take into the equation the number of viewers that the competing channels vie for and the total amount of overall *attention time* available. US producers exported to Europe $ 350 million worth of television programming in 1984, while the equivalent value for 1989 was almost triple – $1 billion (Smith 1993: 101). Hence, the benefits of EC television liberalisation for the Americans have been and will continue to be astronomical.

Had the EC in its TWF policy not imposed or prohibited domestic quotas – as was forcefully sought by ACT in the first revision process – the overwhelming majority of the business and revenue increase, if not its totality, would have been reaped by Hollywood. This is simply because US programming is by far the cheapest (its production costs only 15% of the cost of an average European work) and it is, consequently, the most popular with broadcasters. It makes particularly good business sense to new entrants in this market who logically want to avoid upfront production costs. But while this makes perfect business sense for broadcasters, it would have converted EC household screens into home video shops for American and other overseas productions. This was precisely the goal of the MPEAA, in their GATS battle. Certain Europeans, on the other hand, terrified of this threat, campaigned for the exemption of the sector from GATS altogether. But this was to no avail.

---

[140] As was noted in Chapter 3, on the first revision of the TWF Directive, the issue of production and investment quotas had resurfaced and at that time investment quotas found more support. For a further discussion on the distinction between production and programming or screening quotas, see EIM 1987 monograph 8, Chapter X.

This highlights the conflicting (mutually exclusive) goals between the pressure (1) to create viable new broadcasters (2) to boost the domestic hardware industry, and (3) to pursue the objective of cultural diversity (by boosting independent production industries), all in a general climate of deregulation and within a dysfunctional EC framework legally and decision-making-wise. For the EC policy the need to help new broadcasters was clearly paramount, though this entailed the risk of damaging or even destroying domestic programme producers and the values of traditional broadcasters. Thus, by including quota provisions in the 1989 transfrontier Directive, the EC protectionists sought to slightly moderate the impact that aggressive liberalisation and global competition would have on content, at a time when multilateral negotiations were under way and a global agreement on services loomed large. Meanwhile, the 'stand still' and 'roll back' principles inserted in the UR ministerial declaration obliged the contracting parties not to add any new trade restrictions in the issues under negotiation (NUR 1986: 3).

The American Offensive against European Quotas

Quotas were an unbearable thorn in the side of American interests. The US attack on Article 4 was immediate. US Trade representative Carla Hills filed a formal complaint against EC quotas with the GATT dispute resolution mechanism (Smith 1993: 106). She criticized the provision as a protectionist measure inconsistent with the EC's GATT obligations, and subsequently requested consultations with the EC. Similarly, the US House of Representatives denounced the quota which supposedly favoured European works, as a violation of the General Agreement (ibid). In addition to that, the government of the US threatened to take retaliatory action against the EC if export quotas were not abolished (Filipek 1992: 346). The US offensive was based on the assumption that TV programming constituted a 'good' and not a 'service' and that it is, therefore, covered by the rules of the original GATT agreement. Thus it alleged that through the transfrontier Directive provision the EC violated three fundamental GATT principles: (a) the principle of national treatment (Article III), (b) the Most Favoured Nation (MFN) principle (Article I), and (c) Article XI which bans quantitative restrictions.

However, even those asserting that TV programming is a good and not a service had to admit that the GATT provisions failed to define 'goods' or to distinguish them from 'services'. This absence of definitions meant that matters would have been complicated in any attempt at a dispute settlement panel (Smith 1993).

The US position was utterly contradictory. While it argued that TV programming was a *good* it had at the same time submitted offers to liberalise TV programming in the *services* section of the ongoing talks of the Uruguay Round. Consequently, it treated the audiovisual as supplying both products and services! The Directive would have contravened GATT principles if audiovisual services had indeed been regulated by the GATT. In reality the Directive grants favourable conditions, i.e. MFN treatment, to all non-EC signatories of the Council of Europe.

The European Defense

Americans tried to define TV programming narrowly rather than defining the notion of broadcasting broadly. They argued that since TV programmes have a physical, material support (video) as are films on celluloid, they constitute a good and are therefore covered, like films, by the GATT (Filipek 1992: 350). The EC, consistent with earlier ECJ rulings as well as with its relevant Internal Market provisions, countered that TV programmes are not bought and sold for ownership, but that exhibition rights are leased for screening a specified number of times over a certain period and they, therefore, constitute a service (ibid: 351).

The EC's reasoning and second line of defence was built around the notion of *cultural specificity*, and of cultural exceptions already negotiated, in the case of both cinematographic works and the US-Canada trade agreements (EIM 1987: 46). As has been indicated earlier, paragraph 10 of Article 3 of the General Agreement and the whole of Article 4 of the GATT are devoted to the exceptions concerning films. These exemption provisions permitted governments to impose screening quotas with a view to defending public morals (GATT 1986).

In its resolution of 15.07.1993, the EP, a proponent and consistently strong defender of quotas, on its part, asserted that the audiovisual sector was an important facet of European culture and that liberalisation of trade must safeguard "higher interests and the European culture in particular". It further asserted that future technological progress would lead to the moving image becoming the main medium for culture in the 21st century. This was an allusion to media convergence and the possible danger of a loophole being created by the liberalisation of telecommunications. The EP made the further point that: "the United States (exports worth $3-4 billion) and the Community ($250 million) means that the European policy...could not in all honesty be regarded as a barrier to trade" (EP 1993a). The problem here is that invocations to honesty are not worth anything in the domain of global and fiendish competition for market shares and profits. The Commission also invoked the OECD Code on Invisible Operations, which like GATT Article 4, recognises the cultural importance of the audiovisual sector and allows screening quotas in its Codes Annex on Films (Filipek 1992: 352).

The Community's response to American allegations that the article was violating free trade rules ultimately hinged on the distinction between what is legally as opposed to politically binding. An inspired Commissioner Martin Bangemann sought to pacify the alarmed European operators and their American programme and software suppliers, the MPEAA, by stressing that the quotas Article was merely *politically binding*. Correct though this was, technically, it embodied not only a self-defeating comment, but also a contemptuous regard for the EU parliament, for the defenders of cultural exemptions and for broadly shared European sensibilities. On their part, the implacable American commentators argued that it is irrelevant whether the nature of the Directive is politically or legally binding and that what matters under GATT rules is the *de facto* discriminatory effect of a policy (Smith 1993: 122-123).

Despite the soundness of these arguments, in practice the European Community was pursuing *contradictory policies* at international level. It proved incapable of making its mind up about a single course of action, and in his address to the EP on 11.10.1989, Commissioner Bangemann stated that the Commission would not take action against any member state for non-compliance with Article 4 except in extreme cases (Filipek 1992: 353).

Cultural Issues in the GATS

As a result of these conflicting approaches, the EC Commission draft proposal for the GATS negotiations contained no offers of special concessions relative to liberalisation and market access to the audiovisual sector. This was contrary to the US draft proposal which, having absolutely nothing to lose, offered relevant concessions. During the Tokyo Summit Meeting of the G7 on 7 July 1993 the USA, EU, Canada and Japan announced a preliminary agreement on market access. This facilitated the resumption of the then stalled UR negotiations in the early autumn of 1993, and with regard to the audiovisual, secured a pledge to continue working towards satisfactory solutions "for all aspects of the sector" (*GATT Focus*, Aug/Sept. 1993: 3).

This meant that the EC Commission had finally succumbed to irresistible external pressures and had opted for the inclusion of the audiovisual in the negotiations. This event marked a decisive shift of strategy from that of seeking to exclude the sector from GATS rules completely, to one of seeking to secure cultural specificity exemptions or special treatment, as was demanded by the professional lobbies (*Independent* 28.9.1993: 13). To exclude the sector entirely from the multilateral liberalisations of the GATS would have been, according to external affairs Commissioner Leon Brittan, politically unacceptable.

On 15 December 1993 the Uruguay Round of GATT/GATS was concluded successfully. The accord which heralded a new triumph for neo-liberalism provided a package of rules for the conduct of trade in services based on old GATT principles, but also on new rules and mechanisms (*GATT Focus*, Dec. 1993: 2). GATS, for example, established a framework for a process of *constant liberalisation*. This enhanced deregulation was justified in terms of exploiting growth markets and fending off any possible protectionist measures by governments in the absence of a multilateral framework (*GATT Focus*, Nov. 1993: 3). It was also predicated on the assumption that the job creation potential in services, in both developed and developing countries, should not be underestimated. Despite pressures and a variety of negotiating manoeuvres on both sides, the GATS did not immediately impose constraints on potential, protective, audiovisual policies.

This temporal respite was celebrated as a success of the EC and France in particular. It should be clear, however, that the audiovisual *de jure* is not exempted from GATS and particularly that no overall exceptions were granted with respect to it (Wagner 1994: 64-68).

> The audiovisual industry is fully covered by the GATS with no special status, culturally or otherwise; it is accordingly subject to Article XIX of the agreement which reads: Members shall enter into successive rounds of negotiations, beginning not later than five years from the date of entry into force of the Agreement establishing the WTO and periodically thereafter, with a view to establishing a progressively higher level of liberalization.' (GPEAP)

Out of three possible options – (1) that the GATS has nothing to do and should not deal with cultural issues, (2) that television programming, just like cinema in GATT Article 4, gained an explicit exemption *mutatis mutandis*, and (3) that television be included in the multilateral services liberalisation package of GATS – the third option was agreed upon, but with a deferral of time. From the point of view of European protectionists, this was the worst possible option. Nevertheless, it was celebrated triumphantly in the media as a 'success'. Therefore, the general rules adopted apply in principle to all services, and the Final Act of GATS thus covers the audiovisual sector (*GATT Focus*, Dec. 1993: 7).[141]

By the mid-1990s world trade in international commercial services was worth over $1000 billion a year and was growing at 12% per year. Production of non-government services was estimated at $10,000 billion worldwide in the mid- 1980s, while in the mid-1990s it exceeded $12,000 billion. It was noteworthy that international trade in services excluding trade by local affiliates was thought to amount to as much as ten times this figure (GATT 1992: 19).

Ostensible Stalemate

There are certain elements and aspects that could be invoked to present the outcome as a stalemate. These included the following:

(a) Up to the last instant of the negotiations, the US insisted that (1) the quota upper limit be 51% and apply on a 24-hour basis rather than on prime time only; (2) that it be restricted to Hertzian transmissions, leaving the more lucrative satellite, cable and new transmissions with no quota protection for the individual channel; and (3) that pay-per-view and video-on-demand (VOD) services be excluded from quotas and that American artists get royalties from levies raised on blank video were unacceptable (*Financial Times*, 15.12.1993: 6). These maximalist, not to say preposterous,

---

[141] The new GATS framework comprised a) the framework agreement regarding principles such as the Most Favoured Nation, National Treatment and the progressive liberalisation of market access; b) annexes which refer to particularly sensitive areas such as telecommunications and financial services and the free movement of persons; c) schedules of concessions for market access expected were to be submitted by all contracting parties by April 1994 for the Marakesh Ministerial Conference (*GATT Focus*, Dec. 1993).

demands by Mr Jack Valenti, the American USDC negotiator, were thus rebuffed.

So for the moment EC member states can still maintain or reinforce protective measures, for developing European audiovisual space, and exemptions from the MFN principle. Thus preferential co-productions between EC and non-EC European states and programmes such as MEDIA and Eurimages were not deemed to violate GATS rules (Wagner 1994). However, exemptions to MFN Article II might be reviewed every two years and could not exceed a period of ten years (that is, 2003) (GATT 1993a: 26). In the medium and long term, then, risks could not be avoided. It is noteworthy that the applicability of the general principles of the GATS has some crucial implications for the sector.

GATS applied to all telecommunications services other than basic telephony. This implies that Fixed Satellite Services (FSS) and Direct to Home (DTH) activities are perfectly legal, when using tele-communications frequencies rather than broadcasting frequencies and transmitting from outside the EU and the Council of Europe where the transfrontier regulations (Directive and Convention) apply. To stop this method of circumventing quota protection, reservations and exemptions should be required for telecommunications services in order to preclude 'back door' outlets both *de jure* and *de facto*. In any case, technical convergence and digital enhancement have already enabled a variety of video transborder and transatlantic services to be provided.

The theoretical question was whether the EC Commission would ever sue an American satellite channel using the Fixed Satellite Services (FSS) narrowcast band for broadcasting (or for narrow-casting), as was latterly discussed regarding video services on the Internet, for example from outside EC territory, and if so, on what grounds. Given that the free flow of information is enshrined in the EU, would not such a move make it clearer that two mutually exclusive rights had been declared?

(b) A ruling by the Independent Television Commission (ITC) enabled BT and other prospective telecommunications operators to offer VOD services nationwide *without* the requirement of any specific license

(*Broadcast*, 1.10.1993: 1 & 8.10.1993). It was considered that even these services fall under the remit of Article 1 of the Directive and should therefore respect quotas (M. Hewitt, of ITC, interview, 10.3.94). A question that is more difficult to answer and to justify politically is: how is monitoring to take place? Is it going to be another form of *self-regulation*? Since video on demand constitutes an individual service, would it be compatible with the principle of freedom to receive and impart information (of Article 10 of the ECHR) and, if not, on the basis of which public policy – moral, national security or industrial sovereignty – could it be curtailed? This condition then entailed that the liberalisation of telecommunications services at multilateral level would enable any foreign telecommunications operator to offer similar services. There is no legal or technical problem as long as relays or transponders are not involved within European territory.

Under the codes of the International Telecommunications Union (ITU), television services are said to be 'broadcast' while telephony, point to point communications, are dubbed 'narrowcast'. When narrowcast operations become massive and take on such a large scale, it makes little difference what the service is called. The crucial thing is what this new deregulated service does to your 'protected' market, given the technological advances and above all the convergence of the media. Trade creation benefits the competitor, while trade diversion is neutralised by multilateral liberalisation. Besides, if a European government cannot restrict foreign and domestic telecommunications operators from offering video on demand services both *de jure* and *de facto*, then quotas simply create a competitive advantage for the competitors to the disadvantage and detriment of domestic, incumbent, generalist broadcasters. The one certain effect then would be both to scupper the domestic market and to leave culture with only the protection of rhetoric. The way the quotas articles have been handled by EC policy-makers was thus boomeranging against the aspired European Audiovisual Space.

(c) The Americans were expected to reactivate their formal complaint against quotas. This was particularly likely from the moment that the

GATS now covered the audiovisual in principle. Moreover, the dispute-settling mechanism has become more efficient now. Furthermore, the GATS agreement included the principle of *continuous liberalisation*. There could even be litigation over the issue of definitions. The view that "TV programming is a good" may resurface on the initiative of a US subsidiary or a European firm. For example, Mr Jack Valenti expressly reserved all his rights to legal action since diplomacy had failed.

(d) Since market access was denied to them, US firms started making vigorous use of bilaterally–arranged, foreign, direct investment (FDI) and establishing subsidiaries in order to distribute Hollywood productions freely and to foster advantageous co-productions. This entailed the direct capital flows particularly into certain welcoming and attracting member states (e.g., Ireland). However, "FDI is a policy-induced substitute for direct trade" (Peterson 1987: 26) not a market-led development.[142] This is of dubious value particularly when dealing in cultural matters. Is FDI a lesser form of 'cultural imperialism' than overseas trade? Buena Vista, the international arm of Walt Disney, has already signed co-production agreements with four European broadcasters, TF1, ARD, RAI and TVE. These agreements were prompted by the need to ascertain that their product qualify as European (*Broadcast*, 1.10.1993: 32) and the need for capital flows into the now ailing European broadcasting organisations, commercial or psb.

How consistent, then, would a criterion of cultural purity be which recognises as European something that is co-produced between Turkey (a member of the COE) and Germany, while being suspicious of a co-production between Ireland and the US? In any case, Hollywood can overcome such problems via the two-tier, flexible, specialisation strategy of cheap offshore production.

This demonstrates that it is difficult to sustain an exclusive definition of European 'cultural origin' on geographical grounds. A radical, cultural definition must be based on the political-economy of human, civil and

---

[142] "America hies to free trade when it is convenient and turns to protection when it isn't." (Zysman 1983: 277).

social rights. Such a definition would recognise and claim firstly the right of self-projection and of cultural localisms to all groups. It would construct a European cultural distinction on the basis of such values as pluralism, equality of freedom, diversity, and respect for political, ethical and religious sensibilities in the democratic political tradition. This cultural and political definition was equally threatened by both local and global commercial domination; secondly it should defend the right to local production and right to work and express oneself artistically, culturally, politically in each and every locality which is threatened by conglomerations and rationalisations, irrespective of origin. The issue is evidently not one of nationality and geo-commercial origin but of a commercial and unaccountable concentrated domination.

(e) Private broadcasters, notably the ACT, work against quotas. This is the strongest lobby in the European economic and political arena (Kaitatzi-Whitlock 1994). If quotas do not make business sense and channel owners consider that these cannot remain economically viable, and if at the same time the logic of commercial viability predominates, why then should they support cultural quotas? The members of ACT, Fininvest, CLT, TF1, ITV and SAT-1 unanimously opposed domestic quotas in 1989 (Stuart 1989: 6-7). At a briefing to sector representatives by EC Commissioner Leon Brittan, ACT remained unmoved by this European battle against America's (the external competitor) attempts to liberalise the EU's audiovisual culture.

(f) With the proliferation of television channels there would be a marked shortage of European programming. Therefore, the EC Directive was in danger of shooting itself in the foot by imposing screening (rather than investment) quotas. The economic and cultural paradox was that the Directive provided for multiple channels without ensuring the necessary content e.g. by production quotas. This was exacerbated by including the vague expressions "where practicable" and "by appropriate means" in the TWF Directive.

A Short and Overestimated Respite

The EC has been a pioneer in enshrining the free flow of information as a central principle governing current international relations. The impact of this principle was to be felt in the worldwide audiovisual domain without frontiers that we all started to experience since 1989. Having first restructured and *ipso facto* commercialised the market, thus contributing to the creation of many voracious new channels, the EC hesitantly requested the implementation of quotas of European works. It is, however, naïve to expect that any commercial broadcaster would risk his/her viability and profits by respecting legally non-binding measures.

This ambivalent and in effect negative position *vis-à-vis* the cultural sector was hardly a strong negotiating basis in the GATS controversy. The EC failed to commit itself and to stand up for its audiovisual sector by accepting its inclusion in principle in the liberalisation agreement on services, which was concluded on 15 December 1993. The MPEAA, vigorously supported by the USDC, would, naturally, like to capture the entire European cash cow. The US has not achieved its goal for total market openness and control in the EC; this has erroneously been celebrated as an EC victory, but in fact it merely secured a breathing space of five years. In addition to the technological and economic convergence of ITC sectors using satellite frequencies, the non-implementation of the quotas provision as well as FDI and ingenious methods of defining foreign produced programmes as European works have all paved the way for the feared American 'cultural imperialism' and the complete capture of the European audiovisual stock programming market by Hollywood.

Are Open Systems Common Markets?

A system is defined through its relation to its environment and, hence, necessarily also through the boundary that separates it from its environment and from the rest of the world. The crucial challenge for regional integration in the EU has been for this regional system to withstand global integration trends and exchanges while maintaining its homeostasis, its distinct socio-political physiognomy and its viability. Yet, the challenges of globalisation have been extremely harsh on Europe. In this chapter I have presented the global environment that was taking shape at the time the Community was initiating its involvement in communications policy.

The fundamental ideological tenet of this formative phase was a world-wide *laissez-faire* attitude. With satellite communications and other highly pervasive and globally expansive media, the economic elites of western countries could foresee the enormous economic and political gains that could be made. The battle in the UN and in the other international and transnational organisations (ITU, OECD, GATT/WTO) was between those who fought for preserving and defending the national terrain, and those who wanted to break up national spaces and boundaries and to create a unified global territory of entrepreneurial activity.

I have correlated the EU policy in this field with the movements of these international and global policy-makers, and examined the impact of such global, political, technological and economic trends on regional policy-making in the EU. Setting the larger global context within which the EU found itself provides a perspective of the complex difficulties faced and the constraints towards alternative or effective action. Overarching guidelines and trends expose the contradictions or the political paralysis in the face of the inexorable movement of the forces of capital against political forces.

A regional 'super-power', the EU, was forced to rush into a policy without yet having the necessary institutional equipment to tackle the situation. The aim behind those precipitate and certainly forceful moves was to share the anticipated profits and the reaping of either novel or still unexploited markets. The rationale upon which both the regional and global strategies of the information- rich were predicated was the principle of freedom of expression. This was hastily equated or transmuted with the 'free flow of information' for commercial exploitation.

The *raison d'être* of the GATT/GATS liberalisations was precisely to capture lucrative but as yet inaccessible markets. The particular controversy case of the US *versus* the EU reveals that the EU, once again, became a victim of its own strategic choices. EC countries, as members of the G7, were also in the forefront of those promulgating globalisation and deregulation. However, the quotas controversy shows that the EU became the prey of its ally the US, who intended to milk it for all it could. There were no restraints on what the US sought to capture from the European audiovisual market. By conceding this strategic victory to its opponent in GATT, the EU has in fact ended up with a thoroughly contradictory and confused policy of being both liberalist and protectionist at the same time. By the same token, the EU deprived the field of public communications and television from any meaningful political uses.

But the subjugation of the field of communication to commercial interests has also failed economically. Rather than providing jobs and investments, the EU has surrendered its 'Internal Audiovisual Market' to its trans-Atlantic ally and opponent.

Changes in GATT/WTO, ITU, and global capital movements are constraining factors that cannot be neglected, but the most politically debilitating factors have come from within the EU itself: the ambivalence of its decision-making formulas, its crypto-nationalisms, and the hegemonic role of certain larger member states. Europe has shown itself divided between the national (and supra-national) and the global and between a pro-political approach to politics and the pro-market approach to 'resolving problems'.

Chapter 8

THE COMMUNICATIONS DEFICIT AND THE DISEMPOWERMENT OF EU CITIZENS

How is the EU represented by existing media and what are the actual forms that such coverage takes? Are national and transnationally broadcast media guided by the needs of citizens and the obligations that arise out of the proclamation of European citizenship? Is reporting about Europolitics adequate and constructive in terms of the criteria of democratic politics?[143] What kind and how complete a political communication environment do these media furnish for citizens?

Evidence suggests that national media fail severely in providing the requisite attention to and space for decision-making or political developments at the supra-national level. This remarkable failure raises many questions. Apart from establishing the facts and the empirical data about this phenomenon, it is also necessary to locate its deeper causes and the effects. In this final chapter I focus on the communicative environment which we have been experiencing, both as national and as European citizens, since 1989, when the EC effectively decided to '*organise the political*' by entering the controversial and strategic domain of policy-making on communications.

To start with I present how national media have reported on the European Union as a whole, on political output at that supra-national level and on the institutional constellation of the EC/EU. I also discuss the relation that thus emerges between on the one hand the national media as active, depicting agencies and the EU institutional complex as a

---

[143] Such criteria are for instance set out by scholars such as Jürgen Habermas, Norberto Bobbio, Benjamin Barber, Robert Dahl and so many others. See also Chapters 1 and 2.

passive, depicted agency, subject to journalistic choices as to information dissemination or restriction. Two elements are particularly salient and are, therefore, analysed extensively. The first is the extremely scant attention given to Europolitics. I argue that under-mediatisation or the practice of ignoring European affairs constitutes an active factor against 'citizens' rights' to information about their common public affairs. Such a communicative reality politically handicaps citizens both in their capacity as nationals but also in their capacity as European citizens. I further elaborate on the resulting phenomenon of European ignorance of European affairs that accrues from such a lack of information and low-mediatisation, two mutually reinforcing phenomena. I subsequently raise the question of the lack of a pan-European channel that should have remedied the gaps in political communication left by commercial and national media.

Moreover, I discuss the effects and the further implications that such failures as ignorance, the lack of information and low or negative visibility of the EU have on the European integration project. I argue that all these failures are policy-induced by the very policy-agency under discussion: the EC/EU. But the European integration project is not the only concern here. Larger and more important values of democratic politics such as the universal right to political communication are in jeopardy. The compound effect is *depoliticization*. If the political communication framework is paralysing the body politic, undermining the foundations of the Community and its democratic future, why does the EU persist with its communications policies?

The 'Topic of Europe' in the National Media

In a study about the role of national media in European affairs, in 1993, Jürgen Gerhards observed that the development of the European *public sphere* was lagging behind the processes of transferring competences, controls and resources from the nation-state to the supra-national constellation of the EU. This, he argued, took place in two ways: first, the central focus of attention in the mass mediated public space continued to hinge exclusively around what happened in the nation state territory; nationally-based and nationally-oriented media primarily reported from national arenas. Secondly, even when national media actually did report from Brussels, this happened from the specific 'perspective' of the interests of a distinct nation-state. Such filtered reporting then bore a weak relation or no relation at all to a 'common European interest' (Gerhards 1993: 92-93). The Treaty of the European Union, adopted at Maastricht, had just been ratified in 1993, so one might rush to disagree with Gerhards about his 'precipitate' inference about the 'lagging behind' of the public sphere in comparison to "transfers of national competences to the EC" (ibid).

Yet, subsequent national and international comparative research projects and surveys came to concur systematically with Gerhards' observations. A long-term survey was carried out by Frank Brettschneider and Markus Rettich at *Media Tenor*, which covered the most prominent print and television media in Germany[144] for a period of seven years (1998-2004). This study is quite revealing of the utterly negative relation between national media and Europolitics (Brettschneider & Rettich 2005: 31-33). This work makes is a significant contribution to this issue not only because it is one of the rare, longitudinal studies examining media conduct. It is also crucial because it covers the most prominent print and broadcast media in Germany, a country whose centrality for the European integration project is commonly admitted. Apart from everything else, in pan-European attitude surveys, Germany – despite a marked recent decline – continues to score among the most positive pro-Europe

---

[144] A group of nine major German media were studied. Among them were four serious newspapers: *Suddeutche Zeitung, Frankfurter Algemeine, Die Welt, Frankfurter Rundchau* and one tabloid, *Das Bild*. Under study were also the news and current affairs programmes of four television channels *ARD, ZDF, RTL*, and *TVSat*. See Media Tenor, 1/2005: 30-33, www.mediatenor.com.

member states, unlike the UK, which figures steadily among the strongest Eurosceptics.[145]

As Brettschneider and Rettich ironically state, "European integration has not quite arrived at the editors' doorsteps. Never since 1998 has coverage on the European Union made up more than 9 per cent of total coverage in the seven prime time news programs and the 5 national newspapers analysed." (Brettschneider and Rettich 2005: 31). As a result of this editorial snubbing, European topics attract scant, selective and short-lived attention.[146] Moreover, this occurs primarily in the context of *outstanding occasions*: for instance, in 1998, when the European monetary union was finalised, or in 1999, when the EU financial scandal broke out.

The preliminary adoption of the European Constitutional Convention on October 29, 2004 in Rome was certainly one such outstanding occasion. Yet it was hardly highlighted by the press, thereby resulting in ignorance about it. In respect to this Habermas had envisaged that the adoption of a Constitution by the EU can function as a "unique opportunity of transnational communication, with the potential for a self-fulfilling prophecy" (2001: 16). However, as was demonstrated by the referenda in France and the Netherlands (2005), the European Constitution, instead of becoming a self-fulfilling prophecy, provoked a rejection. Rather than igniting 'transnational communication' and a broad debate about it, through interpenetration between national media, or over a pan-European TV channel, it was in fact ignored and condemned to obscurity; to a handling by an elitist enclave that carefully shut citizens out of its preparation.

---

[145] In opinion polls from the autumn of 2004, 60% of German people thought that the EU was "a good thing", while 12% considered it "a bad thing". By contrast, only 38% of British respondents thought that the EU was "a good thing" while 22% regarded it as "a bad thing". Comparatively, the percentage of those who view the EU positively is lowest in the UK, throughout the 25 member states. Germany ranks among the higher ones, but the highest is Luxembourg (85%) (Commission 2005: 72-73).

[146] About 1,000 journalists are accredited correspondents at the EU, around 140 are from the German media. Thus, many German media do not have their own correspondents in Brussels.

The negative findings of the German longitudinal study are also confirmed by other comparative or national cases or other relevant evidence. A content analysis of how the Dutch media cover 'Europe' and Europolitics by Semetco and Valkenburg (2000) establishes that in its coverage of the 'topic of the EU', the Dutch television resorts merely to 'episodical frames' and to reports of isolated singular events. Conversely, broadsheets tend to use 'thematic frames', and also to provide some contextual and background material (Semetco & Valkenburg 2000).

As regards news and current affairs stories in the German media, the coverage on Europe is characterised as "rare, primarily event-related, low on background and generally related from a national perspective" (Brettschneider & Rettich 2005: 31-33). But even when looking into commentary and opinion items, these analysts observe that the 'topic of EU' is not faring better there either in terms of numbers of items (frequency) or in terms of quality (serious analysis or favourable overtones).Therefore, in the kinds of items where readers would anticipate explanatory analysis regarding the significance of political developments, instead of enlightening or interpretative contributions, they read commentary which "gleefully makes fun of Brussels bureaucrats" (Brettschneider & Rettich 2005: 32, Gerhards 1993).

Another aspect that the study focuses on is the 'hierarchy' of importance between the institutions of the EU as this is constructed by the agenda-setting function of the German media. Which of the European institutions is portrayed most frequently and, thereby projected as the protagonist in European politics? The study finds that the European Commission is by far the most and the best mediatised EC institution. This press attitude corresponds to a familiar pattern in reporting politics in general. In the domestic context as well a very strong dominance of the executive is manifest in media coverage. This relative journalistic 'bias' in favour of the Commission is further corroborated by Olivier Baisnée, who shows that EP press conferences are normally not well attended. Indeed he remarks that these are attended by Brussels correspondents only whenever a Commissioner is also present (Baisnée 2004: 231). Besides, it transpires that Commissioners themselves seem to be aware of this positive discrimination they enjoy in comparison to the EP (Baisnée 2004, Smith 2004).

Thus, oddly perhaps the institution with the poorest and the most negative 'image' appears to be the EP, the only internationally elected body in the world. It is notably pointed out that that the EP is allowed to 'exist' in the pages and in the spaces of national media almost exclusively during Euro-election years. As a result, while the EP was visible in the election years of 1999 and 2004, it appeared to play practically no role whatsoever in the interim, non-election years. Significantly, however, even then, "the coverage of Parliament does not reach the same prominence as the EU Commission" (Brettschneider & Rettich 2005: 32).

Both from the EP's and the European citizens' point of view, the lack of public presence of such a decisive factor in Europolitics as the EP, at least since 1993, has serious repercussions in terms of influencing the content of their decisions; no citizen can influence a decision that s/he does not know about. Consequently citizens are alienated from day-to-day Europolitics which nonetheless concerns and affects them.

It must be acknowledged that from the citizens' point of view, even Euro-elections seem displaced; they appear too dispersed, at a distance, over a wide-spread continental domain. But, if the media do not make this prime political event visible in all its facets, then they are guilty of rendering it invisible, semi-visible or incomprehensible: out of sight out of mind. Thus, the EP is gradually evolving into something of a second-rate political entity. This degradation is certainly evident when comparing the participation rates in national and European elections. The drop in citizens' participation in Euro-elections over the last decade is a particularly worrying case in point.

The other interesting observation made in the German study is that the 'scornful' treatment of the EP by national media is more or less uniform. Different media do not vary significantly from one another in their ignorance of the EP. As a general rule, "the media only rarely see an occasion for reporting positively on the work of the EU parliamentarians" (ibid: 32). Reporting on EU integration, in general, rises during election years. It is, thus, inferred that while Euro-elections have a catalysing affect on public perception of the topic of 'Europe', the event of the Euro-elections *per se* was not properly reported (Brettschneider & Rettich 2005: 33). Besides, according to Jochen Peter (2004: 148), whenever television did cover the Euro-electoral campaign, this usually occurred in the less-prioritised items of the news bulletins. It was observed for instance that EP issues never "led the news". Surprisingly, perhaps the mediatic degradation of the EP is comparable in both commercial and public channels. "Even public television aired more pieces on the European Soccer Championships (which only started on June 12) than on the European parliamentary elections." Besides, European Parliamentarians are "evaluated more negatively than federal and state politicians, who voice their opinions on Europe." (Brettschneider & Rettich 2005: 33).

This uniformly marginalizing attitude towards an elected, and unique in its kind, institution is most perplexing. To start with, unlike the Council of Ministers, the EP is in constant operation. Moreover, in the light of the 'democracy deficit' debate, the EP is the most transparent and the most accountable institution of all four, if we also include the ECJ (Sbragia 1993). Such a 'hostile' media projection, then, cannot be explained logically, nor is it justifiable. On the other hand, as has been seen in a number of the media policies analysed in previous chapters, the EP has pioneered in political communication and in media democracy policy issues; in this vein, it has often taken radical and disagreeable positions against major commercial operators in its attempt to safeguard the public interest. More particularly, in the case of the frustrated policy towards pluralism and control of media concentration, the EP positioned itself against the views of ACT and of the European Association of Newspaper Proprietors (ENPA-CAEJ). In this light it could be argued perhaps that effacing the political role of the European Parliament, particularly by such commercial media is not entirely accidental. In any case the study of this uneven relation crystallises the formidable dependence of the political order on the media order in post-1989 Europe.

Generally, however, the EP appears to be sharing the roughly similar grey 'fate' of non-mediatic existence as the European Commission and the Council of Ministers. It should be noted, however, that even if the members of the Council do not attract general or continental-size media attention, as such, nevertheless, each Council member enjoys adequate publicity in his/her governmental capacity within the domestic framework by the nationally 'fixed' media. In this, then, they find themselves in a comparatively advantageous communicative position in relation to the EP and the Commission.

Commissioners appear to be utterly disappointed by the kind of 'press' the central bureaucracy of the EC gets. Indeed, many commissioners have criticised the media coverage of the EU, sometimes in quite harsh terms. Some will even go as far as to accuse journalists of a form of "European Treason". For example, a member of De Silguy's[147] cabinet lamented that "in five years of work on a crucial issue, we never once made the headlines on the 8 o'clock news'." (Smith 2004: 8, Fn. 12). Significantly, the crucial issue in question was an historic event: the introduction of the common currency, the Euro. As is also underlined by Peter Ludes, below, a comparative study in five European countries established an inexplicable lagging behind of the national media on the reporting of such a crucial event in the life of Europeans (ibid: 216-7).

Given this systematic snubbing of EU processes, it is astounding to read in the Commission's recent Plan-D that its dreams for re-invigorating democracy, dialogue and debate should be realised and also take place on television. "Finally, the debates can only be a success if the mass media are engaged in the process, in particular television." (Commission 2005a: 3).

Here then we observe a confluence of three interesting but incompatible realities which reveal a logical caveat and political impotence. (1) The EU as a theme is belittled by the media. (2) EU politicians do not dare to regulate television through 'must carry rules'. (3) The EU launches a Plan-D which it relegates to the mass media, notably television, and whose success is predicated on their engagement.

---

[147] Commissioner for the economic and financial affairs' portfolio.

"The current crisis can be overcome by creating a new consensus on the European project, anchored in citizens' expectations." (ibid: 3), the Plan-D strategy goes on. In the circumstances, however, of communications policy paralysis, the 'crisis' is most certainly here to stay.

The Inadaquacies of Existing Transfrontier Channels

Over the last 20 years a host of transnational channels have sprung up to occupy the market space that was opened up by new technologies such as satellite and digital telematic systems. Today there are more than one hundred transnational channels operating in Europe. Significantly, however, over 80 per cent of these channels hold a license from the UK Ofcom Authority. Britannia apparently now rules the airwaves! These channels vary in a number of ways: transnational transmission scope, language, type of programming output, type of ownership (private vs. public) and indirect or direct commodification (advertising vs. subscription channels). Chalaby (2002: 186) notes that "among the transnational channels that are pan-European in scope, 17 are particularly prominent" in the sense that they have a strong distribution in at least five EU countries and that they demonstrate an expansive strategy. Among them figure Arte, BBC Prime, BBC World, Bloomberg, Fox Kids, MTV, Eurosport, Cartoon Network, TV5, CNN International, Sky News and Euronews. These channels are transmitted to about 24 territories and are received by approximately 40 million households in the EU. The great majority of these channels are commercial in nature and most of them are mono-thematic. Significantly, these are for the most part dominated by entertainment contents (e.g. music, film or sport).

The overwhelming majority of these channels are commercial enterprises which by extending into the transfrontier territory are mainly or exclusively seeking to expand their market basis. As such, they are neither interested in nor suitable for serving the objectives of a European political communication as they are rather in the business of selling

Europeans to advertisers and advertised from the global market. As such, not only do they not promote civic and political goals or desiderata, but they even work against them. One classical way of obtaining this result is by occupying viewers' total attention span with broadcast material of the 'lowest common denominator' and by aspiring to 'entertain us to death'.

To assess the nature and the extent of *transnationality* and to classify the differences of degree between these channels we can apply certain criteria. These should include (a) the range of transmission in a territorial sense, but also the scope in a geo-political or geo-linguistic sense; (b) the type of ownership and management; (c) the type of content in the sense of internal pluralism, pluralism in content sources and of reflecting the observed needs across Europe, rather than applying a show-business, supply-side policy; (d) the language of transmitted contents, i.e. in the *lingua franca* (English), in local languages or in both; (e) the profile and strategy including business strategy or the profile of a distinctively psb channel; and last but not least, (f) the content of current public affairs and of a participatory political culture, which is the specific prerequisite at issue here.

On the basis of these criteria we can single out just two channels which demonstrate a relatively more complete 'transnationality': Arte and Euronews. Both of these are positive on most of these counts, though in varying degrees.

Euronews ,a news-only, satellite-transmitted channel, is definitely the most transnational of the two as it broadcasts in five languages simultaneously (Purvis 1999: 36), across 16 countries and it is *multi-nationally* owned. Euronews was originally launched by eleven members of the European Broadcasting Union (EBU) later joined by another eight members. Together they hold 51% of the shares while the remainder 49% is owned by the London–based, news-production company ITN (Purvis 1999: 36; Machill 1998, Maggiore 1990: 73).

In spite of this advanced degree of transnationality, Euronews is still far from being a channel that fulfils the necessary criteria of a truly transnational, supra-national or pan-European channel that would be committed to the citizens of the EU or to the politics of Europe at large. To start with, it neither reaches nor is it interested in reaching all or most European viewers. In fact, in its promotion profile, it stresses the fact that its focus is on "high-income earners and businessmen." More specifically, it states that it is targeting the top 20% of households, by income, in 16 countries as measured by European Media and Marketing survey (EMS). Thus, the most fully–fledged, transnational, continental channel reaches about a quarter of European citizens, while its basic criteria of targeting them are class-bound and economic. Evidently the supply of the channel's broadcasting content is shaped accordingly.[148] Compared to Europa TV in terms of output programming, Euronews is pluri-national rather than non-national (Theiler 2001). Moreover, as stated by Schlesinger, "stylistic constraints and limited resources have led to a rather characterless journalism, heavily tied to pictures rather than analysis, with little that is characteristically European about its news agenda" (1994: 42).

Their news menu is limited to business and global news or snaps of high Euro-politics. Such an editorial strategy is certainly influenced, if not dictated, by the need to compete with channels such as CNN. Nevertheless, Euronews, which took off with EU financial support, prides itself as holding the position of "Europe's own news channel, providing world news from a European perspective" (Purvis 1999: 37). In regard to European affairs, it also features regular Commission-sponsored programmes about the EU policies and institutions which cross the boundary between "neutral information and 'infomercial'-type of self-promotion" (Theiler 2001: 9). This signifies also that Euronews does not stand up to the most elementary psb principles, for example of universal access and internal pluralism.

Therefore, in the existing nationally- and transnationally–shaped, mediatic constellation, it is precisely the possibility of a unitary and universal form of addressing Europeans which is lacking in terms of both networks and contents. Thus, effectively, in the post-1989 and post-TWFD era, a common electronic public space has been denied to citizens,

---

[148] Information derived from the Euronews web-site.

due to deregulation, harsh commercialisation, competition for audiences and the trend towards lowest–common- denominator programming.

In such circumstances the potential for creating a common European public space, in the foreseeable future, is extremely slim. Even if one agrees with Habermas on what is needed for the EU to meet its present challenges, the means for providing the solution to these needs, in the present circumstances, are elusive. Thus, the impasse over such political *desiderata* persists, seemingly beyond the concerns of European media owners, and even the journalistic communities, whose frame of reference is also nation-centric, or vaguely global, and also of politicians. The latter are particularly constrained when they have to operate "against the economic and journalistic interests of the broadcasters" (Hoffmann-Riem 1992: 163). Consequently, while civil society tends to be neutralised in regard to such goals, media agencies appear to disregard them. Civil society cannot achieve very much, on its own, as it itself requires to breathe publicity the air of publicity, in public space and time. In particular, on such a large continental scale, this may be provided exclusively by interactive, electronic, television broadcasting networks. In other words, civil society is not getting the mediatic support and disseminating power which it desperately needs first for its survival and secondly for its activism.

What is needed is a specific communication system attached to the new political entity and to its corresponding civil society. This is all the more critical as this political system is still constituting itself and developing in both ambitious and peculiar ways. The low-key approach adopted in the early years of the Customs Union, in communicative terms, may well be the opposite of what is currently required. Indeed, as Thompson (1995: 14), who projects the ideas of Max Weber, argues "the capacity of a state to command authority is generally dependent on its capacity to exercise two related but distinct forms of power, which I shall describe as coercive power and symbolic power." The EU in its current phase of development seems to rate very low – if at all – on the latter count.

Small Audiovisual Exchanges between Europeans

One of the recurring findings of the implementation studies on the TWF Directive is that there are extremely low exchanges of transfrontier programming between national channels of different member states. As has been shown in Chapter 4 (TTR 1994, GPEAP 1994, Holznagel 1993) non-national broadcasts in each member state predominantly originate in the US and to a minute degree from other European producers, or from elsewhere. This is another significant manifestation of the 'mutual rejection' of fellow Europeans. Europeans' notorious ignorance about European affairs and institutions – the basic profile of the Union and its composite parts – is thus further augmented by not watching programmes made in other European countries.

This looks like a peculiar European 'allergy', yet it is more a market-driven than a sociological condition. The fact that the market was left effectively unregulated thanks to the notorious 'where practicable' phraseology of the 'quotas' articles transformed audience ratings companies into the sole controllers and the true regulators of all TV programming. But a basic community survival instinct suggests that the people of the EU need to learn about each other. One of the key characteristics in screening quotas was the striking neglect of the need for the inter-penetration of 'European works' into each others' TV systems, both in cultural and business terms. This (potential) real interest, although taken up in the policy rhetoric, was then abandoned. Cultural integration is supposedly desired, but the accepted equation of 'European production' with 'national productions' makes this a remote possibility.

The makers of the TWF policy can thus boast that the largest single common programming type now viewed by Europeans on national or 'transfrontier' television consists of exports from Hollywood. And both the last and the ongoing revision of the TWF Directive guarantee the perpetuation of this situation. As Collins stresses, during the elaboration process of this Directive some of its internationalist integrationist aspects were actually dropped (Collins 1994: 67). A proactive role for states to promote cultural interpenetration actively by encouraging the 'presence of other European cultures' (Commission 1986a: 24) in the domestic TV programming of each member country did not gain support. Instead of cultural integration, emphasis was placed on cultural distinctiveness and diversity (Collins 1994), as though these two were absolutely mutually exclusive. This rather facile and simplistic navigation between policy priorities ended up, in fact, as a non-community-building policy. The wave of reactions from introverted 'nationalists', thus tied in well with the powerful commercial pressure to set up and adopt this policy without any serious analysis of its deeper political implications and its long term socio-cultural effects. Rather than European integration, national introversion and nationalistic approaches were reinforced under the umbrella of *diversity*.

James Curran identifies three reasons why television is still quite nationally oriented: (a) that viewers prefer to watch nationally-made programmes[149] (b) that consumers preferences are reinforced by political power, notably by national policies of governments (e.g. public finance), and (c) economic reasons: "much of the staple of national television output – such as news, chat shows, game shows and sport – is relatively cheap to produce." (Curran 2004: 193). Papathanassopoulos stresses that "localisation is a strong strategy for survival" and that "there is no channel with an international strategy that has not tailored its content and schedule to cater for local differences" (2002: 161). Thus political economy ties in well with socio-cultural inertia and national governments will to frustrate proactive policies and to keep constantly regressing to the *status quo*.

With so little inter-European penetration of programming contents, why would anybody hope, with Jürgen Habermas,[150] that this would occur with live or ephemeral material like on-line news or the daily press? This is unrealistic. Thus, a policy process which took off on the hype of 'cultural

---

[149] This is concurred by de Bens and Smaele (2001), who observe that demand for stock and fiction programming (soap operas, situation comedies and drama) is nationally/culturally determined.

[150] See relevant discussion in Chapter 1.

integration' thus produced the opposite result in terms of policy for TV programme screenings. "The draft Directive had prioritised unity, the Directive emphasised diversity" (Collins 1994: 67). So it appears that both political and cultural integration were useful only as opportune invocations for the justification of the EC's intervention in this policy domain and the control of communications by the fiercest of market forces.

Effacing Politics and Depoliticization

One could expect at least from public television, especially in view of Euro-elections, "that the media (a) inform about (sic) topics that are relevant, thereby creating interest in the election and showing alternatives; (b) that they vet the democratic process and (c) provide space and airtime to European integration", argue Brettschneider & Rettich (2005: 33). In short, that the media serve the simple and minimum democratic requirement of "providing information, articulation, control and platform for public discourse" (ibid). The actual coverage did not meet this expectation, though these are the absolutely minimum requirements for politically reliable and democratic media.

Whenever the problem of the inadequate representation and airing of EU affairs in national media is raised, media owners and news editors tend to claim that such issues are not covered because the public does not care about them (Panagiotarea 2005, Stangos 2004). In other words, they claim that the people (viewers, listeners and readers) do not create demand for such issues. Similarly, in a survey among German journalists at the beginning of the 1990s, 47% of the editors interviewed responded that it was not their job to promote the emergence of a European sense of community (Shoenbach 1995: 27 cited in Brettschneider & Rettich 2005: 33). This editorial stance, which is shared rather broadly and is of an explanatory but also a defensive nature, in fact confuses political activism (Europeanism) with professionalism. Unless journalists admit that they no longer have any role to play in democratic polities, such stances and responses are – democratically – indefensible. As Brettschneider & Rettich aptly argue, "one should expect from the media that they [at least] cover relevant issues and offer the people an opportunity to find out about world events, in order to then form their own opinions. When it comes to Europe, they basically fail to do so." (2005: 33).

Citizens and civil society members who retreat *en masse* from politics and even from their electoral rights/obligations may then justifiably claim that the great majority of people are *naturally* disinterested about a political regime which ignores them patently and which does not learn about them or inform them via the requisite communication system. Undoubtedly, the problems identified by the long-term German study are not restricted only to that country. Indeed, evidence from other member states or from relevant analyses on EU matters suggests that this is a general problem afflicting most member states.

On the basis of a comparative study of the press coverage on the introduction of the Euro currency in Germany, France, the UK, the Netherlands and Switzerland, Peter Ludes (2004: 216-7) establishes the failure of national media to cover this historic European-wide policy choice adequately. He remarks particularly that the "media coverage of the Euro, lags behind the prerequisites of long term trust", which is implicit in such a major leap ahead as the giving up of the national currencies and the adoption of an entirely new one. Overall, he also assesses that "national frames and concerns overshadow European perspectives" and that nationally oriented mass media "inadequately convey the historically new phase of monetary and economic European Union". So, "despite the considerable convergence of living conditions in the EU, mass media distribution and usage may well differ more fundamentally" (ibid). Thus, Ludes' conclusions concur with most of the other evidence concerning the phenomenon of national media effectively ignoring or significantly downplaying important EU issues. These media not only fail to reflect reality accurately, but in fact distort it. What emerges, then, here, is a *discrimination* against *Europolitics*. Even if we assume that this is not an intended outcome but a collateral one, the damage is still too important to be left un-remedied.

Biased but Saleable News

National media do not only neglect or unduly play down important European affairs. In fact, some of them drastically counteract European integration by the ceaseless supply of systematically biased reports. A comparative content analysis between British and Romanian newspapers on how these covered the issue of enlargement of the EU with the accession of the ten new member states in May 2004 is highly representative. This comparative approach per se is interesting as it is also original. However, the most striking element documented in this study is the sheer anti-Europeanism and the nationalism of the British press. In her analysis Ruxandra Trandafoiu argues that the widespread phenomenon of Euroscepticism, which is largely cultivated by national and often explicitly nationalistic media, shows that the idea of a 'united Europe' is not to be taken for granted at all.

The generous, but somewhat elitist, idea of a united European continent, she says, has never managed to be translated into popular language. A lot of media in many European countries, of which the UK is, arguably, the starkest example,[151] are so Eurosceptical and even explicitly anti-EU that it is difficult to anticipate a time when the media will be bringing the European project to the eyes and ears of the people of Europe in an objective and a more positive light (Trandafoiu 2005). The concern here is about how and why *Europeanness*, that is, the discourse on what it entails to be European, has paradoxically ceased to assist the

---

[151] This is a discourse analysis of the English press at the time of the 2004 EU enlargement. It is based on a selection of London-based newspapers, the tabloids *The Sun* and *The News of the World*, the mid-market papers *The Daily Mail* and *The Mail on Sunday*, and the broadsheets *The Independent*, *The Independent on Sunday*, *The Financial Times* and *The Business*. The papers were monitored over a period of two weeks, Monday 26 April to Sunday 9 May, one week before and one after the enlargement on May 1st 2004.

building of a European identity. Quite to the contrary, in fact, Europeanness today seems to be used by various national media precisely to boost nationhood in tandem with Euroscepticism.

"It is hard to bring Europe to most editors' attention, unless it is about scandals or problematic cases. There are reasons for doubt that this coverage adequately reflects politics in Brussels and Strasbourg." (Brettschneider & Rettich 2005: 33). The dynamics and the working practices of 'negativism' and of 'sensationalism' are deeply ingrained in the political-economy framework of competition. Thus, the routines of editors and journalists are admittedly counterproductive in this respect. These dynamics are reinforced by various ethno-centric, nationalistic approaches or simply stances rebuffing Europeanness as competition often assumes the format of national antagonisms. In order to even start looking for a common perspective, rather than projecting Europeans through the 'us against them' filter, such attitudes would need to be cleared away. As already mentioned, however, this is hardly a matter of editorial choice or policy. Editors in fact admit to self-censorship, censorship proper and 'manufacturing' of 'events', crises and scandals (Goldberg 2002, McManus 1994, MacGregor 1997, Tumber 2004). This in itself proves the superordinate control by commercial criteria of the profitability of a media company via the profitability of sensationalism. Here then we observe several forces at work for the production of bias. The problem of negativism in press coverage is inherent in the political economy of this – by now wholly – competition and profit-driven sector. This condition, profitable though it is, is also politically corrupting and thoroughly affects public policy (Tumber 2004).

This, then, is a manifestation of how the term *Europeanness* is constantly loaded with negative connotations. It is, thus, associated with the set of the 'unsolvable problems' of the 21st century, as it is blamed for the possible loss of (national) identity. The problem is manifest in the role of 'nationalist' or 'nation-centred' media. The crucial question arising out of this account is: what needs to be done for national media "to change their role so as for them to translate Europeanness into a popular, but not populist, language? How can national media help in the construction of an inclusive and meaningful European identity rather than the contrary?" (Trandafoiu 2005).

Such questions were of course answered indirectly by the German editors in interviews referred to above. The problem is not mainly one of journalistic agency and, hence, convincing the members of a key agency group. Since the media are in the business of producing profit, they could not care less how they go about doing it. The structure of competition – for sales, advertising revenue and 'saleable news items' – is the *automatic pilot* which sets the rules of this game. In this respect the media ceases to play the classical political game of primarily brokering information. It chiefly brokers huge chunks of capital and this cannot be 'changed' by any moral persuasion of journalists or editors.

The pattern of 'negativism' in media coverage results from the compulsion of the media to attract the largest shares of audience. This harsh political economy of advertising-dependent media in its turn results in 'strong news selection' and *agenda-setting* practices (McCombs 1972).

Programming and editorial policies of commercially-driven and advertising- financed media, notably TV stations, are predominantly determined by what is saleable. Populism is thus to a large extent sustained structurally. Ever since the enforcement of the TWF directive and the establishment of the so-called transfrontier 'European Audiovisual Space' (EAS) the vast majority of media belong in this category. Over the last decades, the TWF policy has converted advertising into the *de facto* and official censor of all information flows and into the strategic controller of this domain. This means that commercial media also largely set the intra-sectoral agenda of what will be published. These mega-censors of our time are profit-driven and 'have to' resort to sensationalism, negativism and infotainment. This condition means that such media are effectively in the business of producing ignorance structurally. Their output compounds the primary problem of ignorance produced by (a) minimally useful information and (b) the lack of dedicated pan-European media. Moreover, the majority of the media that broadcast transnationally are also nationally-oriented and driven by the same competitive dynamics.

On top of this, media moguls exchange favourable visibility to 'co-operating' governments for industrial policy favours. Thus, there is a strategy of a mutual exploitation between top politicians and the 'select few' of media proprietors.[152] Overriding even the agenda-setting thesis, scholars refer to controlling media practices in relation to politics in general. In this conception, the media not only set the terms for the political, but they colonize the space of politics and control both the news agenda and the power game (Meyer 2004). As a result of such market-driven processes, "political consciousness has also been profoundly affected by the 'mediatisation' of life both at work and at home, as well as of party politics." (Leys, 2001: 36). It is hardly surprising then that the former mass parties have by now "been converted into elite organisations of a new type and party membership and electoral participation have declined" (ibid: 36).

Given this dark and threatening set up, the inevitable question that is posed for the leadership of the EU is whether any political entity can condition its visibility, its transparency and the dialogical facilities of its constituent parts on the basis of whether these activities sell according to the criteria of commercial media and their public imitators. The fact that such media *are not delivering* democratic, political, communication framework should then be a matter for a different communicative policy, arguably a policy based on a different market structure and additionally on 'must carry rules'. The very legitimacy of EC institutions rests on their visibility, transparency and accountability and on the provision of communicative facilities to citizens. And in politics legitimacy is existential.

---

[152] Such previleged relations have been remarked on by the press for instance about the relationships of Kirch and Bertelsmann with Kohl and between Murdoch with Thatcher and with Blair.

In Search of a Medium for Pan-European Political Communication

Without condoning the biasing practices of national media or underestimating their responsibility, it is wrong to place all expectations on national media for informing European citizens or for offering them spaces for dialogue. For a number of reasons, some of which have been discussed in Chapter 1, these objectives are quite beyond the capabilities of the national media. Only a supra-national, independent, non-profit-making medium, which would be exclusively politically accountable, can assume such a strategic role.

National media including national psbs have their own agendas, some of which run directly counter to the political integration of the EU. The UK maintains for example a thriving BBC World Service, funded by its Foreign Office. This broadcasts political news programming to 'the world' in several languages many of which many European. Yet, the UK actively subverted the attempt to even try establishing a similar service for all Europeans. This is evident in its obliging the BBC to withdraw from its participation in the Europa TV project. The same applied also for the withdrawal of France's Antenne 2 (Theiler 2001: 5, Maggiore 1990: 71). As a consequence there arose a strongly negative climate against establishing and supporting something like a *European Broadcasting Corporation* (EBC) in the form of the Europa TV. The invocation of such criteria as 'national sovereignty' and 'cultural diversity' is, then, quite useful as it is also opportunistic in serving hegemonic goals.[153]

Thus, the lack of information on national media is just one of the factors which contribute to ignorance. Moreover, this is up to some extent unavoidable as the scope of those media is merely local, regional or national. By definition, such media cannot tackle, let alone resolve, a

---

[153] "There are, however, indications that such scepticism regarding the EU's audiovisual Europeanization agenda did indeed extend beyond the ranks of its most explicit opponents. This came to the fore in the widespread lack of enthusiasm for Europa TV" (Theiler, 2001: 25, Footnote 14). The attitude of the UK within the EU in most if not all communications policy matters has been utterly hegemonic. (See for example Kaitatzi-Whitlock 1998 and 1996).

communicative gap the political-geographic expansion of which is larger than the area of their own coverage. Neither can such expectations be met by commercial (national or transnational) media, as the main objective of those is profit through competition. This being in the nature of commercial media, the third factor, the absence of a pan-European public channel, that would be free of national considerations, obsessions or commercial burdens is all the more critical. It is, then, the responsibility of a more overarching, pan-European agency to fill these gaps. The absence of a channel *dedicated* to the pan-European coverage of Euro-political affairs is certainly a greatly missed opportunity for the European Union.

The Frustrated Pan-European Channel

The concept of a pan-European channel appeared for the first time in one of the very first motions by the then fledgling European Parliament. The original EP motion of 1980 accurately stated the problem facing the EC: "reporting of European community problems by national radio and television companies and the press has been inadequate, in particular, as regards integration" (EP 1982). It is amazing to see that 25 years later, the same situation stands today. As has been shown and discussed in the previous units of this chapter, narrow 'national approaches' or biases and under-mediatisation still plague the coverage of the 'topic of the EU'. When drafting the original EP proposal for an initiation of a common audiovisual policy, the relevant EP report argued that: "Information is a decisive, perhaps the most decisive factor in *European unification*" (Hahn Report 1983: 7). In line with this argumentation, in fact, the Hahn report and the associated resolution proposed the establishment of an *ad hoc* transborder television channel for broadcasting on common pan-European affairs and transmitting them to all Europeans. This was an exciting idea as such to many but when it came to implementing it, things were less bright and Europeanism ceased being stimulating (Dacheux 1994: 192-3).[154]

That proposition came to nought, although some interesting attempts were made in that direction.[155] The EP and those sections of the Commission that favoured proactive policies persevered in establishing a pan-European channel. Eventually, two concrete attempts towards this end materialised. The first was the *Eurikon* experiment and the second *Europa TV*.

Fifteen European broadcasters gathered forces in 1983 and cooperated with the EC, also under the auspices of the EBU, in an experimental supply of television programming in simulated broadcast conditions. The Eurikon experiment lasted for five weeks and five of the fifteen broadcasters involved also assumed the responsibility of contributing programming. Each of these five broadcasters also had the responsibility of running the programme for one week. The experiment entailed that programming was supplied to invited viewers in a closed-circuit video system and to a specialist panel that was expected to monitor and assess this operation and to conduct audience research as well (Collins 1993a: 165-166).

The menu of Eurikon featured roughly the entire repertoire of a generalist psb channel – news and current affairs programming, documentaries, feature films, music, sport, light entertainment, and children's' and religious programmes (Negrine & Papathanssopoulos 1990). The launching of Eurikon starkly exposed the existing divergences between national cultures and tastes. It also demonstrated reluctance on the part of the 'public' to cross over to an alternative cultural output of non-national origin. Linguistic barriers, interest disparities and stylistic heterogeneity were most perplexing for the proponents of this project, i.e.

---

[154] "...une télévision publique européenne, car la 'culture participe au processus de prise de conscience de l' Europe'. " Dacheux 1994: 192).

[155] As has been discussed in Chapter 2, this was the original demand of the EP in the early 1980's, on the action of which the EC grasped the control of communications policy. This demand, however, still persists.

the Commission and the EP. In effect, they could find no common 'vector' between the styles of the national segments. As a result, conclusions as to how to proceed towards a potential pan-European television plan in the future did not materialise. The Eurikon project was a first test to assess the feasibility and viability of a transnational channel. Even though five weeks hardly constitute an adequate time scale, in a way the Eurikon experiment can be viewed as the pilot project for the concept of Europa TV.

Notwithstanding the negative results of Eurikon, three years later, a bold new initiative followed: Europa TV. This first publicly-funded, pan-European channel started broadcasting in October 1985. Though original aspirants had been many more, eventually only five European public service broadcasters, from Germany, Italy, Ireland, the Netherlands and Portugal, participated to form the consortium for this operation. Financially, Europa TV depended on funding from the Commission of the EC, the Dutch government, the broadcasters themselves involved in it and – as was anticipated – advertising revenue. The budget assigned to this path-breaking channel for its first three-year period was set at 35 million Swiss francs.

Linguistically, Europa TV catered for the languages of the participating broadcasters. The ambition of Europa TV was for it to be genuinely pan-European on a number of counts: geographical scope, blend of output programming, and management. "In many respects Europa TV lived up to the expectations that had previously been spelled out" for it (Theiler 2001: 5, Maggiore 1990: 71) by the EP and the Commission.

In terms of programming content, it broadcasted a menu similar to Eurikon. However, the key emphasis here was that news and features would be presented not from a national but from a distinctly 'European perspective'. To this effect, editorial and news gathering teams were structured in order "to avoid the dominance of any single national group" whereas "[a] comparative approach became the essential feature of Europa news portrayal. A non-national perspective was encouraged by all available means." (Maggiore 1990: 71). One of the key challenges faced by

Europa TV was the compiling of an enticing programme policy. Because Europe is culturally and linguistically fragmented, this was a critical imperative. Significant common issues for Europeans are certainly not exhausted in narrowly defined policy matters such as those are reported from the Brussels journalistic arena. Yet, the goal to create and transmit contents of *common interest* for such a broad Union proved both quite challenging and elusive.

In terms of style of policy-making, among the significant features of the Europa TV project was that "broadcasters such as the BBC and France's Antenne 2, decided – or were made to decide by their respective national authorities – not to participate in the project" (Theiler 2001: 5). In November 1986, just over one year after its launch, that promising channel folded up, urgently pressed to do so by financial failure and indebtedness. According to Negrine and Papathanassopoulos (1990), at the time of folding up, its accumulated debt came to £3.7 billion. Even if the immediate reason for the failure of Europa TV was a matter of faltering finances, this was far from the only reason. This politically and culturally promising experiment failed through lack of economic and political support, but was also actively undermined, indeed sabotaged.[156] "Many national governments [refused] to secure the Union-wide distribution of its signals and adequate funding." (Theiler 2001: 3).

The failure of Europa TV, like that of Eurikon, was blamed on the unwillingness of viewers in a linguistically and culturally fragmented continent. So the tool (pan-European TV) that was supposed to be the vehicle for Europeanising the public was anticipating a ready made Europeanised audience right from the start! Rather than being assisted patiently and slowly arriving at a new condition, European viewers had to prove *a priori* that they were at that destination in great numbers! But this is absurd. It is to confuse *means* with *ends*. Even plain observation of human inertia indicates that individuals prefer, at first, to continue with their acquired habits and routines. This is exactly why incumbent

---

[156] For more details, see also Zimmer, 1989, European Institute for the Media, 1988, Lange & Renaud, 1989.

companies and practices usually have comparative advantage over newcomers. Rupert Murdoch was cross-subsidizing Sky Channel for years from the profits of his other companies. Yet, certain European governments expected Europa TV to be self-financing – by one third – even in its first year of operation.

At an initial phase, the success of a channel of such a character cannot be predicated either on massive viewerships or on economic viability in the sense of covering even part of its costs through advertising revenue. Such a channel ranked as a real challenge and an innovation in many ways and was bound to come up against all sorts of difficulties. Most innovations take years before they are broadly adopted (Rogers 1962). In other words, a project like that could not be undertaken half-heartedly or be abandoned as easily.

So, the main criticism to be made in the face of the twin fiasco of both these bold projects is that European politicians themselves betrayed the goal of European integration by abandoning the project for a European political communication. National egoisms and national hegemonic stances prevailed once again. [157] "The Europa TV experience showed the need for initiative at the root, i.e. in relation to the training of journalists", argued Maggiore (1990: 71) who thus restricted his emphasis mainly to limited agency factors.

In respect to the difficult issue of finding interesting common contents to attract various European national viewers, a point can be made about the absence of innovativeness and participatory formats in the supplied programming. An experimental approach was required in every meaning. Hesitation or inability to overcome traditional patterns or standard paternalistic formats may also be blamed for the fiasco. Citizens, particularly the young, do not only have informational gaps. They also

---

[157] As pointed out "it is difficult to assess the extent to which such opposition enjoyed the tacit support of other member states. Since the countries mentioned (and especially Denmark) seemed so staunchly set against the Commission's audiovisual aspirations, governments which shared similar reservations could afford to exercise restraint in their display of overt opposition and yet be assured that the commission's efforts would remain fruitless" (Theiler 2001: 25fn14).

have primary needs for dialogue. Citizens need to express and exchange their views on crucial issues. In other words, communication rights involve not only issues of the spread of information and knowledge but also matters of opinion and views on how things could be done alternatively. Unless people are taken seriously, they will not respond. Members of the general public in such circumstances possess no particular motivation "to engage in the required cognitive investment. More profoundly still, their reticence to change is compounded by the fact that so few efficient symbolic mechanisms exist which might encourage a rearticulation of their habitual framework of references" (Forêt 2003: 82).

For this to be accomplished, apart from a common language of communication, a common or at least converging political culture is also required. And this can only emerge slowly through systematic perseverance and cultivation. It cannot appear automatically. Osmosis between Europeans can only arise out of the potentiality of shared spaces for dialogue and from integrated processes of 'political will' formation. Consequently, so far, the discrepancies between Europeans as individuals and as nationals are growing rather than being bridged, and this is happening in the name of diversity.[158]

There are no Democracies without Democrats

Whatever the reasons, the lack of pan-European media that provide political information corresponding geographically to the EU constitutes a crucial problem for any democracy. The agencies of the EU, particularly the Commission and the EP, are weakened, and citizens alienated from the political process. This brings up a serious challenge that has often been a matter of concern. Both EU parliamentarians and Commission politicians and functionaries are concerned about their lack of 'public

---

[158] Common symbolic manifestations are other important aspects of a shared political culture, but such celebrations, rituals, and common bank holidays are also, as yet, rather scarce in the EU. See also Forêt (2003).

image' and their withering legitimacy. Such concerns peak whenever there are negative popular manifestations which demonstrate the loss of legitimacy such as the recent negative referenda in France and in the Netherlands (2005).

The Treaty of the European Union at Maastricht provoked a rise in popular disaffection and this became an issue in 1993-1994. The then Commissioner of culture at DG X Joao de Deus Pinheiro set up a strategic special Unit to take care of matters concerning the public image of Community institutions and of the Commission. This special Unit encompassed *inter alia* also a 'users council'. Moreover, it proceeded by ordering an *ad hoc* investigation of such growing civilian disaffection and the formulation of proposals for politically pertinent measures in the face of this challenge. Indeed the brief of the 'committee of wise men' chaired by the Belgian MEP Willy De Clercq was to produce a policy draft for the entire college of Commissioners. The De Clercq report was submitted promptly in the spring of 1993 and amounted to a strategy which would enable EC institutions as well as member states to respond to the needs, the concerns and the hopes of European citizens at a decisive moment for the process of European integration (De Clercq 1993: preamble). There was a special effort to examine the European situation from the perspective of citizens or even to bring citizens back into the game, if not into the epicentre, of European developments.

Yet, in the climate of the new rise of neo-liberal forces with the Bangemann group and APEWIS, and the pressures for further liberalisation and privatization De Clercq's recommendations appeared to be 'too political'. Thus, just as with the concurrently presented Think Tank Report (see chapter 3), Commissioner Pinheiro did not dare to translate any of the recommendations of the De Clercq report into actual policy proposals.[159]

It should be highlighted that the neutral or negative reception of the De Clercq report by the press (Tumber 1995: 517) itself contributed to the abandoning of the idea of any action on it. But, as we have seen, the

---

[159] See also Tumber (1995: 517), Stavrakakis (2004: 29), Smith (2004).

press is generally mean or negative about Europolitical developments. Hence, to expect any different press coverage for such a 'radical' and an alternative step would be, to say the least, odd. Reactions against such measures were arguably more deep seated and more compelling. One needs only to be reminded of the climate of the then emerging 'global coherence' among the members of the G7 (See also chapters 6 and 7).

Since the still-born De Clercq report, no communicative initiative or political communication strategy has been designed or adopted by the EU from the perspective of its citizens. Given that the diminishing legitimacy of EU agencies is by now galloping, they may end up by employing PR programmes to keep this tendency in check. Thus twenty years after the Hahn report, the situation regarding 'the national control of mass mediated information' remains fully in tact. The only difference now is that the control of the media is still mainly national and almost entirely in the hands of commercial media barons.

The media can thus be seen to exercise power over political entities on a number of levels. (1) They control the agenda of output contents in the media they own and so they can efface or give substance to the 'public existence' of political agencies such as the Commission and the EP. (2) They influence the conduct of such 'public image starved' political agencies, as these go out of their way to attract the slightest media attention. And finally, (3) the media control the agenda of policy-making itself in the field of communications.

Producing Citizens' Ignorance at a Profit

Since the under-mediatisation and mis-representing of Europolitics is now a well-researched and demonstrated reality, it needs to be addressed in political terms. The production of ignorance it implies impacts directly on European political culture and *mores* that prevailed until recently. *Knowledge is power,* while ignorance means powerlessness as well as political impotence. Hence, this communicative deficit is subversive of the European polity, but eventually also for the member states that comprise it.

According to the Eurobarometer survey of 2003, when EU citizens were asked if they consider themselves informed or not about political decision-making and the institutions of the EU, 71% answered "little or not at all informed" and 25% "adequately informed". The equivalent Eurobarometer figures for 1973 were 63% and 25% respectively (Peel 2004: 13).[160] So despite the recent media explosion and information cornucopia, more Europeans – three quarters of the total population – are dissatisfied with their political information today.

The widespread political ignorance of Europeans has been attested by various surveys and analyses (Peel 2004: 13, Meyer 2005, Golding 2005). But are national media the key or the only perpetrators of this? And does the observed ignorance apply just to Europolitics or does it increasingly pervade the entire spectrum of political issues? The fact emerging from the 2004 Eurobarometer survey was that "there is still an awful lot of ignorance about the EU – and often more in the old member states than in the new." (Peel 2004: 13). Gullibility is a function of ignorance and the growth of naive mystifications, xenophobia, nationalism, racism and new 'superstitions' is not unrelated to a certain brand of commercial television 'culture' which aims to 'entertain' or to *infotain* us at any cost. Thus, we observe a demonstrable ignorance of EU affairs among EU citizens, an ignorance that is testified by a broad spectrum of sources.

Surprisingly, "the 'knowledge gap' research has revealed that the spread of television consumption to more and more people involving larger segments of their time does not equalize the stock of politically relevant knowledge among subgroups of society, but instead widens such gaps between them" (Meyer 2002: ix). Such a *knowledge gap* is primarily due to the prevailing tendency of commercial television to show torrents of homogenised contents of the lowest common denominator (Kaitatzi-Whitlock 2004). If this continues, the problem of ignorance will become

---

[160] For recent data on the decreasing popularity of the EU see also http://europa.eu.int /comm/ public opinion/archives/eb/eb63/eb63 en.htm.

increasingly dense and widespread. From the early 1990s, analysts were already pointing to a growth in capital formation and in the administrative and the regulatory development of the EU without commensurate public knowledge (Hjarvard 1993: 90, Gerhards 1993: 99-101). But democracy cannot live on just economic growth. It requires knowledge and communication. The problem of modern citizens and capitalism is to reconcile the two.

The surveys and content analysis studies discussed here testify to the lack of due reporting on European Union issues. But national media are not entirely to blame for the prevalence of such ignorance. Ignorance-producing factors include (1) the arguably intentional under-mediatisation of Europolitics in the national news media both commercial and psbs; (2) the biased and systematically Eurosceptical media contents as a function of commercial saleability; (3) insignificant audiovisual production and other cultural exchanges between European countries; (4) the absence of appropriate Pan-European Media.

Depoliticization and other Structural Implications

Disaffection, a distancing from and lack of interest in EU politics was clearly demonstrated in the Euro-elections for parliamentary representatives in May 2004. This is undoubtedly also linked to the demonstrably low level of media coverage on supra-national EU affairs and the lack of accessibility of EU citizens to common EU media. The former indicates the lack of an *imagined common European identity*, while the latter the direct contemporary causes for it. This – to say the least – constitutes a severe political problem. But until the two alarming referenda of 2005, it persisted unchallenged. This impasse perfectly suits the interests of those economic and socio-political forces that, either because of their globalist or commercial and concurrently nationalist preferences, work against the political integration of Europe: the creation of a more accountable and stronger power formation. However, in many

European countries there is something more worrisome than disinterestedness. There is a growing *anti-Europeanism* which often reflects very legitimate worries. This is evidenced by the dismissive referenda in Denmark, Norway and Switzerland and the notorious anti-Europeanism of the UK. Plainly, in these countries, *nationalism* or *ethno-centrism* prevailed over *Europeanism* (Mazower 1998).

In spite of a common European television policy, originating in the famous TWF Directive of 1989, today there is no common European public sphere, nor any clear sense of European identity. As is shown by a number of Eurostat surveys, the phenomenon of disinterestedness keeps growing as well along with that of ignorance. Thus, participation in the electoral process for the EP of June 2004 dropped dramatically throughout the 25 EU member states. The level of absenteeism was over 50%, for the first time in its history. Such a level of absenteeism, in the core democratic institution of the EU, is an alarming measure of political crisis and the ideological confusion of the EU. Participation was quite high in the two recent referenda in France and Holland in May 2005, but returned huge percentages of disapproval for the European constitutional convention. People are clearly disaffected with the way Europolitics are run and with the undignified treatment they receive as citizens.

Given the under-mediatisation of European affairs, the lack of media networks to address these needs and active communication rights of citizens and the perpetuation of ignorance and the effects of it, the long term structural implications for the EU are ominous. Consequently, communicative deficits can only be remedied if the original decision to put the control of the communications into the hands of private and unaccountable agencies is reconsidered.

By the same token, depoliticization derives from the EC's policy-making in communications. But the observed phenomenon of depoliticization is not just a produced affect. It is itself transformed into a cause of socially and politically undesirable ideas and conduct such as xenophobia, introversion, fear of the others etc. Depoliticization, indifference and cynicism become the growing ingredients for future boomerang effects.

The Disempowering of European Citizens

Control is vital for community and polity building and for the 'fair' negotiation and allocation of all power. As Karl W. Deutsch (1963) expertly argues, citizen feed-back processes of control are a *sine qua non* for the function of the democratic political system. Similarly, Edgar Morin (1986), and Norbert Wiener (1949) also stress the fundamental notion and function of control for the sustainability, the equilibrium, of any system. It is imperative that political control be granted to and shared among communities and citizens. Drawing on findings of political psychology, Stanley Renshon (1979) stresses that the need for personal control is existential. To this Seligman et al. additionally assert that people are "happier, healthier, more active, solve problems better, and feel less stress when they are given choice and control" (Seligman et al. quoted in Shapiro 1999: 240).

For a regeneration of politics and any power shift to happen, Habermas puts his hopes on organised civil society. However, the means to organise in today's large, social, continental-sized, community constellations are largely provided and colonised by the media. Individuals, in fact, are not considered as proper citizens at EU level, as the prior qualification of employment insert a derogation on citizenship as this applies to national constitutions.

What can citizens do to stop this from continuing or to change such premises? In order to achieve anything in the way of large scale organisation, citizens need to dispose of their free and unhindered public space – a public space which is not privately owned nor commercially controlled. Hence, in the prevailing circumstances, most notably at EU level, citizens are locked out; they are excluded from the temple of democracy.

Europeans are faced with an absence of common, pan-European networks. This void is usually blamed on the linguistic fragmentation of Europe, which is indeed a serious barrier. But, if this can be overcome for parliamentary and political discussions and decision-making, it can also be overcome for pan-European information media, as is shown in the case of Euronews. The true cause is that mass-mediated information is controlled by global media barons and other self-interested actors both at national and transnational levels. Hence, the intermediate political agency of the EU is submerged. It is not surprising then that analysts doubt the viability of a Unified Europe. If about 80% of the decisions which determine our lives as Europeans are taken in Brussels, the malaise may recover when dedicated overarching pan-European information networks materialise. If these networks do not materialise then the 'ever growing gap between being influneced by something and participating yourself in its change' (Habermas 1994 quoted in Chryssochoou 2005: 88) will never be bridged. Neither will there be chances to create a European *demos* and a polity.

The *mediatic deficit* is a crucial composite part of the *democratic deficit* as political accountability is directly linked to publicity and to transparency. In its turn, the *democratic deficit* makes people suspicious and dismissive. "The opacity of decision-making processes at the European level, and the lack of opportunity for any participation in them cause mutual mistrust among citizens" (Habermas 2001: 14-15). For decades, the democratic deficit and political accountability to electorates was considered one of the thorniest problems of the EC.[161] Implicit in the *media deficit* and the *democratic deficit* are two strong undercurrents that undermine the advance of the project of the Union. Such challenges and pressures stifle the process of the Union's political integration, which has resulted in the creation of a politically unaccountable and low key entity. The point made then here is that the position against the political integration of the EU is neither endurable nor defensible.

---

[161] This problem was most intense until 1992 when the EP acquired increased co-decision powers. This has improved further since thereby superseding a circumscribed legislative role for the EP.

Chapter 9

CONCLUSIONS

In this study I have analysed key aspects and crucial moments of European policy-making in the field of communications in order to establish whether and to what extent the EU has attempted and succeeded in safeguarding the political-communication prerequisites of a democratic polity in the making. A novel political entity of 25 states and 457 million inhabitants (Commission 2005), which has been proclaimed a 'Union' and accorded European citizenship in 1992, appears still today to lack an overarching, commonly- and universally–accessible, minimum system of political communication. This entail that very many of its citizens not only cannot learn about their European *res publica*, their common political system in Brussels, but also about each other. This deficit means that European citizens cannot dialogue in common public *fora* about their common affairs. They have no means to symbolically and discursively approach each other or even liaise among themselves. Can this be deemed to be a democratic political union? Even if modelled on the least demanding theoretical model of "democracy as a marketplace" Meyer 2002: 4-5), it still falls short on fundamental democratic premises.

The proclamation of the Union and of European citizenship in 1992 gave a prime opportunity to correct the aberration and the shortcomings of the 1980s, which had, ostensibly by default, led to a market-driven regime. Communications policy on television could now be grounded anew on constitutional political values. However, as my analysis indicates, the EU, intergovernmental system repeatedly failed utterly to defend the functions of political communication: (1) through the revisions of the TWF Directive (2) through the frustrated 'pluralism' and anti-concentration of ownership policy, (3) through the issue of the allocation of control of conditional access TV systems and (4) through the adoption and pertinent action on the recommendations of the De Clercq report.

Instead, on the one hand exclusively pro-market and on the other hand nation-centred policy options have continued systematically to prevail throughout the 1990s and up to the present. The epitome of the failure of this approach is that the supra-national political system, as a political and policy producing subject (Commission, EP, Council and ECJ), is itself the prime victim of a peculiarly European pathology of being rendered *incommunicado*. These political and policy entities are largely effaced by the media. This condition, however, deprives Europeans of even the most elementary crucial political information and, thus, erodes the last vestiges of the system's effective transparency and legitimacy. So, is this system political, in liberal democratic terms? Are the policies the system itself produced and is still producing compatible with its self-proclaimed 'political identity' or with the idea of European citizenship?

The *thesis* of this book is that communications policy-making, element (A) of the dialectical triangle, is the means by which politics and the political are organised. The type of communications policy pursued in the EU over the last two decades undermined both element (B) at EU level and politics as such element (C), in the broad sense. The *specificity* of political communication in the context of a constellation as peculiar as the EU – which accrues in a cross-division at two levels (see Figure p. 48) – was never addressed nor was it catered for at both these levels. In fact, communications policy was exploited to turn the terms of the agenda upside-down. It was used in order to privatise and to commodify the domain of communications and of the most popular and accessible mass medium, television. By the same token, it pursued and successfully achieved the now lamented and feared condition of de-politicization.

If we look at the Figure on page 48 again, we see that in the beginning of the 1980s most member states[162] found themselves in the position of

---

[162] With the exception of Italy, Luxembourg and, to some extent only, the UK, member states had no privately owned and advertising-financed channels.

Box 1, that is, using television broadcasting mainly or exclusively for political, cultural and non-profit purposes.

In a positive appreciation of the democratic-political role of electronic media, after the 'Europeanization' of the electronic communications media in the 1980s, both in individual member states and in the EU as a whole, both aspects of communication (political/economic) should have been safeguarded. That is, both the political and the economic aspects and roles of television should be guaranteed at both the national and the supra-national, pan-European levels and, thus, all four boxes of the Figure should have been operable. What we observe, instead, is that the role of broadcasting that was forged and that prevailed is just limited to those in Boxes (2) and (3).

Consequently, first, commercial, profit-seeking channels have come to dominate over or to eliminate political and cultural ones at both national and transnational levels. Moreover, at national level these commercial channels threaten to subvert the residual, political-communication functions, which have managed to survive usually in the form of the psbs. Secondly, sustainable communication channels of pan-European scope for addressing supra-national, political-communication needs were never allowed to materialise. Consequently, the overall political-communication functions are decreasing dramatically, with dire consequences in terms of depoliticization. The accruing condition of depoliticization entails not only the proliferation of apolitical genres, but also of the commodification of citizens themselves.

The second significant division in the European constellation in respect to political communication, derives from the very nature of the political entity in question, split as it is between the national level and the overarching supra-national level. This specificity of the EU, inevitably, presupposes that that dual nature of communication (political/economic) must be preserved and guaranteed concurrently at both levels of this political formation, the national and the pan-European. Yet, as we have observed (in chapters 5 and 6 for example) the intervention of the EU in communications policy has totally failed to deliver democratically and politically indispensable premises.

But, where exactly does the communicative deficit originate and, most crucially, why is it continuing to plague EU citizens and politics?

The original aberration was to do with the placement of the media sector, by the EC communications policy (element A), in the Internal Market framework. This strategic choice determined that the field of communications be handed over, by the leading politicians of the time, exclusively to market forces and explicitly for profit and growth. Attempts to rescue some vestiges of political communication at least at the nation-state level, through the acknowledgement of public-service broadcasting in the pertinent Protocol of the Treaty of Amsterdam, could hardly make up for that strategic mistake and the structural hurdles that it established. In addition, because psbs operate at national level and, by definition, are nation-centred in their approach, they can never compensate for the crucial deficit in pan-European political communication (Box 4 of my schema).

The loss of several political battles by the EP and the other 'pro-political', integration forces to the fierce neo-liberal camp, which was in the ascendance ever since the 1970s, not only in Europe but world-wide, cost European politics dearly. Yet, the very first involvement of the EU in this policy field took off in response to EPs calls for the creation of pan-European communications channels and for establishing a common, political-communication space. Rather than political communication, through its 'Flagship of the Single Market', the notorious Green Paper on Television Without Frontiers, the Commission succeeded in turning everything upside-down leading to a phenomenal aberration. With unshakable arguments grounded in pertinent ECJ jurisprudence and in the shortcomings of the TEC, it launched the most ferocious attack on the political-communication systems upheld at that time by the member states.

In this way, proponents of that Green Paper won two victories in one blow: first, to liberalise, to completely commodify and deregulate the electronic media market across the Community and, secondly, to effectively subvert the nation states' sovereign prerogatives on electronic communications. This dual victory of the ultra-neoliberal forces within and outside Europe entailed essentially the privatising of the control of the communications sector across the board. In effect this entailed the 'feudalising' of a vast amount of political, social and economic power. Silvio Berlusconi and Rupert Murdoch are just the most notorious cases in point. This power conversion inevitably entailed that there would be no ground for political demands to be expressed. It also meant that demands for civic and participatory political communication would never be given any realistic opportunity within the EU polity, despite the fact that interactive technologies are by now completely amenable for such practices. Such an objective, in the form of a counterfactual, is totally adverse to strategic neo-liberal and monopolistic goals. Effective monopoly holders – in all market segments – relentlessly maintain the sole control and the exploitation of the entire communications space.

Commercial tendencies, such as the trend towards 'infotainment', put severe pressure on previously existing forms of political communication in the member states. Thus, it assessed that the victory of the Green Paper on transfrontier television, and thereby on European politics, set the terms of the game for a long time to come. Twenty years later the same forces rule and exploit Europe's public domain, depriving it of the chances for building up political communication and of sustaining European citizenship.

Both the absence of an elementary, common, political-communication framework and the continued refusal to introduce pertinent, 'must carry rules' thereof, in the ongoing revision of the TWFD, testify to a control of the agenda by those forces which counteract EU citizens' political-communication rights. Similarly the refusal to introduce provisions in favour of interactive uses of mass media by citizens for a pan-European, communication potential for civic purposes is another case in point.

Overall, the policy instances I analysed show that European and global ultra-neoliberal forces are exploiting both the communications field and

European citizens as their proprietary feudal terrain. The two revisions of the TWF (one still on-going), and the attempt at a policy for 'pluralism and the control of media concentration' demonstrate the formidable power of economic agency over political agency. These developments reveal that economic forces alone control the political agenda, hence the 'divorcing of politics from power'. The grip of television, and the media more broadly, over European citizens, thus, seems overwhelming, perhaps even terminal. The EP and its allies continued to be defeated in the continuing policy-making battles of the 1990s. Their policy proposals were either entirely frustrated or at best a weak, symbolic recognition.

In the face of such pervasive, neo-liberal incursions, certain member states reacted defensively by launching strategies hinging on the notion of diversity. In trying to save what could be saved, the notion of *diversity* conferred some protectionist brakes. However, if we carefully consider the notion of cultural diversity, for a Union which ostensibly is aspiring to full integration, in fact, it constitutes a regressive, nation-centred ideology. It is a contradiction in terms to aim at political integration while at the same time working to preserve or to reclaim 'national otherness'.

Strategically, the 'diversity' argument is as subversive of the European integration project as is the commodification of politics. The 'diversity' argument can, therefore, only be appreciated as a last minute tactical ploy to prevent the complete take-over of the media field by cultural imperialists and global, feudal, media barons, for example by rescuing the psbs. Regarding European integration, the tactics of national, cultural protectionism is counter-productive, while it does not face up to or deal with the problems of the commodification of citizens or of depoliticization.

Pluralism and diversity are important and valuable conditions in a self-respecting democracy. However, for these values to exist and to thrive, a different market structure is required, one that is kept constantly under political check and that does not commodify viewers and citizens. Alternatively the rhetorical invocation of such notions serves purely ideological ends. It is most characteristic that the consultation process for the pluralism and media-concentration checks, almost unanimously called for bold EU intervention and tight regulation in order to establish a decent minimum balance between the dominant oligopoly of market forces and all other interested parties, stake-holders and citizens.

Yet, through its 'decision not to decide' on this issue, the EU virtually declared itself powerless against the oligarchy of market forces. Judging by the recent developments in the ongoing revision process the neo-liberal grip on the communications domain in the EU seems to be still as unshakeable as it is destructive for the formation of a political union. Commission cabinet members do not hesitate to declare that 'the best mechanism for value allocation in this market is competition". The implications of the failure to regulate the sector against trends towards media monopoly are ominous, politically embarrassing, and lethal.

The *deficit in political communication* is, thus, a key constitutive element of the *democratic deficit* of the EU today. Unless some severe re-orientation takes place in the vital domain of political communication, a European, democratic, political entity will not come into existence and depoliticiza-tion will keep growing, as will their collateral damage. In the words of the Chancellor of the Weimar Republic, Hermann Müller, in 1930 "a democracy without democrats is an internal and external danger".[163]

The communicative deficit along with the derivative democratic deficit, thus, combine to mock and demoralise citizens, provoking cynicism and reactionary attitudes, un-democratic mind-sets that lead to the dangerous depoliticization. The EU as a political construct and Europeans as its citizens have everything to gain from communications policies to strengthen the European democratic process, among which the establishment of a pan-European channel to fill the gaps created by nation-centred and commercial media. Otherwise we can only look forward to the further growth of ignorance, nationalism and gullibility.

---

[163] Quoted in Mark Mazower 'Dark Continent' (1998: 22).

References

(includes interviews and EU documents)

Agence Europe, 'Mr Monti plans next year to propose directive on access to media ownership'. 28.9.95: 7

APEWIS – see Commission (1994a).

Apter, David E. (1977) 'Introduction to Political Analysis', Cambridge Mass., Wintrop.

Aristotle (1962) *Politics* Trans. Sir Ernst Barker, Oxford, OUP.

Aristotle (1992) *On Rhetoric* Trans. George A. Kennedy, Oxford, OUP.

Ayer, D., et al. (1982) 'The Business of Motion Pictures', in G. Kinden (ed.) *The American Movie Industry*, Southern Illinois University Press.

Bachrach, Peter & Nelson S. Baratz (1970) *Power and Poverty: Theory and Practice*, Oxford, OUP.

Bachrach, Peter & Nelson S. Baratz (1962) 'The Two faces of Power', *American Political Science Review*, 56: 948.

Bachrach, Peter & Nelson S. Baratz (1963) 'Decisions and Non-Decisions: An Analytical Framework', *American Political Science Review*, 57: 632-642.

Bagdikian, Ben (1983) The Media Monopoly, Boston, Beacon Press.

Baisnée, Olivier (2004) 'The politics of the Commission as an information source', in Andy Smith (ed.) *Politics and the European Commission* (pp. 134-155), London, Routledge.

Baldi, Paolo (ed) (2004) 'Broadcasting and Citizens' European Association for Viewers Interests (EAVI), EACTV Project, Rome: Edizioni Eurispes.

Baldwin F., McVoy D.S & Steinfeild C. (1996) *Convergence: Integrating Media, Information and Communication*, London, Sage.

Baltzis Alexis & Sophia Kaitatzi-Whitlock (eds), (2005) *Innovations and Challenges in European Media,* Thessaloniki, University Studio Press (in Greek).

Barber, R. Benjamin (1984) *Strong Democracy: Participatory Politics for a New Age*, Berkeley, University of California Press.

Barker, P. (1988) *Satellite Broadcasting in Western Europe*, MA Dissertation, London, City University.

Barnett, S. (1991) 'Why Satellite Television is Pie in the Sky', *The Independent (Media)* London, 17.7.91.

Barnett, S. (1993) 'Cross-media Ownership: Who is the Ring Master in the Information Circus?', *Intermedia* Jan/Feb 1993, Vol 21 No 1.

Baumann, Zygmunt (2005) *Each Time Unique*, Lecture at the London School of Economics, www.lse.ac.uk/collections/LSEPublicLecturesAndEvents/ events /2005/htm. 8.11.2005.

Bell, Daniel (1973/6) *The Coming of Post-industrial Society*, Perseus Books.

Berstein, Serge and Pierre Milza, (1994) *Histoire de l'Europe, Etats et identité européenne*, (Vol 3) Paris, Hatier.

BEUC (1986) *Bureau Européen des Unions de Consomateurs*, 'BEUC is disappointed by the C.EC proposal on transfrontier Television', press release, 10.6.86.

BEUC (1995) interview by the author with BEUC officials Carsterns and Mosca – 2.12.1995.

Blumler, J.G. (1992) *Television and the Public Interest*, London, Sage.

Bobbio, Norberto, (1993), The Future of Democracy, Thessaloniki, Paratiritis (in Greek).

Bourdieu, Pierre (1997) 'Sur La Télévision', Paris: Lieber-Raisons d'Agir.

Boyd-Barrett, O. & P. Braham (1990) *Media, Knowledge and Power*, Routledge, London (first published by Croom Helm, 1987).

Brettschneider, Frank, & Markus Rettich (2005) 'Europe – A quantité négligeable', *Media Tenor* (1/2005)

Broadcast, 1.10.93 (Baker & O'Carroll).

Broadcast, 1.11.94, 'Parliament Blasts EC Ownership treatment'.

Broadcast, 10.10.91 (Moullier).

Broadcast, 18.6.93: 122, 'TV spent outpaces economic growth'.

Broadcast, 18.6.93: 18, 'New era for broadcasters'.

Broadcast, 8.10.93 (A. von Gamm).

Burgelsman, J. C. & C. Pauwels (1991) 'Growing Convergence between Broadcasting and Telecommunication: Policy Problems at the level of the Commission of the EC', *Telematics and Informatics*, Vol. 8, No 3: 5-141.

Burgelsman, J. C. (1995) 'Assessing information technologies in the information society: the possible relevance of communication science and research'. in Calabrese et al (eds.) *Information Society and civil society. Contemporary Perspectives on the changing World Order*, West Lafayette, Purdue University Press.

Cable & Satellite Europe 'Yes it was a fudge' (editorial) August 1991: 42.

Cable & Satellite Europe 'Down to the Wire', July 1991: 16.

Cable & Satellite Europe, January 1990.

Cave, M. (1989) 'Regulating a Partly-Deregulated Broadcasting System' in Hughes & Vines (eds) *Deregulation and the Future of Commercial Television*, Aberdeen University Press.

Cawkell, Tony, (1988), *The Telecommunications Power Game*, Oxford-New York-Amsterdam, Elsevier Advanced Technology Publications

Chalaby, Jean (2002) 'Transnational Television in Europe: the Role of pan-European Channels', European Journal of Communication, Vol. 17(2): 183-203.

Chryssochoou, D. N. (2005), *Towards a European Res Publica*, Athens Papazisis (in Greek)

Cockfield, Lord V.P. (1986) 'The future of Television in Europe', *EBU Review Programmes, Administration Law*, Vol XXXVII, No 6 Nov. 1986.

Cohen, Bernard (1963) *The Press and Foreign Policy*, Princeton NJ, Princeton University Press.

Collins R. & Murroni C. (1996) *New Media, New Policies*, Polity Press, Cambridge.

Collins Richard, (1993a), Public service Broadcasting by Satellite: Eurikon and Europa, Screen, 34 (2), 162-175).

Collins, R. (1993) *Audiovisual and Broadcasting Policy in the European Community, London, University of North London Press*

Collins, R. (1994) *Broadcasting and Audiovisual Policy in the European Single Market*, London, John Libbey.

Collins, R., N. Garnham & G. Locksley (1987) *The Economics of Television*, London, Sage.

Colombo, Fausto (ed.) (2004) *TV and Inetractivity in Europe: Mythologies, Theoretical Perspectives, Real Experiences*, Milan, Vita & Pensiero-Strumenti..

Commission (1983) *Realities and Tendencies in European Television: Perspectives and Options* (25.3.83) X/12/83 COM(83)229, Brussels.

Commission (1984) Green Paper: *Television Without Frontiers*, 8827/84, COM(84)300, 23.05.84, Brussels (GPTWF)

Commission (1985) *Completing the internal market*, White Paper, COM(85)310.

Commission (1986) *European Broadcasting*, 6739/86 (March 1986) COR 1 COM(86)146, Brussels.

Commission (1986a) *The European Broadcasting Policy (Scope and purpose of the proposal for a Directive)*, Explanatory Memorandum, Bulletin of the European Communities Supplement, 5.6.86.

Commission (1988) *Towards a larger European Audio-visual market*, European File, C.EC, Luxembourg, February 1988, 4/88.

Commission (1989) *Europe – 1992: the report on the Single European Market*, Communication from the Commission, Brussels, Vol.1: 325 1.10.89.

Commission (1992) *Europe and the Technologies of Information and Communication.* (Booklet) EEC DG XIII, Office for Official Publications, Luxembourg: 28.

Commission (1992a) *A Television for tomorrow* (Booklet) DG XIII, Office for Official Publications, Luxembourg.

Commission (1992b) *Pluralism and Media Concentration in the Internal Market (an assessment of the need for Community action)*, Green Paper, COM(92)480.

Commission (1993) *Complementary Questionaire relating to the Green Paper 'Pluralism and Media Concentration in the Internal Market'*, COM(92)482, Brussels.

Commission (1993a) *Proposal for a Directive of the European Parliament and of the Council on the use of standards for the transmission of television signals (including repeal of Directive 92/38/EEC)*, COM(93)556 -COD 476, 15.11.93.

Commission (1993b) *Communication from the Commission to the Council and the European Parliament, a Framework for Community policy on Digital Video Broadcasting.* COM(93)557. 17.11.93.

Commission (1993c) DG for economic and financial affairs, *The European Community as a World Trade Partner*, No 52 1993, Brussels.

Commission (1993d) *Suggested Guide-lines for the Monitoring of the TWF Directive*, Brussels 15.02.93.

Commission (1993e) *Conclusions of Hearing on Concentration* 26-27.4.93.

Commission (1993f) *Reply to a written question No. 2597/92 Mary Bannotti* OJ C 195/14, 19.07.93.

Commission (1993g) *Livre Vert de la Commission 'Pluralism et concentration des Médias dans le Marché interieur – Evaluation de la nécéssité d'une action communautairé', Commentaires des parties intéréssées*, DG XV/E/5, Bruxelles, Volume I: *Contributions des fédérations européennes*, 29.04.93 – Volume II: *Commentaires des parties Intéréssées autres que les fédérations professionelles européennes*, 29.04.93 – Volume III: *Fédérations européennes*, 26.07.93 *Réponses au questionnaire complémentaire du 28 juillet 1993* – Volume IV: *Fédérations européennes*, 01.02.94 – Volume V: *Commentaires des parties intéréssées autres que les fédérations professionelles européennes, 09.02.94.*

Commission (1993h) *Proposal for a Directive of the European Parliament and of the Council on the use of standards for the transmission of television signals (including repeal of Directive 92/38/EEC).*COM(93)556 – COD 476, 15.11.93.

Commission (1993i) *Growth, Competitiveness, Employment: The challenges and their confrontation for the Transition to the 21st Century.* White Paper, COM(93)700, Brussels 5.12.93. ('The Delors White Paper').

Commission (1994) *Communication to the Council and the European Parliament on the Application of Articles 4 and 5 of Directive 89/552/EEC Television Without Frontiers*, COM(94)57, Brussels.

Commission (1994a) *Action Plan on Europe's way to the Information Society*, (APEWIS), COM(94)347, 19.7.94. Brussels.

Commission (1994b) *Green Paper on European Audiovisual Programming* COM(94)96, Brussels. (GPEAP)

Commission (1994c) 94/922/EC: *Decision of 9 November 1994 relating to a proceeding pursuant to Council Regulation (EEC) No 4064/89 (IV/M.469 - MSG Media Service)* (only the German text is authentic) *OJ. L 364 , 31/12/1994 : 0001 – 0021.*

Commission (1994c) *Rapport sur l'Application de la Directive, elabore conformement a l'article 26*, COM(94)524 and 524/3, Brussels.

Commission (1994d) *Communication from the Commission to the Council and the European Parliament, Follow-up to the consultation process relating to the Green Paper on 'Pluralism and media concentration in the internal market – an assessment of the need for community action'* COM(94)353, 05.10.94.

Commission (1994e) *Amended Directive proposal on the use of standards for the transmission of television signals, (including repeal of Directive 92/38/EEC).* COM(94)455 – 94/476 COD, 25.10.94.

Commission (1995) *Pluralism and media concentration in the internal market, Questionnaire No. III concerning a possible initiative on media ownership,* DG XV unit E/5, Jan 1995.

Commission (1995a) *Revision de la Directive Television sans Frontieres 89/552/CEE Version revisee du document COM(95)86/2* COM(95)86/3, Brussels.

Commission (1995b) *Communication de la Commission au Parliament Européen et au Conseil relative à la Révision de la Directive 89/552/CEE Visant a la Coordination de certaines Dispositions Legislatives, Réglementaires et Administratives des Etats Membres Relative à l' Exercise D'Activités de Radiodiffusion Telévisuelle 'Télévision Sans Frontières', Rapport d'application et éxposé des motifs, Proposition de révision.*

Commission (1995c) Marcelino Oreja statement – internal document 17.3.1995.

Commission (1997) *Television Without Frontiers,* OJ L202 30.7.1997.

Commission (1999) *Communication from the Commission to the Council, the European Parliament, the European Economic and Social Committee and the Committee of the Regions, on principles and guidelines for the Community's audiovisual policy in the digital age* (COM (1999) 657 Article 10(1).

Commission (2000) *Directive of the European Parliament and of the Council of 8 June 2000 on certain legal aspects of information society services, in particular electronic commerce, in the Internal Market* (Directive on electronic commerce), 2000/31/EC.

Commission (2002a) *Audiovisual Policy,* www. europa.eu.int/comm/avpolicy/ regul/regul_en.htm (accessed 5 Feb. 2003)

Commission (2003) *Fourth Report to the Council and the European Parliament on the Application of the TWF Directive* Brussels, C.EC 06-01-2003

Commission (2003a) *Communication from the Commission to the Council, the European Parliament, the European Economic and Social Committee and the Committee of the Regions, on principles and guidelines for the Community's Audiovisual Policy,* Brussels (15.12.2003) COM(2003)784 final.

Commission (2004), *Interpretative Communication on certain aspects of the Provisions on Televised Advertising in the 'TVWF' Directive,* Brussels, 23.4.2004 (C-2004) 1450.

Commission (2004/5) *Proposal for a Directive of the European Parliament and of the council Amending Council Directive 89/552/EEC on the coordination of certain [rovisions laid down by law, regulation or administrative action in Member States concerning the pursuit of television broadcasting activities* (approved 13.12.2005).

Commission (2005), *Key Facts and Figures: about Europe and the Europeans,* Brussels DOR Press & Communication

Commission (2005a) *Communication from the Commission to the Council, the European Parliament, the European Economic and Social Committee and the Committee of the Regions. The Commission's contribution to the period of reflection and beyond: Plan D for Democracy, Dialogue and Debate* COM(2005)494 final, Brussels 13.10.2005

Council (1989) *Directive on the co-ordination of certain provisions laid down by law, regulation or administrative action in member states concerning the pursuit of television broadcasting activities*, (TWFD) EEC/552/89, 3.10.89. OJ L 298/23, 17.10.89.

Council (1989a) *Regulation of on the control of concentrations between undertakings*, EEC/4064/89, OJ L 395/1-12, 21.12.89.

Council (1993) *Resolution of July 1993, on the Development of Technology and Standards in the Field of Advanced Television Services.* OJ C 209/1, 3.8.1993.

Council (1993a) *Decision of 22.7.1993, on an Action Plan for the Introduction of Advanced Television Services in Europe. (93/424/EEC)* OJ L 196/48, 5.8.93.

Council (1994) *Commissioned Report by the High Level Group on the Information Society, Europe and the Global Information Society, Recommendations to the European Council:* 1-35, Brussels 26.05.94.

Council (1994a) *Resolution of 27.6.1994, on a framework for Community policy on digital video broadcasting*, OJ C 181/3, 2.7.94.

Council (1995) *Directive of 24.10.1995 on the use of standards for the transmission of television signals, repealing Directive EEC/92/38.* OJ L 281/51-54, 23.11.1995.

Council (2005) www.europa.eu.int/comm/dgs/information_society/directory/index_en.

Council of Europe (1991) *Which Way Forward for Europe's Media?*, 3rd European Ministerial Conference on Mass Media Policy, Sub-theme 1 – Media Economics and political and cultural pluralism, Working Party on CDMM (9-10 Oct. 1991).

Council of Europe (2003) *Conclusions regarding the TWF Directive*, (OJ C 13, 18.1.2003: 1).

Crick Bernard (2002), *Democracy: a very short introduction*, Oxford, OUP

Cuprie, E. (1984) *Advertising, Cable and Satellite*, Manchester, European Institute for the Media.

Dacheux, Eric, (1994), Les Strategies de Communication pPersuasive dans l' Union Europeene, Paris, L' Harmattan – Logiques Sociales.

Dahl, R. A. (2000) *On Democracy*, New Haven, Yale University Press.

Dahlgren, Peter, (1995), *Television and the Public Sphere: Citizenship, Democracy and the Media*, Sage, London

David, P. A., & Shurmer, M. (1996), 'Formal Standards-Setting for Global Tele-communication and Information Services', *Telecommunications Policy*, Vol. 20 (10), December, 789-815.

De Bens, Els & Hedwig de Smaele, (2001), *The Inflow of american Television Fiction on European Broadcasting Channels Revisited*, European Journal of Communication, Vol 16, No 1: 51-56

De Clercq, Willy (1993) *Reflections on the information and communication policy of the European Union.* Report of experts presided over by Willy De Clercq MEP, March 1993.

De Jonquires, G. (1994) 'Brittan wants rights on WTO agenda', *Financial Times*, London, 24.03.94.

Delors, J. (1994) European Audiovisual Conference keynote speech July 1994, Brussels, DG X.

Deutsch, W. Karl (1963) *The Nerves of Government*, New York, The Free Press

Doutrelepont, C. & P. Eeckhout (1994) 'Rules of the Game after the Uruguay Round', *Sequentia*, Sept/Oct 1994, Vol 1 No. 1.

Druesne, G. & Kremlis, G. (1990) *La Politique de Concurrence de la Communauté Economique Européenne*, Presses Universitaires de France.

Ducatel, Kenneth, Commission cabinet member, interviewed by the author, 28.11. 2005.

Dupagne, M. (1992) 'EC policymaking: The case of the 'Television Without Frontiers' directive', *Gazette*, 49: 99-120, Netherlands, Kluwer Academic Publishers.

DVB, 'DVB Agrees Final Elements of Conditional Access Package', press release, 7.3.95: 1, Frankfurt.

DVB, 'Television for the Third Millennium: Going Ahead With Digital Television', DVB Project Office, September 1995, Geneva.

DVB News 'Draft Digital Terrestrial Specification approved by DVB Steering Board', & editorial, June 1995: 1-2.

Dyson, K. & P. Humphreys (eds) (1990) *The Political Economy of Communications*, London, Routledge.

Eberle, Carl-Eugen (ZDF Legal Department) interviewed by the author, 12.10.1995.

EBU, (2002), *Media With a Purpose: Public Service Broadcasting in the Digital Era*, The Digital Strategy Group of the EBU, Version DSG 1.0, November 2002, Geneva

EC (1987) *European Community Treaties* Abridged Edition, Brussels-Luxembourg.

EC/EU (1992) *The Treaty of the European Union*, Brussels-Luxembourg.

ECJ (1973) *Sacchi case*, No. 155/73, 1974.409. ruling: 30.4.74.

ECJ (1980) *S.A.Compagnie Générale pour la Diffusion de la Télévision Coditel, and Others v. S.A. Ciné Vog Films and Others*, Case No. 62/79, 18.3.80.

ECJ (1980a) *Procureur du Roi v Marc J. V. C. Debauve & Others*, Case No. 52/79, 18.3.80.

ECJ (1988) *Vereniging Bond van Adverteerders & Others v. State of the Netherlands*, Case No. 352/85, 26.4.88.

ECJ (1989) *Stichting Collectieve Antennevoorziening Gouda et autres et Commissariaat voor de Media*, Case No. C288/89, 30.8.89.

ECJ (1989a) *German TV Films: The Community v Degeto Film GmbH and Others*, Case No. IV 31.734, 15.9.89.

ECJ (1990) *Re. the Application of the European Broadcasting Union (EBU)*, Case No. IV, 32.150, 5.10.90.

ECJ (1991) *ABC/Generale des eaux/Canal+/WH Smith TV*, Case No. 91/CF, 244/06, 10.9.91.

ECJ (1992) *Prior notice of concentration Sunrise*, Case No. IV/M.176, 13.1.92.

ECJ (1992a) *Commission Decision relating to a proceeding pursuant to Article 85 of the EEC Treaty – Screensport/EBU Members*, Case No. IVI32.524, 19.2.92.

ECJ (1992b) *La Cinq SA V. Commission of the European Communities, Case No. T-44/90, 24.1.1992 & Appeal* Case No. C-98/92P, 27.3.92.

Eco, Umberto (2003) 'The EU Between Renaissance and Decline', La Republica/'Bibliothiki', (Literary supplement of Eleftherotypia) 11/07/2003: 16-21.

Economist, 'HDTV – All Together Now', 29.5.93: 74.

EIM (1987) *Towards a European Common Market for Television: Contribution to a Debate*, European Institute for the Media and the European Cultural Foundation, Manchester, Media Monograph No 8., Manchester University.

EIM (1988) *Europe 2000: What kind of television?*, Television Task Force, (president: Valéry Giscard d'Estaing) European Institute for the Media and the European Cultural Foundation, Media monograph No 11, Manchester University.

ENPA (1995) European Newspapers Association study and consultation to the EP's Media Committee.

EP (1979) *Resolution on Misleading Advertising*, OJ 140/23) 5.6.79.

EP (1980) *Motion for a resolution on radio and television broadcasting in the European Community*, EP Doc. 1-409/80

EP (1982) *Resolution on Harmonisation of provisions related to TV Advertising*, EP Doc. 1-187/82.

EP (1982a) *The Hahn Report and the Resolution of 12.03.82, on Radio and Television Broadcasting in the European Community, European Communities Official Journal*, OJ C 87/109 – 112, 05.04.1982.

EP (1982b) *Resolution on the Consequences of TV Advertising*, EP Doc. 1-120/ 82.

EP (1983) *Resolution on the promotion of film-making in the Community Countries*, OJ C307: 16-19.

EP (1985) *Resolution of 10.10.1985 on the adoption of a framework-Directive regarding a policy in the audiovisual sector,based on the Green Paper of the C.EC for the creation of a common audiovisual market, particularly by satellite and cable.*OJ C 288/113, 11.11.85.

EP (1988) *Amended Proposal for a Council Directive Concerning the Pursuit of the Broadcasting Activities*, Legal Affairs Committee, OJ C 110/21, 27.4.88.

EP (1990) *Resolution on media takeovers and mergers*, OJ C 68/137-138. 15.02.90.

EP (1992) *Media Concentration and diversity of opinion. Part A: Motion for a Resolution*, Rapporteurs: B. Fayot & D. Schinzel 27.4.92 (A3-0153/92) EP 152.265, EP Session Documents, Report by the Committee on Culture, Youth, Education and the Media.

EP (1993) *Working Document on COM(2)480 final*, Committee on Culture, Youth, Education and the Media.

EP (1993a) *Resolution on the cultural aspects of GATT*, EP 174.419, PV 23 II, 15.07.93.

EP (1994) *Resolution on the Commission Green Paper 'Pluralism and Media Concentration in the Internal Market'*, OJ C 44/179, 14.02.94.

EP (1994a) *Debate on Pluralism and Concentration of Ownership* Verbatim reports of Session proceedings, 19/20.1.94: 345-356.

EP (1994b) *Opinion of the European Parliament issued on 19.4.1994.* OJ C 128/54, 9.5.94.

EP (1994c) *Debate on Pluralism and Concentration of Ownership* Verbatim reports of Session Proceedings, 25/26.10.94.: 101-120.

EP (1995) *Decision of the European Parliament taken on 13.6.1995.* 10/EP 192.O34: 10-15, OJ C 166, 3.7.95.

EP (1995a) *Draft Opinion of the Committee for external economic affairs,* EP 211.287 revised.

EP (2002) *Report on Cultural Industries* (2002/2127 (INI)) Committee for Culture, Youth, Education, Media and Sports, Raporteur: Mirsini Zorba, RR#503959EL.doc PE 312. 547 pp 7/7, 13/13 & 14/14.

EP (2005) *Report on the application of Articles 4 and 5 of Directive 89/552/EEC (the "TV Without Frontiers" Directive), as amended by Directive 97/36/EC, for the period 2001-2002 (2004/2236(INI))* "Weber Report", EP 357.689/V02-00, A6-0202/2005 of 21 June 2005

ESC (1985) *Opinion on the Green Paper on the establishment of the common market for broadcasting, especially by satellite and cable.* ESC(85)776, 25.9.85.

ESC (1987) Opinion on the draft proposal for the Directive Television Without Frontiers, OJ C 232, 31.8.87/29 p p 29 ESC (1991) *Communication to Parliament and the Council on encouraging audio-visual production in the context of the strategy for high definition television* ESC(91)1470 Brussels 24.7.91.

ESC (1993) *Opinion on the Green Paper 'Pluralism and Media Concentration in the internal market',* OJ C 304/07, 10.11.93.

European Communities (2005) 'Treaty Establishing a Constitution for Europe', Luxembourg: Office for Official Publications.

European Consumer Law Group (1990) *Transborder TV Advertising and the consumer interests,* Working Paper (Xerox) London, City University.

European Report, No. 1703, 14.9.91, 'Brittan Flattens Reports on new Merger Threshold Proposal'.

European Union (1997) Treaty of Amsterdam amending the Treaty of the EU, the Treaties establishing the European Communities and certain Related Acts, Luxembourg: Office for Official Publications (TEU)

Eurostat (2004) www. europa.eu.int/comm/eurostat/newcronos/reference/display.do ?screen=detailref&language=en&product=EU_yearlies&root=EU_yearlies/ yearlies/I/I5/ir031

Fauks, Keith (1994) 'What Has Happened to Citizenship?', *Sociological Review,* Nov. 1994.

Fayot & Schinzel report (see EP 1992).

Fayot, Ben (MEP, *Rapporteur*) interviewed by the author, 29.11.1994.

Ferguson, M. (ed) (1986) *New Communication Technologies and the Public Interest: comparative perspectives on policy and research,* London, Sage.

Ferguson, M. (ed) (1991) *Public Communication the New Imperatives: Future Directions for Media Research*, London, Sage.

Filipek, J. (1992) Culture Quotas: The Trade Controversy over the European Community's Broadcasting Directive, *Stanford Journal of International Law*, 28.323 1992: 324-370.

Financial Times 11.2.93 – see Bradshaw, D. et al.

Flynn, B. (1993) 'Canal+ bets on Digital TV', *Advanced Television Markets*, Oct. 1992: 2.

Forêt, F. (2003) 'Espace public européen et mise en scène du pouvoir', in E. Dacheux (ed) *L'Europe qui se construit*, St-Etienne, Publications de l'Université de St-Etienne.

Fox, B. (1995) 'The Digital Dawn in Europe', *IEEE Spectrum*, April 1995: 50-53.

Frangos, S. (1995) 'War rekindled: Brussels vs Hollywood', *To Vima*, 5.2.95: E17 (in Greek).

Garitaonandía, Carmelo, Emilio Fernádez Peña & José Oleaga (2004) 'Coping with Audiovisual Plenty on TV and Virtual Purchase on the Internet', *New Directions in European Media*, European Sociological Association – Media Research Network, Aristotle University Conference Proceedings, CD-ROM, Thessaloniki, Aristotle University.

Garnham, N. & V. Porter (1994) *Evidence to the Review of Cross-Media Ownership*, CCIS, University of Westminster, London.

Garnham, N. (1986) 'The Media and the Public Sphere', in Golding, P. et. al. (eds) *Communicating Politics*, Leicester University Press.

Garnham, N. (1990) *Capitalism and Communication: Global culture and the economics of information*, London, Sage.

Garnham, N. (2000), *Emancipation, the Media and Modernity*, Oxford, OUP

GATT (1986) *The Text of the General Agreement*, Geneva, Centre William Rappard.

GATT (1992) *GATT Activities 1991*, Geneva.

GATT (1993) *GATT Activities 1992*, Geneva.

GATT (1993a) *The General Agreement On Trade In Services (GATS) and Related Instruments*, GATT December 1993, Geneva.

GATT (1993b) *The Uruguay Round : A Giant Step For Trade and Development, And A Response To The Challenges Of The Modern World*, Geneva.

GATT Focus, 'News of the Uruguay Round of Multilateral Trade Negotiations' (1986, 1992, 1993)· Geneva.

Gerhards, Jürgen (1993)*Westeuropäische Integration und die Schwierigkeiten der Enstehung einer europäischen Öffentlichkeit*, FS III, 92-101, Berlin

Gillespie, A.E., & M.E. Hepworth (1985) 'Telecommunication and Regional Development in the Information Economy: a Policy Perspective' *PICT Policy Research Papers*, No 1 (August 1985).

Goldberg, Bernard (2002), *Bias: A CBS Insider Exposes How the Media Distort the News*, Washington D.C. Regnery Publishing, Inc.

Golding, P. & G. Murdock (eds) (1986) *Communicating Politics*, Leicester University Press.

Golding, Peter (2005, in press) 'Eurocrats, technocrats, and democrats: competing ideologies in the European Information Society', in *Innovations and Challenges in European Media*, A. Baltzis & S. Kaitatzi-Whitlock (eds), Thessaloniki, University Studio Press (in Greek), also to be published in *European Societies*.

GPEAP – see Commission (1994b)

GPTWF – see Commission (1984)

Grimm, D. (1997) 'Does Europe Need a Constitution?, In P. Gowan & P. Anderson (eds.) *The Question of Europe*, London, Verso.

Guardian "Yes, it was a No" May 31st 2005

Gurevitch, M. et al. (eds) (1982)*Culture Society and the Media*, London, Methuen.

Gyllenhammar, Per, (1994) 'Let us Liberalise Cross-media Ownership', *Intermedia* June/July, Vol. 22 No 3.

Habermas, Jürgen (1989) *The Structural Transformation of the Public Sphere*, Cambridge, Polity

Habermas, Jürgen (1995) 'The market against politics' *Eleftherotypia*. 25.2.96.

Habermas, Jürgen (2001) 'Why Europe Needs a Constitution', *New Left Review*, 11: 5-26.

Habermas, Jürgen (2003 / 1998) *Die Postnationale Konstellation; Politische Essays*, Frankfurt, Suhrkamp.

Hagen, Lutz (ed) (2004) *EuropäischeUnion und mediale Öffentlichkeit*, Cologne

Hahn Report (see EP 1982a).

Ham, C. & M. Hill (1984) *The Policy process in the modern capitalist state*, New York, London, Harvester Wheatsheaf.

Hanada, Tatsuro (1999) 'Digital Broadcasting and the future of the Public Sphere', *Studies of Broadcasting*, Vol. 34: 9-40.

Hartley, T.C. (1988) *The foundations of European Community law*, Oxford, Clarendon Press.

Healy, M. (1993) 'Operators speak on digital TV', *Advanced Television Markets*, 11/1993: 12.

Hellman, Heikki (2001) 'Diversity – An End in Itself? Developing a Multi-Measure Methodology of Television Programme Variety Studies', European Journal of Communication, 16(2): 131-154.

Hennebert, Bernard (2003) *Mode d'emploi pour telespectateurs actifs*, Brussels, Labor.

Hewitt, M. (ITC Deputy Secretary) (1994) Interview with the author 10.3.1994

Hilve, P., Rosengren K. E. & Majanen P. (1996) *Quality in Programming: Commercial and Public Service Diversity, Media and Communication Studies, University of Lund* (unpublished paper), Lund.

Hjarvard, Stig (1993) Pan European Television News. Towards a European Political Public Sphere? in Drommond, Phillip; Paterson, Richard & Willis, Janet: *National Identity and Europe*, London, British Film Institute

Hoffmann-Riem, W. (1992) 'Trends in the Development of Broadcasting Law in Western Europe', *European Journal of Communication*, Vol. 7 (1992): 147-171, London, Sage.

Hoffmann-Riem, W. (1992b) 'Defending Vulnerable Values: Regulatory Measures and Enforcement Dilemmas: 173-201 in *Television and the Public Interest*, J. G. Blumler (ed) London, Sage.

Holtznagel & Orlandi (see Orlandi).

Humphreys, P. (1988) 'Satellite Broadcasting Policy in West Germany – Political Conflict and Competition in a Decentralised System', in R. Negrine (ed) *Satellite Broadcasting, The Politics and Implications of the New Media*, London, Routledge.

I&T Magazine (1994) 'Advanced television between the lines' No. 14: 5-9 (A.W. Brown).

I&T Magazine (1995) 'TV standards Directive signals TV lift-off towards information society', October-November 1995, No. 18: 3.

Independent, 28.9.93.'Appeal from European Film and Programme Makers, Performing Artists and Producers for Cultural Exception in the Gatt'.

Iosifidis, Petros, Jeanette Steemers & Mark Wheeler (2005) *European Television Industries*, London, British Film Institute.

IRIS, Legal observations of the European Audiovisual Observatory, October 1994, Vol. 1, No O.

ITC (Independent Television Commission) (1995) 'ITC to draw up code on conditional access for subscription television' 18.07.1995, London.

Juneau, P. (1989) 'Television Without Frontiers?' *EBU Review, Programme, Administration, Law* Vol XL, No 3 May 1989.

Kaidatzis, Akritas (2005) 'European Citizenship in the European Constitutional Convention', Symposium: *European Constitution: Challenges and Prospects*, Evrigeneio, Centre for International European Economic Law, 11-04-2005, Thessaloniki (in Greek).

Kaitatzi-Whitlock, Sophia (1994) 'European HDTV Strategy: Muddling Through or Muddling Up?', *European Journal of Communication*, Vol. 9, No. 2, London, Sage.

Kaitatzi-Whitlock, Sophia (1996) *European Audiovisual Policy: An Elusive Target*, PhD Thesis, Westminster University, London, (British Library).

Kaitatzi-Whitlock, Sophia (1998) 'HDTV and Standardization Policymaking in Europe', in M. Dupagne & P. Seel, *High-Definition Television: A Global Perspective* Iowa, Iowa State University Press.

Kaitatzi-Whitlock, Sophia (1999) 'The Right of Reply and Self-regulation in Television', in *The Constitution, (To Syntagma)*, Vol. 25, Nos 3-4, Athens, Sakkoulas (in Greek).

Kaitatzi-Whitlock, Sophia (2000) 'Implementing Strategies for Digital Pay Television in Europe: the case of Greece' *Telematics and Informatics*, Vol. 16, 2000: 151-176, Oxford, Elsevier Science-Pergamon Press.

Kaitatzi-Whitlock, Sophia (2000a) 'A Redundant 'Information Society' for the European Union?' *Telematics and Informatics*, Vol. 17: 39-75, Oxford, Elsevier Science - Pergamon Press.

Kaitatzi-Whitlock, Sophia (2002) '*Six Arguments Against the Notion of Cyberdemocracy*', IAMCR Barcelona, Technology Policy Section. Also in Roi Panagiotopoulou, (ed) *The Digital Challenge: The Media and Democracy* (2003) Athens, Typothito-Dardanos (in Greek).

Kaitatzi-Whitlock, Sophia (2003) *The Domain of Information*, Athens, Kritiki (in Greek).

Kaitatzi-Whitlock, Sophia (2004) '*Miserabile Visu*. How and Why Lowest Common Denominator Programming Dominate Television Broadcasting', in *Media and Culture*, V. Laokratis (ed.) Athens, Entelecheia (in Greek).

Kaitatzi-Whitlock, Sophia (2004a) 'Banking on Interactivity' COST A20 Research Project, in Fausto Colombo (ed.), Milan, Vita & Pensiero, Universita Cattolica.

Kaitatzi-Whitlock, Sophia (2004b) 'The state cannot abide by its own laws and keep market forces under control', 27.12.2004: 63-68, Athens, *Marketing Week* (in Greek).

Kaitatzi-Whitlock, Sophia (2006) 'The role of the media in the European Public Sphere and the creation of a Common European Citizenship' in *Innovations and Challenges in European Media*, Alexis Baltzis & Sophia Kaitatzi-Whitlock (eds), Thessaloniki, University Studio Press (in Greek), to be published in English in *European Societies*.

Kaitatzi-Whitlock, Sophia & Alexis Baltzis (eds), (2005) '*Innovations and Challenges in European Media*, Thessaloniki, University Studio Press, (in Greek).

Kallinikos Jannis, (2001), *The Age of Flexibility – Managing Organisations and Technology*, Lund, Academia Adacta,

Keane, J. (1991) *The Media and Democracy*, London, Polity Press.

Keane, J. (1991a) *Democracy and Civil Society*, London, Polity Press.

Kellner, Douglas (1990) *Television and the Crisis of Democracy*, Boulder Colorado. Westview

Keohane, O.R. & S. Hoffmann (eds) (1991) *The New European Community, Decision making and Institutional Change*, Oxford & San Francisco, Westview.

Leclercq, T. & B. Flynn (1994) 'CA stalls digital directive', *Advanced Television Markets*, June 1994: 7.

Leclercq, T. (1994) 'MEPs oppose Simulcrypt, *Advanced Television Markets*, May 1994: 4.

Leys, Colin (2001), *Market-Driven Politics: Neoliberal Democracy and the Public Interest*, London, Verso

Lhoest, H. (1983) *The Interdependence of the Media*, Mass Media Files No 4, Strasbourg, Council of Europe.

Lichtenberg, Judith (ed.) (1991) *Democracy and the Mass Media*, Cambridge Studies in Philosophy and Public Policy, Cambridge University Press.

Lindblom, C.E. (1959) 'The Science of Muddling through', *Public Administration Review*, 1959, and discussion of this article in *Public Administration Review*, 24, 1964.

Locksley, G. (1987) 'Direct Broadcast Satellites: the media-industrial complex in the UK and Europe', *Telecommunications Policy*, June 1987: 193.

Ludes, Peter (2004) *Eurovisions? Monetary Union and Communications Puzzles', in 'European Culture and the Media* (2004) Bondebjerg, Ib, & Golding, Peter (eds) Bristol: Intellect Books.

Lukes, Steven. (1974) *Power: a Radical View*, London, Macmillan Education.

MacGregor, Brent (1997) *Live, Direct and Biased: Making Television News in the Satellite Age*, London, Arnold.

Machill, Marcel (1998) 'Euronews: The First European News Channel as a Case Study for Media Industry Development in Europe and for Spectra of Transnational Journalism Research', *Media Culture and Society*, 20(3): 427-450.

McNair, Brian (1998) *An Introduction to Political Communication*, London: Routledge.

Maggiore, Matteo. (1990) *Audiovisual Production in the Single Market*, Brussels, CEC.

Malangre, K. (1993) 'Working Paper on the Green Paper Pluralism and Media Concentration in the Internal Market (an assessment of the need for Community action)', COM(92)480 final, Legal Affairs Committee, 28 September.

Manousaki, Elengo (2004) Commission DG Research, Presentation at the National Centre for Research & Technological Development, Thessaloniki, 04/11/2004.

Mathews, J. (1989) *The Age of democracy: the politics of post-fordism*, Oxford, OUP.

Mazower, Mark (1998) *Dark Continent: Europe's Twentieth Century*, London, Penguin.

McAlpine, A. (1995) 'Are politicians voting for the end of Democracy?' London, *The European* 6-12 January 1995.

McCombs, E. Maxwell & Donald L. Shaw (1972) 'The Agenda Setting Function of Mass Media', *Public Opinion Quarterly*, 36 (2) 1972 : 1976-1987.

McLaughlin, A.M. et al. (1993) 'Corporate Lobbying in the European Community', *Journal of Common Market Studies*, Vol 31, No 2 June 1993.

McManus, J. (1994) *Market Driven Journalism: Let the citizen beware*, London, Sage.

McNair Brian, (1995): An Introduction to Political Communication. London:, Routledge

McQuail, D. (1986) 'Is media theory adequate to the challenge of new communications technologies?', in M. Ferguson (ed) *New Communication Technologies and the Public Interest: comparative perspectives on policy and research*, London, Sage.

McQuail, D. (1986a) 'Policy perspectives in new media in Europe' in M. Ferguson (ed) *New Communication Technologies and the Public Interest: comparative perspectives on policy and research*, London, Sage.

McQuail, D. (1987) *Mass Communication Theory*, London, Sage.

Messerlin, P.A., (1993) 'The EC and Central Europe: The missed rendez-vous of 1992?" *Economics of Transition*, Vol 1 (1): 89-109.

Metaxas, A.-I. D. (1979), *Political Communication* Athens, Sakkoulas (in Greek).

Metcalfe, S. (1986) 'Information and some economics of Information revolution', in M. Ferguson (ed) *New Communication Technologies and the Public Interest: comparative perspectives on policy and research*, London, Sage pp. 37-50.

Meyer, Thomas, with Leo Hinchman (2002) Media Democracy – How the Media Colonize Politics, London, Polity Press

Michael, J. (1986) 'Information Law, Policy and the Public Interest', in M. Ferguson (ed) *New Communication Technologies and the Public Interest: comparative perspectives on policy and research*, London, Sage, pp. 102-121.

Moravcsik, A. (1991) 'Negotiating the Single European Act' in O. R. Keohane, & Stanley Hoffmann (eds) *The New European Community, Decision making and Institutional Change*, Oxford & San Francisco, Westview Press.

Morgan, G. (1992) 'A Compressed Market?' *Advanced Television Markets*, September 1992: 10-11.

Morgan, G. (1993) 'Picking Up the Bits', *Advanced Television Markets* (Montreux) 1993: 36.

Morgan, G. (1995) 'EU Plans its digital rules', *Advanced Television Markets*, June 1995: 1-2.

Morin, Edgar (1986) *La methode – 3 La Connaissance de la Connaissance*, Paris, Seuil.

Mosco, Vincent & Janet Wasko (1990), Democratic Communications in the Information Age, Toronto, Garamond Press

Mouffe, Chantal (1993), *The Return of the Political*, London, Verso

Mouffe, Chantal (2000), *The Democratic Paradox*, London, Verso.

Mouffe, Chantal (2005) *On the Political*, London, Routledge.

Muller-Romer, F., *Radio and TV Broadcasting*, Hans-Bredow-Institut, Special reprint, International Manual of Radio and TV, 1992/1993.

Murdoch, G., & P. Golding (1986) 'Unequal Information: Access and Exclusion in the New Communications Market Place', in M. Ferguson (ed) *New Communication Technologies and the Public Interest: comparative perspectives on policy and research*, London, Sage: 71-83.

Murdock, G. (1982) 'Large Corporations and the Control of the communications industries', in Gurvitch M. et al (eds) *Culture, Society and the Media*, London, Routledge: 118-150.

Murdock, G. (1984) 'Cultural Policy and Consumer Choice in the 'new' television Age: from Rhetorics to realities', *in Technological Development and Cultural Policy*, Council of Europe Symposium, 9-10 November 1983, Strasbourg: 40-48.

Murdock, G. (1991) 'Redrawing the Map of the Communications Industries: Concentration and Ownership in the Era of Privatization', in M. Ferguson (ed) *Public Communication and the New Imperatives*, London, Sage.

Negrine, R. & S. Papathanassopoulos (1990) *The Internationalisation of Television*, London, Pinter.

Negrine, R. (1988) 'Satellite Broadcasting : An Overview of the Major Issues', in R. Negrine (ed) *Satellite Broadcasting, The Politics and Implications of the New Media*, London, Routledge.

Nieminen, Hannu (2000), *Hegemony and the Public Sphere*, Turku, Turku University Press

Noel, E. (1988) *Working together: the Institutions of the European Community*. Office for Official Publications of the EC, Luxembourg.

Nohrstedt, Stig-Arne, Rune Ottosen, Sophia Kaitatzi-Whitlock & Christina Riegert, (2000) 'From the Persian Gulf to Kosovo – War Journalism and Propaganda', *EJC* Vol 15 (3) London, Sage.

NUR (see GATT, News of the Uruguay Round).

Oreja, Marcelino (1998, April 8) *For a modern audiovisual policy in the European Union*, Speech at the closing plenary of the European Audiovisual Conference, Birmingham, UK, URL: www.europa.eu.int/eac/speeches/oreja2.html

Orlandi, C., & B. Holtznagel (1993) *Transposition of the EC 'Television Without Frontiers' Directive: Advertising, Sponsorship and Programme Quotas*, Hamburg, Hans Bredow Institute.

Padovani, Claudia & Kaarle Nordenstreng (2005) 'From NWICO to WSIS: another world information and communication order?: Introduction', *Global Media and Communication*, Dec 2005; 1: 264-272.

Papadimitriou, Giorgos (1999) 'European Unification and the National Constitution', in Napoleon Maravegias amd Michaelis Tsinisizelis, (eds) *The Integration of the European Union*, Athens, Themelio.(in Greek)

Panagiotarea, Anna (2005) 'Why is news about the European Union Absent from National Channel Networks?' in *Innovations and Challenges in European Media*, Baltzis, A. & Kaitatzi-Whitlock, S. (eds), op. cit.

Papathanassopoulos, S. (2002) 'European Communications', Athens: Kastaniotis (in Greek).

Papathanassopoulos, S. (2002a) *European Television in the Digital Age: Issues, Dynamics and Realities*, Oxford, Polity.

Papathanossopoulos, Stelios, (2005), *Television in the Twenty-first Century*, Athens Kastaniotis (in Greek)

Peacock, A. (1986) *On the financing of the BBC*, Commission Report, HMSO, London.

Peacock, A. (1989) Introduction to G. Hughes & D. Vines (eds) *Deregulation and the Future of Commercial Television*, Aberdeen University Press.

Peel, Quentin (2004) 'A summer of Heated Haggling for Barroso', Financial Times, 29-07-2004: 13.

Peter, Jochen (2004) ‚Kaum Vorhanden und Eher Negativ – Die Alltägliche Fernsehberichterstattung über die Europäische Union in internationalen Vergleich', in Hagen 2004 pp 146-161 (above).

Peterson, J & E. Bomberg (1999) *Decision-making in the EU*, London, Macmillan.

Peterson, J. (1987) *International Trade In Information*, CCIS, London, University of Westminster (formerly Polytechnic Of Central London).

Peterson, J. (1988) *The Uruguay Round and the Implications for Cultural And Information Services*, CCIS Working Paper No 1, London, University of Westminster, (formerly Polytechnic Of Central London).

Pinheiro, Joao de Deus, speech at EAC conference, 30.6.1994.

Popper, Karl & John Condry (1994) *La Télévision: un danger pour la démocratie*, Paris, Anatolia.

Porter, V. (1994) 'State Licensing and the Freedom of Expression in Broadcasting', *Media Law and Practice*, Vol. 15, No 1, 1994: 26-27.

Porter, V., & S. Hasselbach (1991) *Pluralism, Politics and the Market Place (The Regulation of German Broadcasting)* London, Routledge.

Porter, Vincent (1996) Interview with the author 26.06.1996

Pressley, J. (1994) 'UIP expects EU to renew Competition-Law Exemption', *Wall-Street Journal*, 1.7.94.

Pryce, R. (1994) 'The Maastricht Treaty and the new Europe', in A. Duff, J. Pinder & R. Pryce, *Maastricht and Beyond*, London, Routledge.

Purvis, Stewart (1999) 'Euronews Improves Output and Distribution under ITN', EBU Yearbook 1999: 36-37.

Raboy, M., & B. Dagenais (eds) (1992) *Media, Crisis and Democracy (Mass Communication and the Disruption of Social Order)* London, Sage.

Raboy, Marc, Ed. (2002) *Global Media Policy in the New Millennium*. Luton (UK), University of Luton Press.

Radaelli, M. Claudio (1999) *Technocracy and the European Union*, London, Longman.

Randall, Jeff (2002) *The fallout from ITV Digital's collapse* BBC News 1.6.2002

Renaud, J-L. (1994) 'The Commission follows the DVB: at a distance', *Advanced Television Markets*, November 1994: 11.

Renshon, A. Stanley (1979) 'The Need for Personal Control in Political Life: Origins, dynamics and Implications': 41-64, in *Choice and Perceived Control*, Perlmuter C. Lawrence et al (eds.) New York, Lawrence Erlbaum Associates.

Richardson, J, G. Gustafson & G. Jordan (1982) 'The Concept of Policy Style', in J. Richardson (ed) *Policy Styles in Western Europe*, London, Allen & Unwin.

Rogers E.M. (1962) The diffusion of Innovations, Glenco Illinois, Free Press.

Rosen Jay, Taylor Paul (1992), *The New News Versus The Old News: the Press and Politics in the 1990s* New York, Twentieth Century Fund, Inc.

Rouard, D. (1994) 'Sur La Piste d'un Eurocartel de la Television.', *Le Monde*, 25.11.94.

Sabater, Fernando, 'Lessons of Abyss: there is more to culture than modernisation of the markets', El Pais/Bibliothiki, Literary supplement of Eleftherotypia 11/07/2003: 16-21.

Sabine H. G. & Thorson, T.L., (1973), A history of Political Theory, Hinsdale, Illinois, Dryden Press

Sachpekidou, E. R. (1990) *Free circulation of Television Services in the European Economic Community*, Thessaloniki, Sakkoulas (in Greek).

Sanchez-Tabernero, A. (1993) *Media Concentration in Europe: Commercial Enterprise and the Public Interest*, Media Monograph No 16, Dusseldorff, EIM.

Sarikakis, Katharine (2002) 'Supra-national Governance and the Shifting Paradigm in Communications Policy-making: The Case of the European Parliament', in Mark Raboy (ed.) *Global Media Policy in the New Millennium*. 77-91, Luton, Luton University Press.

Sarikakis, Katharine (2004) *Powers in Media Policy – The Challenge of the European Parliament*, Oxford, Peter Lang.

Sbragia, Alberta (ed.) (1992) *Euro-politics: Institutions and Politics in the 'New' European Community*, Washington D.C., Brookings Institution.

Scharpf, W. Fritz (1997) *Economic Integration, Democracy and the Welfare State*, Journal of European Public Policy, 4: 2 (March) pp 219- 242.

Schattschdeider, E.E. (1960) *The semi-sovereign People – A Realist's View of Democracy in America,*, Hinsdale Illinois, Dryden Press.

Schiller, D. (1990) *Communications And The European Single Market: A view from The United States*, Los Angeles, University Of California.

Schiller, Herbert (1969) *Mass Communication and American Empire*, New York, Kelly.

Schiller, Herbert (1976) *Communication and Cultural Domination*, White Plains, N.Y., Sharpe.

Schlesinger, Philip (1994), *Europe's Contradictory Communication Space*, Daedalus, 123(2), 25-52.

Schoenbach (1995) *Der Beitrag der Medien zu Europa. Rezeption und Wirkung*, in Erbring (1995): 27-38

Schoof H. & Watson Brown A. (1995) 'Information Highways and Media Policies in the EU', *Telecommunications Policy*, Vol.19, No 4: 325-338 Elsevier Science Ltd.

Schott, J.J. (1991) Trading Blocs and the World Trading System, in *The World Economy*, Vol.14, No 1.

Seligman, Martin E.P. et al, (1979) 'The Psychology of Power – Concluding Remarks' in Lawrence C. Perlemutter (ed), *Choice and Personal Control*, Hillsdale NJ, Lawrence Erlbaum, pp. 347-368.

Semetco, Holli A. & Valkenburg, Patti (2002) *Framing European Politics: A Content Analysis of Press and Television News*. Journal of Communication 50: 26-28.

Sepstrup, P. (1989) 'Implications of current Developments in West European Broadcasting', in *Media Culture and Society*, Vol. 11 : 29-54 London, Sage.

Sepstrup, P. (1993) *Transnationalization of Television in Western Europe*, London, J. Libbeys (Academia Research Monographs Series).

Servan-Schreiber, J.J. (1967) *Le Defi Americain*, Paris, Denoel (English edition: 1968).

Severin W. & Tankard, J. (1992) *Communication Theories: Origins Methods and Uses in the Mass Media*, New York, Longman.

Shapiro, Andrew L. (1999) *The Control Revolution*, New York, PublicAffairs, Perseus.

Sharp, M. & K. Pavitt (1993) 'Technology policy in the 1990s' *Journal of Common Market Studies, 31(2) June*.

Shönbach, Klaus (1995), 'Der Beitrag der Medien zu Europa: Rezeption und Wikung', in Lutz Erbring, *Zu Zukunft das Tageszeitung* Schriftenreihe der Deutschen Gesellschaft für Publizistik- und Kommunikationswissenschaft Band.21, Verlag: Konstanz, UVK Medien/Ölschläger, 27-38.

Sifounakis, Nikos (President of the EP Committee for Culture etc.,) interviewed by the author, 29.11.2005.

Silj, A. (1992) *The New Television in Europe*, London, J. Libbey.

Smith, Andy, (2004) *Commissioners and the prospects of a European public sphere: Information, representation and legitimacy*, Paper presented to the conference *Citizenship and Democratic Legitimacy in Europe*, University of Stirling, 5-6th February, 2004.

Smith, C.N. (1993) 'International trade in television programming and GATT: an analysis of why the European Community's local program requirement violates the General Agreement on Tariffs and Trade', *International Tax and Business Lawyer*, 10: 97-137.

Smythe, W. Dallas (1977) 'Communications: Blindspot of Western Marxism', *Canadian Journal of Political and Social Theory*, Vol. 1. No 3 (Fall 1977).

Snoddy, R. (1994) 'BSkyB and Reuters on verge of partnership', *Financial Times*, 24/25.12.94.

Sony Entertainment Inc. (1994) London Economics Study, London.

Stangos, Philios, (2004), 'The Sophoriphic Action of European News', Eurocentricities, ERT-NET TV, (Greek psb), 9-13 February 2004.

Starr Paul (2004) *The Creation of the Media: Political Origins of Modern Communications*, New York, Basic Books.

Starr Paul (2005) Political Networking, Technology Review, April 2005.

Stavrakakis, Giannis (2004) Prologue to '*The Democratic Paradox*', Chantal Mouffe, Athens, Polis (in Greek).

Stepp, Carl Sessions (1990), *Access in a Post-social Responsibility Age*, in Lichtenberg, Judith (ed.) (1991) *Democracy and the Mass Media*, Ch.6: 186-201, Cambridge Studies in Philosophy and Public Policy, Cambridge, Cambridge University Press.

Stewart, T. P. (1994) *The GATT Uruguay Round: A Negotiating History (1986-1992)* Daventer, The Netherlands, Kluwer Law and Taxation Publishers.

Stiglitz Joseph (2002), 'Globalization and Its Discontents', Allen Lane/Penguin, London

Stuart, J. (1989) European Quotas: Playing Hollywood's Game, *Television Business International* (Jul/Aug 1989) pp. 6-7.

Stüdemann, F. (1996) 'Tiny Duchy with a grand Media design', London, *The European*, 18-24 July.

Styliadou, M. (1997) 'Applying EC competition law to alliances in the telecommunicat-ions sector', *Telecommunications Policy*, Vol 21, No 1: 47-58, Exeter, Elsevier Science.

Swinkels, V. (1988) *Media Ownership Without Frontiers*, MA Dissertation, London, City University.

Taishoff, M.N. (1987) *State Responsibility and the DBS*, London, Pinter.

Tempest, A. (1985) 'The Year of the Green Paper', *EBU Review* Vol XXXVI, No 4, July 1985.

Tempest, A. (1991) 'The playing fields of Europe', *Spectrum*, Autumn 1991.

Theiler, Thomas (2001)'Viewers into Europeans?: How the European Union Tried to Europeanize the Audiovisual Sector and Why It Failed', *Canadian Journal of Communication* Vol 24.

Thompson, John, B. (1995) '*The Media and Modernity: Social Theory of the Media*' Oxford: Polity.

Times, 'BSkyB & Kirch link up to launch digital satellite TV' 9.7.96.

Times, 'Digital era could mean 18 channels', 16.1.95: 4.

Tongue, Carol (1994) interview with the author 10.8.1995

Tracey, M. (1988) Popular Culture and the Economics of Global Television, *Intermedia*, March 1988.

Trandafoiu, Ruxandra, (2005), *Translating Europeanness to the Europeans, A Common 'Language' in the East and West*, in Baltzis Alexis & S. Kaitatzi-Whitlock, (eds), (2005) '*Innovations and Challenges in European Media*, Thessaloniki, University Studio Press, (in Greek).

Troussard, Xavier (DG X official) interviewed by the author, 29.8.1994.

TTR (Think Tank Report – see Vasconcelos).

Tumber, Howard (2004), *Scandal and Media in the United Kingdom: From Major to Blair*, in *Political Scandals and Media Across Democracies*, Tumber H. &Waisbord S. (eds), Vol. I, London, Sage.

Tumber, Howard, (1995), Marketing Maastricht: the EU and News Management, Media Culture and Society, 17 pp 511-519.

Tunstall, J. & M. Palmer (1990) *Liberating Communications*, Oxford, Blackwell.

Tunstall, J. & M. Palmer (1991) *Media Moguls*, London, Routledge.

Tunstall, J. (1977) *The Media are American*, London, Penguin.

TWFD (Television Without Frontiers Directive – see Council 1989).

Van Loon, A. (1992) *National Legislation Analysis*, IViR University of Amsterdam, Council of Europe, CDMM (92) 8, Vol 1, Strasbourg.

Varis, T., (1984) 'The International flow of Television Programs', *Journal of Communication*, No. 34: 143-146.

Vasconcelos, A-P. et al. (1994) *Report by the Think-tank on the Audiovisual Policy in the European Union* Luxembourg, OOPEC.

Venturelli, Shallini (1996), *Freedom and its Mystification: The Political Though of Public Space*, in Braman S. and A. Sreberni-Mohamandi (eds), *Globalisation Communication and Transnational Civil Society*, Cesskill NJ, Hampton Press.

Venturelli, Shallini (1998) *Liberalising the European Media: Politics, Regulation and the Public Sphere*, Oxford, OUP.

*Vima (*Athens Daily) 2.6.96, 'Van Miert rejects.. privatization': E15 (in Greek).

Vima, 21.3.96, 'Albert Frère, the European TV magnate': E8-22(in Greek).

Wagner, M., (1993) 'GATT and broadcasting: Europe stands firm', *Diffusion*, EBU – Winter 1993/94: 64-68.

Ward, David (2004) *The European Union Democratic Deficit and the Public Sphere*, Amsterdam, Ios.

Wasko, Janet (1994) *Hollywood in the information age: beyond the silver screen*, Oxford, Polity.

Weber Max (1978/1986) *Domination by Economic Power and by Authority*, in Lukes S. (ed) *Power* (1986) New York· New York University Press.

Wedell, G. (1985) 'Television Without Frontiers? (Some initial reflections on the GP of the EEC Commission)' *EBU Review, Programmes, Administration, Law*, Vol XXXVI, No 1 Jan. 1985.

Weiler, H.H, Joseph (1995) To be a European Citizan – Eros and Civilization, *Journal of European Public Policy*, 4: 4 (December) pp 495-519.

Wieldman, S.S. & S.E. Siwek (1988) *International Trade in Films and Television Programs*, The American Enterprise Institute, Ballinger Publications.

Wiener, Norbert (1949) *Cybernetics: or Control and communication in the animal and the machine*, Cambridge Mass., MIT Press.

Willard S., Rowland D. Jr & Tracey Michael, *Journal of Communication*, 40 (2) Spring 1990.

Woolcock, S. (1993) 'European *acquis* and multilateral trade rules: are they Compatible?', *Journal of Common Market Studies*, Vol 31, No 4, Dec. 1993, Oxford, Cackwell.

Zeri, P. (1989) 'Television Without Frontiers', *Nomiko Vima*, Vol. 37(4): 692-704 (in Greek).

Zeri, P. (1990) *Private Television (The American Paradigm)* Athens, Papasisis (in Greek).

Zweifel, D. Thomas (2002) *Democratic Deficit? Institutions and Regulations in The EU, Switzerland and the US*, New York, Lexington Books.

Zysman, J. (1983) Governments, markets and growth: financial systems and the politics of industrial change, Cornell Universiy Press

Abbreviations

ACT Association of Commercial Television
ADTT Advanced Digital Television Technologies
APEWIS Action Plan on Europe's way to the Information Society
ARD Allgemeine Rundfunk Deutschlands
AT&T American Telecommunications and Telegraph
BBC British Broadcasting Corporation
BECU Billions of European Currency Units
BEUC Bureau Européen des Unions de Consommateurs
BSB British Satellite Broadcasting
BSkyB British Sky Broadcasting
BSS Broadcasting Satellite Services
BT British Telecom
CA Conditional Access
CAEJ Communauté des Associations d'Editeurs de Journaux de la CEE
CCIR Conseil Consultative International de Radiodiffusion
CCIR International Radio Consultative Committee
CCITT Comité Consultatif International Télegraphique et Téléphonique
CEPI Confederation of European Independent Producers
CICCE Comité des Industries Cinématographiques et Audiovisuelles des Communautés
    Européennes et de l'Europe Communautaire
CLT (Luxembourg TV Channel)
CNN (US TV Channel)
COE Council of Europe
COREPER Committee of Permanent Representatives (of the Council of Ministers)
CSA Conseil Superieure de l'Audiovisuelle (France)
CSCE Council for Security and Cooperation in Europe
DBS Direct Broadcasting by Satellite
DG Directorate General (an administrative division of the Commission)
DHS Direct-to-home Satellite, also DTH
DSB Dispute Settlement Body (of the WTO)
DTH (see DHS)
DTI Department of Trade and Industry (UK)
DVB Digital Video Broadcasting
EAC European Audiovisual Conference
EAS European Audiovisual Space
EAT European Advertising Tripartite
EAVI European Association for Viewers' Interests
EBU European Broadcasting Union
EC European Community
ECHR European Convention on Human Rights,
ECHR European Court of Human Rights
ECJ European Court of Justice
ECOSOC Economic and Social Committee, also ESC
ECS European Communications Satellites
ECSE European Conferance on Peace and Security

ECU European Currency Unit
EEC European Economic Community
EFAP European Federation of Audiovisual Producers
EFTA European Free Trade Association
EGAKU European Council of Trade Unions in Arts, Mass Media and Entertainment
EGTA European Group for Television Advertising
EIM European Institute for the Media
ELG-DVB European Launch Group - Digital Video Broadcasting
EMC European Media Council
EMS European Media and Marketng Survey
ENPA-CAEJ European Newspapers and Periodicals Association
EP European Parliament
EPC European Publishers Council
ESA European Space Agency
ETSI The European Telecommunications Standards Institute
EU European Union
FAEP An association of independant producers
FCC Federal Communication Commission (US)
FDI Foreign Direct Investment
FSS Fixed Satellite Services
GAS General Agreement on Services
GATS General Agreement on Trade in Services
GATT General Agreement on Tariffs and Trade
GP Green Paper
GPEAP Green Paper on 'European Audiovisual Programming'
GPTWF Green Paper on 'Television Without Frontiers'
HD-MAC High-definition Multiple Analogue Component
HDTV High Definition Television
I,T & C Information, Technology and Communications
IAA International Association of Advertisers
IAMCR International Association of Media and Communication Researchers
IBA Independant Broadcasting Authority
ICA International Communication Association
ICC International Chamber of Commerce
IDATE Institut de l'audiovisuel et des télécommunications en Europe (France)
INA Institut national de l'audiovisuel (France)
INTELSAT International Satellite Organisation
ISDN Integrated Services Digital Network, N-ISDN, B-ISDN.
ISI Institute for Scientific Information
ITC Independant Television Commission (UK)
ITU International Telecommunications Union
ITV Independant Television (UK)
MECU Million European Currency Units
MEDIA Measures for the Encouragement of the Development of the Industry of
    Audiovisual Production
MNCs Multinational Companies
MOU Memorandum of Understanding
MPAA Motion Picture Association of America

MPEAA Motion Picture (Export) Association of America
NED 1,2,3 (Dutch TV Channels)
NWICO New World Information and Communication Order
OECD Organisation for Economic Co-operation and Development
PAL Phase Alternation Line
PALplus A strategy group formed in 1989 to develop an enhanced terrestrial
    transmission system compatible with conventional PAL in Europe.
PICT Programme on Information & Communication Technologies (UK)
PPV Pay-per-view
PSB or psb Public Service Broadcaster
RAI Radiotelevision Italiana
RTL (Luxemburger and German TV Channel)
SAT 1 (German TV Channel)
SEA Single European Act
SEM Single European Market, also called the 'Internal Market'
SES Société Européenne des Satellites (Luxembourg)
SME Small and Medium-sized Enterprises
SMIT Studies on Media Information and Telecommunication (Belgium)
SPRU Social Policy Research Unit (UK)
TEC Treaty of the European Community
TEU Treaty of the European Union
TF1 Télévision de France 1
TNT Turner Network TV (US)
TOR Treaty of Rome
TRIPS Trade Related Intellectual Property Services
TTR Think Tank Report (reference: Vasconcelos)
TVE Television España
TWF Television Without Frontiers
TWFD Television Without Frontiers Directive
UIP United International Pictures
UNICE Union National des Industries de la Communauté Européenne (European
    Community Industrial Union)
UR Uruguay Round (of the GATS talks)
USDC US Department of Commerce
VOD Video on Demand
WARC World Administrative Radio Conference
WFA World Federation of Advertisers
WSIS World Summit on Information Society
WTO World Trade Organisation, formerly GATT
WTSC World Telecommunications Standardisation Conference
ZDF Zweites Deutches Fernsehen (Germany)

Appendix

CONSOLIDATED VERSION OF THE TREATY
ESTABLISHING
THE EUROPEAN COMMUNITY

PART TWO – CITIZENSHIP OF THE UNION

Article 17 (ex Article 8)

1. Citizenship of the Union is hereby established. Every person holding the nationality of a Member State shall be a citizen of the Union. Citizenship of the Union shall complement and not replace national citizenship.

2. Citizens of the Union shall enjoy the rights conferred by this Treaty and shall be subject to the duties imposed thereby.

Article 18 (ex Article 8a)

1. Every citizen of the Union shall have the right to move and reside freely within the territory of the Member States, subject to the limitations and conditions laid down in this Treaty and by the measures adopted to give it effect.

2. The Council may adopt provisions with a view to facilitating the exercise of the rights referred to in paragraph 1; save as otherwise provided in this Treaty, the Council shall act in accordance with the procedure referred to in Article 251. The Council shall act unanimously throughout this procedure.

Article 19 (ex Article 8b)

1. Every citizen of the Union residing in a Member State of which he is not a national shall have the right to vote and to stand as a candidate at municipal elections in the Member State in which he resides, under the same conditions as nationals of that State. This right shall be exercised subject to detailed arrangements adopted by the Council, acting unanimously on a proposal from the Commission and after consulting the European Parliament; these arrangements may provide for derogations where warranted by problems specific to a Member State.

2. Without prejudice to Article 190(4) and to the provisions adopted for its implementation, every citizen of the Union residing in a Member State of which he is not a national shall have the right to vote and to stand as a candidate in elections to the European Parliament in the Member State in which he resides, under the same

conditions as nationals of that State. This right shall be exercised subject to detailed arrangements adopted by the Council, acting unanic mously on a proposal from the Commission and after consulting the European Parliament; these arrangements may provide for derogations where warranted by problems specific to a Member State.

Article 20 (ex Article 8c)

Every citizen of the Union shall, in the territory of a third country in which the Member State of which he is a national is not represented, be entitled to protection by the diplomatic or consular authorities of any Member State, on the same conditions as the nationals of that State. Member States shall establish the necessary rules among themselves and start the intern national negotiations required to secure this protection.

Article 21 (ex Article 8d)

Every citizen of the Union shall have the right to petition the European Parliament in accordance with Article 194. Every citizen of the Union may apply to the Ombudsman established in accordance with

Article 195.

Every citizen of the Union may write to any of the institutions or bodies referred to in this Article or in Article 7 in one of the languages mentioned in Article 314 and have an answer in the same language.

Article 22 (ex Article 8e)

The Commission shall report to the European Parliament, to the Council and to the Economic and Social Committee every three years on the application of the provisions of this Part. This report shall take account of the development of the Union. On this basis, and without prejudice to the other provisions of this Treaty, the Council, acting unanimously on a proposal from the Commission and after consulting the European Parliament, may adopt provisions to strengthen or to add to the rights laid down in this Part, which it shall recommend to the Member States for adoption in accordance with their respective constitutional requirements.

Index